The Plight of Rome in the Fifth Century AD

The Plight of Rome in the Fifth Century AD argues that the fall of the western Roman empire was rooted in a significant drop in war booty, agricultural productivity, and mineral resources. Merrony proposes that a dependency on the three economic components was established with the Principate, when a precedent was set for an unsustainable threshold on military spending.

Drawing on literary and archaeological data, this volume establishes a correspondence between booty (in the form of slaves and precious metals) from foreign campaigns and public building programmes, and how this equilibrium was upset after the empire reached its full expansion and began to contract in the third century. It is contended that this trend was exacerbated by the systematic loss of agricultural productivity (principally grain, but also livestock), as successive barbarian tribes were settled and wrested control from the imperial authorities in the fifth century. Merrony explores how Rome was weakened and divided, unable to pay its army, feed its people, or support the imperial bureaucracy – and how this contributed to its administrative collapse.

Mark Merrony is a Supernumerary Fellow at Wolfson College, University of Oxford, and a Fellow of the Society of Antiquaries of London (both in the UK). He specializes in Roman archaeology and history, and has undertaken fieldwork in Britain, France, and the Levant. *Socio-economic Aspects of Late Roman Mosaic Pavements in Phoenicia and Northern Palestine* was published in 2013, and he has authored several peer-reviewed papers on the subject.

Routledge Studies in Ancient History

The Plight of Rome in the Fifth Century AD

Mark Merrony

Routledge
Taylor & Francis Group

LONDON AND NEW YORK

First published 2017
by Routledge
2 Park Square, Milton Park, Abingdon, Oxon OX14 4RN

and by Routledge
711 Third Avenue, New York, NY 10017

Routledge is an imprint of the Taylor & Francis Group, an informa business

© 2017 Mark Merrony

British Library Cataloguing-in-Publication Data
A catalogue record for this book is available from the British Library

Library of Congress Cataloging-in-Publication Data
A catalog record for this book has been requested

ISBN: 978-1-138-04197-4 (hbk)
ISBN: 978-1-315-17409-9 (ebk)

Typeset in Sabon
by Sunrise Setting Ltd, Brixham, UK

MIX
Paper from responsible sources
FSC
www.fsc.org   FSC™ C013985

Printed in the United Kingdom
by Henry Ling Limited

For my mother, father, wife, and family

Contents

Preface

As an archaeologist, with a special interest in the Roman period, one of the questions that crops up in conversation quite often is 'why did Rome fall?' Ever since I was asked this I have not been able to give a definitive answer, although I have had some thoughts about it, and the idea of writing a book on this subject has been rattling around in my mind for some years. Taking all of the literature published into consideration, the demise of Rome has coalesced into fall verses transformation.

I have always been fascinated more by cause than process. Scrutiny of primary texts has, perhaps, made it easier to establish the nature of *what* happened, but deciphering the cause of these events is more difficult. The *why* question is a well-trodden path, and the time is certainly not ripe to readdress this issue, but the multitude of reasons given for the loss of the Roman state over the years makes it as intriguing and relevant today as it was in the eighteenth century. Its timing is also appropriate, written in the two hundred and fortieth year since the publication of Edward Gibbon's first volume of *History of the Decline and Fall of the Roman Empire*.

For reasons that are made apparent in the Introduction, the present book starts early for a study on the fall of Rome – in the Augustan period. Grappling with the primary sources presented a challenge, as did making sense of the vast corpus of archaeological, epigraphic, and numismatic material that is available for interpretation. The written and material records are of course only two layers of the issue, since the Roman empire encompassed such a vast territory and embedded in its long durée are fluctuating cultural, demographic, economic, political, and religious factors to consider.

I am indebted to innumerable archaeological and historical studies that have made this book possible to write, and also the three anonymous peer reviewers whose comments were especially welcome. Any follies that may emerge are entirely my own. This publication will inevitably provoke debate in light of the fact that it deals with such a thought-provoking topic, which has been endlessly discussed, and this will continue to be the case.

Also, at Routledge, I thank Amy Davis-Poynter, Lizzi Thomasson, and Geraldine Martin for helping me develop this project. The academic environment at

Wolfson College, Oxford was an inspiration, and I am grateful to Christopher Howgego, Philip Kay, and Susan Walker, who freely gave their time to discuss ideas related to this book, as did Alan Bowman and Martin Henig, in the congenial atmosphere of the Ashmolean Museum. Thanks also to Alexandra Hamburger and Olympia Bobou for kindly reading and commenting on the manuscript.

Mark Merrony
Oxford, December 2016

Maps and illustrations

Maps

Illustrations

Notes on the sources

Ammianus Marcellinus (c.330–c.395). Latin historian, a native of Phoenicia or Syria, and is generally regarded as a reliable source for those events that he chronicled. He was not a Christian but was liberal in his attitude to the Church and favoured religious toleration. His History was intended to succeed Tacitus, covering the period from the accession of Nerva in 96 to the death of Valens in 378, although the first thirteen books are lost. He drew on various literary sources and his style included a number of excursuses, but he also relied much on his own observation and personal experiences. It is also significant that he aimed at strict truthfulness and avoided exaggeration, does not profess to write without bias, but gives free expression to praise or blame, even on occasion finding fault with Julian whom he greatly admired.

Appian (95–165). Greek origin, a native of Alexandria; little is known about him. His writings chronicle events that occurred long before his time and he has been criticized for a lack of accuracy, depending on earlier sources, such as Polybius, Paulus Claudius, Hieronymus, Caesar, Augustus, Pollio, and quite possibly Paterculus.

Augustine (354–430). Latin theologian, the son of a pagan, Patricius of Tagaste in North Africa. He studied in Africa to become a rhetorician and left for Rome around 383, and lived in Milan a short time after to teach rhetoric. He later returned to Tagaste and founded a religious community there. In 395 or 396 he became Bishop of Hippo, and died there during the Vandal siege. Augustine is no doubt a credible source, and was an eyewitness to the terrible events as they unfolded, but he was of course – akin to Possidius, with whom he was present at the siege – diametrically opposed to the Arian Vandal doctrine, which no doubt coloured his writings.

Augustus (63 BC – AD 14). The emperor wrote his brief autobiography, known as the *Res Gestae Divi Augusti* (*Deeds of the Divine Augustus*) in the year before his death. It is a dignified account of his public life and work. The best-preserved copy is transcribed in Greek, engraved on the walls of the Temple of Augustus at Ancyra (Ankara). It provides details of his public offices, honours, and benefactions to the empire, people, and soldiers and relates his services as a soldier and administrator. It is also a document of propaganda as well as being factual in many elements.

Aurelius Victor (c.320–c.390). Latin pagan historian, perhaps born near Cirta/Constantine in Algeria. Marcellinus informs that he met Julian at Sirmium where he served as an official (361) and it is thought that *De Caesaribus* was written there and that Julian subsequently read it in Naissus, appointing him to the post of governor of Pannonia Secunda. He held the post for perhaps four years and then became prefect of Rome in 388 or 389. He was well informed and not religiously biased. Akin to his contemporary Eutropius, he made use of one main source, the so-called *Kaisergeschichte* (now lost, and weak on historical explanation); although he was also influenced, in part, by Tacitus. His work contains much of his own perspectives rather than historical facts and this made it unpopular, but the *Historia Augusta*, Ioannes Lydus, and Paul the Deacon drew from Victor. His style is confusing, but his emphasis on the need for education, culture, honesty, and respect for tradition make him an exception among other pagan historians, and there is perhaps little reason not to accept his anecdotes as factual.

Candidus (fifth century). Greek historian; little is known about Candidus apart from his residency in Constantinople until 491. He appears to have been a reasonably credible source, having access to official documents. Even taking into account his pro-Isaurian bias he is of foremost importance for the time of emperors Leo and Zeno. However, his style of writing was heavily criticized by Photius, who appears to suggest that his narratives were an uneven collection of disparate elements.

Cassius Dio (c.140–c.230). Greek historian, born at Nicaea in Bithynia, Asia Minor; he entered the Roman Senate in 180, became an advocate under Commodus, served under Pertinax, *praetor* under Septimius Severus, consul around 222 in the reign of Elagabalus, proconsul of Africa under Severus Alexander, governor of Dalmatia and Upper Pannonia, consul for a second time, before retiring in Nicaea. His work comprised 80 Books, covering the era from the legendary arrival of Aeneas in Italy to the reign of *Alexander Severus*. Books 36–60 survive; 36 and 55–60 have some missing content covering 68 BC – AD 47. The lost portions are partly supplied, for the earlier omissions, by Zonaras, and for some later gaps (Book 35 onwards) by Xiphilinus. In the Republican period, his sources were distorted by some writers; a factual basis could be established from others or from public records. For the second phase of his History, his writings are officially sanctioned published reports of events, although he proposes, on occasion, to express his own opinion based on what he has heard and read. The third period, of his own time, records events of which he had first-hand knowledge and his work is more detailed, with access to relevant official documents. He is favourable to Septimius Severus, and not disposed to Commodus, whose cruelty he witnessed at first hand.

Eunapius (c.345–after 414). Greek sophist, he was born in Sardis, Asia Minor and went to Athens to study rhetoric under the Prohaeresius, and returned to his native city to practise sophism. Eunapius' *History* survives only in fragments, although Zosimus' *New History* is largely based on his work. His History was staunchly anti-Christian and the pagan emperor Julian was its hero.

Eusebius (263–339). A Christian writer, *Chronicle*, appears to have been his first work, outlining the history of the world year by year. He drew on earlier sources, as may be expected – Julius Africanus and others, and partly at least – challenging their position. In *Ecclesiastical History* his bias is self-evident. *Life of Constantine* is regarded as a mixture of panegyric and narrative history and therefore controversial for this reason.

Eutropius (late fourth century). Latin historian; held several public offices, many of them illustrious and powerful, secretary under Constantinius II, Julian whom he accompanied on his ill-fated Persian expedition, and Valens. In 369 he became secretary of petitions (*magister memoriae*), from 371 to 372 he was proconsul of Asia, from 379 to 381 he served as prefect of Illyricum under Gratian, and he became a consul under Valentinian II in 387. These personal experiences shaped his detailed but brief history of Rome, written around 370 and commissioned by Valens. The worthiness of the history is traditionally debated, but in more recent years his impartiality has generally been ratified.

Gellius (125–185). Latin author and grammarian; there is no reason to doubt the testimony of Gellius, since he was resident in Rome for most of his life apart from a brief visit to Athens, and he is regarded as a credible source with few defects apart from his obscure style of writing.

Gregory of Nazianzus (c.329/330–c.390). Greek theologian, ordained a bishop and served as head of the orthodox Christian community in Constantinople, where he played a crucial role in formulating the classical doctrines of the Trinity and the person of Christ. A contemporary of Julian, the emperor embittered Christian writers against him after his decree of 17 June 362 requiring every schoolteacher to be approved by the local council and to have that approval officially sanctioned by the emperor. Julian decided that professing Christians were not to be recognized publicly as experts on the Greek language and intellectual heritage that formed cultural fabric of the empire. This resentment was expressed in Gregory's invective against the emperor and probably finished in 364, less than a year after Julian's death.

Herodian (170–240). Greek historian, perhaps from Antioch; he declared at the outset that he intended to write without bias. A senator, an equestrian *procurator*, or an imperial freedman, the most plausible opinions view him in the second role. His references to the finances and economics of the empire were unreliable. If one accepts his word that he was chronicling events between 180 and 238, of which he had personal experience or first-hand information, then he may be regarded as reliable. However, judgements pertaining to the worth of his History have considerable latitude. His use of speeches follows Dio, and veracity distorted by rhetoric and stereotypes, but it is nonetheless a work of its age and useful, despite its deficiencies.

Historia Augusta (fourth century). Our main source from the reign of Hadrian to Numerian; it has generally been regarded as problematic. The various criticisms of it question when it was written, the identity and number of its purported authors, their intent, and its historical substance, although there is also a degree of polarization on its usefulness. For these reasons it is used with caution and with the support of other sources where possible, a convention that is followed in the second and third chapters. There are some cases where it contains unique information, such as a reference to the Antonine Wall. It is now thought of as the work of a single author writing decades after the events that are chronicled, but his sources are probably reliable.

Hydatius (c.400–c.469). Latin theologian, Bishop of Aquae Flaviae in Gallaecia (modern Portugal). His *Chronicle* is the best source for events in the Iberian peninsula in the fifth century, and also sheds light on the Gothic–Roman treaty of 418–419. His perspective was Catholic and of course not favourably disposed to the Arian doctrine.

Ioannes Lydus (490–c.565). He was born in Philadelphia, Lydia, and became a scholar and intellectual at Constantinople in the Justinianic period, serving as one of the *magistriani* (clerks) in the bureau of the *magister memoriae*, one of the emperor's chief secretaries. This work celebrates a deep-rooted history, but it has a certain amount of unsound factual material, although this is a reflection of the intellectual climate of the sixth century. His reference to the value of Trajan's booty from Statilius Crito is intriguing, and Lydus must have been party to an original record, or a later copy.

Ioannes Malalas (c.490–c.575). Greek chronicler; little is known about him. He was probably born around 490 and was perhaps educated at Antioch from where he later moved to Constantinople, possibly after 535.

He refers to a great persecution of Christians in his writing; therefore, it may be distorted by either his own bias or that of an earlier historian on whose work he relied for this period. His credibility as a source has been questioned by some, but more recently it has been recognized that these criticisms do not take into account the extent to which Malalas was conditioned by contemporary knowledge and interpretation of the past and the world around him. For the period before emperor Zeno, he was obliged to rely on the written records of Greek and Latin authors. From the period of Zeno onwards (his own lifetime), he claims reliance on oral information.

Ioannes Zonaras (twelfth century). He was a Byzantine functionary and canonist, and his history is medieval. While in exile from Constantinople, Zonaras culled earlier chronicles and histories to compose an account of events from the Creation to the reign of Alexius Comnenus. For topics where his sources are lost or appear elsewhere in a more truncated form, his testimony and the identification of the texts on which he depends are of great importance. For his account of the first two centuries of the Principate, Zonaras used now-lost portions of Dio. From the point where his History ended to the reign of Theodosius the Great, he drew on new sources, notably John I (429–441) to produce a uniquely full historical narrative of the years 235–395.

Jerome (c.342–420). Latin theologian, born near Aquileia in Dalmatia and educated in rhetoric at Rome by the grammarian Aelius Donatus, returning to his home town in 370 where he established his first society of ascetics before going to Antioch where he was ordained presbyter by Bishop Paulinus. He visited Rome with Paulinus where he became a friend of Pope Damasus, who commissioned him to write a revised Latin version of the Psalms and New Testament; he translated Eusebius' *Chronicle* into Latin. He was a resident in Bethlehem at the time of the Vandal sack of Rome in 410 and his writings are coloured by the terrifying drama of this and those events that led to it. There is no reason to doubt the general veracity of these accounts but it is certainly the case that he was somewhat naïve in his assessment of political events. As a Christian he preferred to interpret the gloom as God's vengeance on a rotten society.

Jordanes (? died 552). Greek historian of Gothic descent; he was an imperial official in Constantinople where he wrote *Getica*. By his own admission he was poorly educated before his conversion to Christianity and this is reflected in the style of this work; it is mainly a compilation of events and personalities, including Attila the Hun whom he describes as the scourge of God and the Visigoth Alaric who thrice sacked Rome. For all its faults it is crucial as the earliest Gothic history that has survived, and it gives much information in this period that is not provided elsewhere.

Josephus (37–100). Jewish historian, writing in Greek; his first work, *Jewish War*, is considered to be his finest, written under the patronage of Vespasian, serving as a warning to the east of the futility of further opposition. The Parthian threat also continued to loom large in this period and there is little doubt that their readership was anticipated as betrayed in a passage on the Roman army. *Jewish Antiquities*, is regarded as the *magnum opus* of Josephus, and contrasts markedly from the *Jewish War*. It was compiled under the oppressive reign of Domitian, enemy of literature and especially historical writing. For this reason it is considered that the work was set aside and only concluded later with the assistance of others. Its purpose was to magnify the Jewish race in the eyes of the Graeco-Roman world through a record of its ancient and glorious history and may be regarded as objective in this sense.

Julius Caesar (102–44 BC). Born in Rome, the career of the soldier and politician was truly meteoric. He served in the Mithridatic wars and in Spain; entered Roman politics as a 'democrat' against the senatorial government; ascended the *cursus honorum*; became the leader of the First Triumvirate (with Crassus and Pompey); conquered Gaul and invaded Britain twice; became forced into civil war; and ultimately became master of the Roman world, implementing reforms before his assassination. Caesar's Commentaries on the Gallic War are thought to have been published early in 51 BC, timed to convey to the Roman people that he was an eminent strategist and statesman, and also to the Senate as a vindication of his campaigns and conquests in defence of the Republic. Collectively, the work is probably a popular edition of the despatches (*epistulae*) sent by Caesar to the Senate each year.

Lactantius (c.240–c.325). Christian, Latin apologist, originally a pagan, possibly born at Cirta/Constantine in Algeria; he moved to Nicomedia where he taught rhetoric and became part of the imperial circle, acquainted with the Tetrarchs, and also Constantine. He converted to Christianity before the Persecutions, and was instrumental in shaping Constantine's religious policy. He is naturally flattering of his patron, and biased to the emperor's pagan predecessors, focusing on their negative aspects. His works are, though, especially engaging in places.

Libanius (314–c.393). A contemporary of Julian and Valens, he was a Greek sophist from Antioch, and one of the last great proponents of Greek paganism who supported Julian, hence the apparent conflation of the two great battles and his sympathy for the outcome of both events. For the purposes of the present book, the translation of *Upon Avenging Julian* is a little difficult to unravel, since at first reading it is hard to establish whether he is referring to the defeat of Julian in Persia or that of Valens at Adrianople, but it appears to praise the performance of the latter in the face of divine providence. It is essentially a defence against Christian writers, such as Sozomen, a Nicene ecclesiastic, who blamed Valens, an Arian Christian, for the catastrophe.

Marcellinus Comes (sixth century). Latin chronicler, born possibly near Skopje in Macedonia, and moved to Constantinople where he served under Justinian I as *kankellarios* before the accession of the emperor in 527 and subsequently received the rank of *comes* (count). His chronicle extended initially from 379 to 518 as a formal continuation of Jerome, adding a sequel down to 534. Its perspective is eastern, with a focus on Constantinople. It provides many interesting and important details, including the first notion of the fall of Rome in 476. There is no reason to doubt his assessment on the gravity of the Hunnic War that afflicted the eastern empire in the fifth century.

Marcus Aurelius (121–180). Emperor and Stoic philosopher, born at Rome, was adopted by his uncle Antoninus Pius. He studied and practised Stoicism, and married Faustina Minor, daughter of Pius, and succeeded him as emperor in 161, sharing some of the burdens with Lucius Verus. *Meditations* comprises reflections written in periods of solitude during the emperor's military campaigns. Originally intended for his private guidance, it remains an important work for students of Stoicism as well as a guide to moral life, and its integrity is widely embraced.

Ovid (43 BC – AD c.17/18) Latin poet, born at Sulmo, modern Solmona in the Apennines, in the year in which the two consuls, Hirtius and Pansa, fell in battle during the civil war which followed the assassination of Caesar, and was a contemporary of Virgil and Horace. He was banished by Augustus to the island of Tomi on the Black Sea. The alleged reason for the sentence was the immorality of his poem *The Art of Love*, but it is thought that it had been published many years before, apparently without creating a scandal at the time, and that the real motive was that he had caused the emperor some grave offence. The *Fasti* was in fact dedicated to Augustus.

Panegyrici Latini (first, third, fourth centuries). The collection of manuscripts that form this corpus are copies of a lost original. The works are speeches of praise and belong to the epideictic oratory or display oratory, and they are panegyrics. Pliny's *Panegyric to Trajan* is the first of these and served as a model for those that followed. The remaining eleven orations are much later in date, ranging from 289 to 389, and are addressed to the emperors Maximian, Constantius I, Constantine, Julian, and Theodosius I. Most of the authors are anonymous and appear to have been Gallic and teachers of rhetoric, several had held, or were to hold, imperial office.

Paterculus (c.20 BC – AD 31). Latin historian in the reigns of Augustus and Tiberius and served as a military tribune in Thrace, Macedonia, Greece, and

Asia Minor, from AD 4 to 12 or 13 as a cavalry officer, and *legatus* in Germany and Pannonia, was *quaestor* in 7, and *praetor* in 15. The weakness of the source is its hasty compilation to commemorate the elevation to the consulship of his friend Marcus Vinicius in 30. However, it may be regarded as the most successful and readable of all the abridgements of Roman history. There can be little doubt that he was well informed as a participant in the War of the Batons.

Philo (25 BC – AD 50). Greek historian; born to a prominent Jewish family in Alexandria, centre of the Jewish Diaspora, and also a centre of Hellenistic culture. He became a philosopher and was trained in Greek and Jewish learning. Philo says he was part of an embassy sent by the Alexandrian Jews to Caligula, carrying a petition to secure the rights of the Alexandrian Jews against Greek persecution, and he was also aggrieved that Caligula was planning on having a statue of himself erected in the Second Temple. Colson suggests this occurred in 39 and that they were received by the emperor in person. There can be little doubt that his writings were not favourably disposed towards Caligula, and it is intriguing that Philo experienced something of his personality, although his writings perhaps contribute in a limited way to his reign.

Pliny the Elder (23/24–79). Latin historian, born at Como and is referred to as 'the Elder' to distinguish him from his nephew. In 23 he studied at Rome before entering military service in Germany and then returning to Rome where he studied law. He rose to distinction towards the end of Nero's reign as *procurator* in Spain and returned to Rome once more, and was admitted into Vespasian's inner circle. He was in command of the fleet at Misenum on the Bay of Naples in 79 when Vesuvius erupted and he subsequently perished. *Natural History* is dedicated to Titus and was completed two years before the author's death. It is an encyclopaedia of astronomy, meteorology, geography, mineralogy, zoology, and botany. It has been criticized as a second-hand compilation from the works of others without critical selection of facts and fiction, although the value of this work is also accepted, since it is diligent, accurate, and free from prejudice. His comment on the magnificence of the Templum Pacis is probably justified but should be tempered with his Flavian sympathies. His knowledge on the extraction of gold in Spain should be considered to be reliable.

Pliny the Younger (c.61–c.112). Latin historian born at Como in Italy and a contemporary of Trajan, and also his predecessors, Domitian and Nerva. He had a successful senatorial career; many of his personal and professional letters survive. Pliny was on favourable terms with Trajan who appointed him consul in 100; his one surviving speech, devoted to thanking the emperor, is known as the *Panegyricus*. Pliny's comment on Trajan's victory should be interpreted in terms of flattery.

Plutarch (c.49–c.121). Greek historian; born in northern Boeotia and educated in Platonic philosophy at Athens. He served as deputy governor of northern Greece and travelled extensively in Greece, Asia Minor, Egypt, and Italy, and lived in Rome for a considerable time where he served as an imperial official, under successive emperors, so he was well informed, dying in the reign of Hadrian. His literary style has been criticized: especially the closing sections of his biographies, which are regarded as often fanciful and contrived and of no historical value. This perhaps does not detract from particular observations of buildings, as in the case of the Temple of Janus.

Porfyrius Optatianus (fourth century). Latin poet, a former citizen of Rome, who lived in exile at Achaea, although it is not clear why he was banished there. He composed a series of poems to Constantine that were essentially panegyrical to win favour with the emperor to coincide with his Vicennalia (twentieth anniversary), celebrated at Nicomedia in 325 and in the following year in Rome. His ploy proved to be successful and he was recalled to the eternal city, so the extant literature tends to cast Constantine and his deeds in a favourable light.

Possidius (370–437). Latin theologian, an eyewitness to the Vandal attack on Calama in 428 who took refuge with Augustine at Hippo in 428. There is little doubt that his testimony is a reliable account of events, although this should be tempered with the reality that the Vandals had recently converted to Arian Christianity and were viewed in the harshest terms by their Catholic 'hosts'; but there is little reason to doubt the violence and plunder that they inflicted.

Priscus (c.410–c.474). Greek historian born at Panion in Thrace, trained as a rhetoretician and became an imperial diplomat. He was particularly well informed and met Attila in person while on a diplomatic mission at his camp in the former province of Dacia in 449. Although he was a Christian writer his chronicles are without religious bias and he is generally regarded as a credible source. His History is a lost work since no manuscript survives that contains all of the eight original works.

Procopius (sixth century). Greek historian, born at Caesarea in Palestine and trained as a lawyer. In 527 he was made legal advisor and secretary of Belisarius, commander against the Persians, and went with him in 533 against the Vandals and in 535 against the Ostrogoths. After 540 he returned to Constantinople. He may have been the Procopius who was prefect of Constantinople in 562, but the date of his death (after 558) is unknown. Procopius' *History of the Wars* and *On Buildings* provide fascinating insights into the reign of Justinian, but were panegyrical in their intent; his *Secret History* does the reverse.

Prosper (c.390–c.456). Latin writer and theologian, he was a native of Aquitaine and perhaps educated in Marseille. Prosper was a disciple of Augustine, embracing his teachings amid the religious controversy of the time. He is a prime source for the Gothic–Roman treaty of 418–419. He moved to Rome on the accession of Pope Leo the Great in 440. His chronicle ends in 455, the year of the Vandal sack, and he was perhaps a credible witness to events.

Seneca (c.4 BC/AD 1–65). Latin historian born at Corduba (Cordova) in Spain, who faced some difficulties, and exile, in the reign of Claudius but became tutor to the future emperor Nero in 49, and then *praetor* in the following year, and the most important public and literary figure at Rome in his reign. *De Providentia* was probably written after his exile and he would naturally have sought to extol the benefits of Roman civilization across large parts of the empire under his patron.

Sidonius Apollinaris (c.430–c.487). Latin historian, born at Lugdunum and of Gallo-Roman extraction. He married Papianilla, daughter of emperor Avitus in whose honour he recited a panegyric at Rome on 1 January 456. He later joined a rebellion, it seems, but was finally reconciled to the emperor Majorian and delivered a panegyric on him at Lyon in 458. In 467 he led a deputation to the emperor Anthemius, and on 1 January 468 recited his third panegyric at Rome. He returned to Gaul in 469 and became Bishop of Auvergne at Clermont-Ferrand. He upheld his people in resisting the Visigoths. After Auvergne was ceded to them in 475, he was imprisoned but soon resumed his bishopric, and was canonized after his death.

Strabo (c.64 BC – c.AD 22). Greek historian and Stoic philosopher, born at Amasia in Pontus. He studied at Nysa in Asia Minor and after 44 BC at Rome. He travelled in Italy and the eastern empire, visiting Rome in 35, 31, and 29 BC, and befriended Athenodorus, a teacher of Augustus. There is some debate as to whether *Geography* was written there or in Amasia, where he spent the remaining part of his life. He was candid about the source of his information, which was based on his own experiences and observations and gleaned from others by word of mouth or in writing. Much of what he recorded was probably written in his homeland. There is little reason to consider that his list of exports from Britain is erroneous, and he may have received this intelligence on one of his visits to Rome.

Suetonius (c.70–c.130). Latin historian, born at Verona in Italy and rose to high office, serving as secretary of studies and director of imperial archives under Trajan and as Hadrian's secretary, although in 119 the emperor dismissed him for his intimacy with empress Sabina. Suetonius conveys strong images of his biographical subjects, they more or less largely agree with other sources. He is negative towards Caesar, Tiberius, Caligula, and Nero; and flattering of Germanicus, and mostly of the Flavians. These views are perhaps explained by assuming that Suetonius simply followed the traditional accounts given by preceding historians on whom he drew as sources of information.

Sulpicius Severus (c.360–c.420). Latin historian born in Aquitania. A member of a prominent family, he studied law in Bordeaux and converted to Christianity around 389 together with his friend Paulinus of Nola. Under the influence of Bishop Martin of Tours he organized a type of monastic life on his estates for himself and his friends. His extant works include *On the Life of St. Martin*, which is an apology of asceticism; and a universal chronicle to 400, which is an important source for the history of the fourth century. The book is an attempt to present a 'breviarium' of history from a Christian perspective but also incorporated pagan writings, including, perhaps, a lost work by Tacitus.

Tacitus (c.56–c.113). Latin historian, born in north-western Italy or southern Gaul and studied rhetoric to equip himself for administrative office. At the beginning of *Annals* is the phrase '*sine ira et studio*', a claim that he is free from bias, and a similar assertion is penned at the beginning of *Histories*. Both works totalled 30 books, but a number are missing. It is well established that his biographical accounts of Claudius, Galba, Otho, and Vitellius tend to be less flattering than those of their Flavian successors under whom he served, with the exception of his portrayal of Domitian's oppressive rule, and his sections on this period were either written in secrecy or after the emperor's death. He was married to the daughter of Agricola, governor of Britannia, so his sentiments tend towards the favourable in this regard.

Themistius (c.317–c.388). A pagan Greek, he was born in Paphlagonia, in northern Anatolia, and trained as a philosopher and rhetorician. Essentially a panegyrist, favourable with several emperors from Constantius II to Theodosius I, but his style is informative of its time and relates some interesting details.

Victor of Vita (fifth century). Latin theologian, bishop of the province of Byzacena. His account focuses on the Arian Vandal persecution of the Catholic Christians in North Africa, so it is in a sense biased to some degree by inherent doctrinal issues. Nonetheless, there is little reason to question the broad credibility of Victor's account of Vandal aggression.

Zosimus (fifth to sixth century). Greek historian; little is known of his life apart from that he was *advocatus fisci* (imperial lawyer) in Constantinople and became *comes* (count). He chronicled from the Augustan period to 410, ending before Rome's sack, and completed his work after 498. For the fourth and early fifth centuries he made extensive and uncritical use of the work of Eunapius and Olympiodorus. He was a pagan and this colours his perspective, viewing the decadence of the empire as a consequence of the rejection of pagan beliefs. He is naturally hostile to Constantine the Great and Theodosius I and favourable to Julian, in the manner of Eunapius.

Abbreviations

AMH	Ammianus Marcellinus, *History*
ARG	Augustus, *Res Gestae*
AVDC	Aurelius Victor, *De Caesaribus*
CG	*Chronica Gallica*
CH	*Chronicle of Hydatius*
CIL	*Corpus Inscriptionum Latinarum*
DRH	Dio, *Roman History*
EC	Eusebius, *Chronicle*
EEH	Eusebius, *Ecclesiastical History*
ETB	Eutropius, *The Breviarium*
HA	*Historia Augusta*
HE	Herodian, *History of the Empire*
HZ	*History of Zonaras*
JJA	Josephus, *Jewish Antiquities*
JJW	Josephus, *Jewish War*
LCL	Loeb Classical Library
LDMP	Lactantius, *De Mortibus Persecutorum*
PL	*Panegyrici Latini*
PNH	Pliny, *Natural History*
SL	Suetonius, *Lives of the Twelve Caesars*
TAg	Tacitus, *Agricola*
TAn	Tacitus, *Annals*
TH	Tacitus, *Histories*
ZNH	Zosimus, *New History*

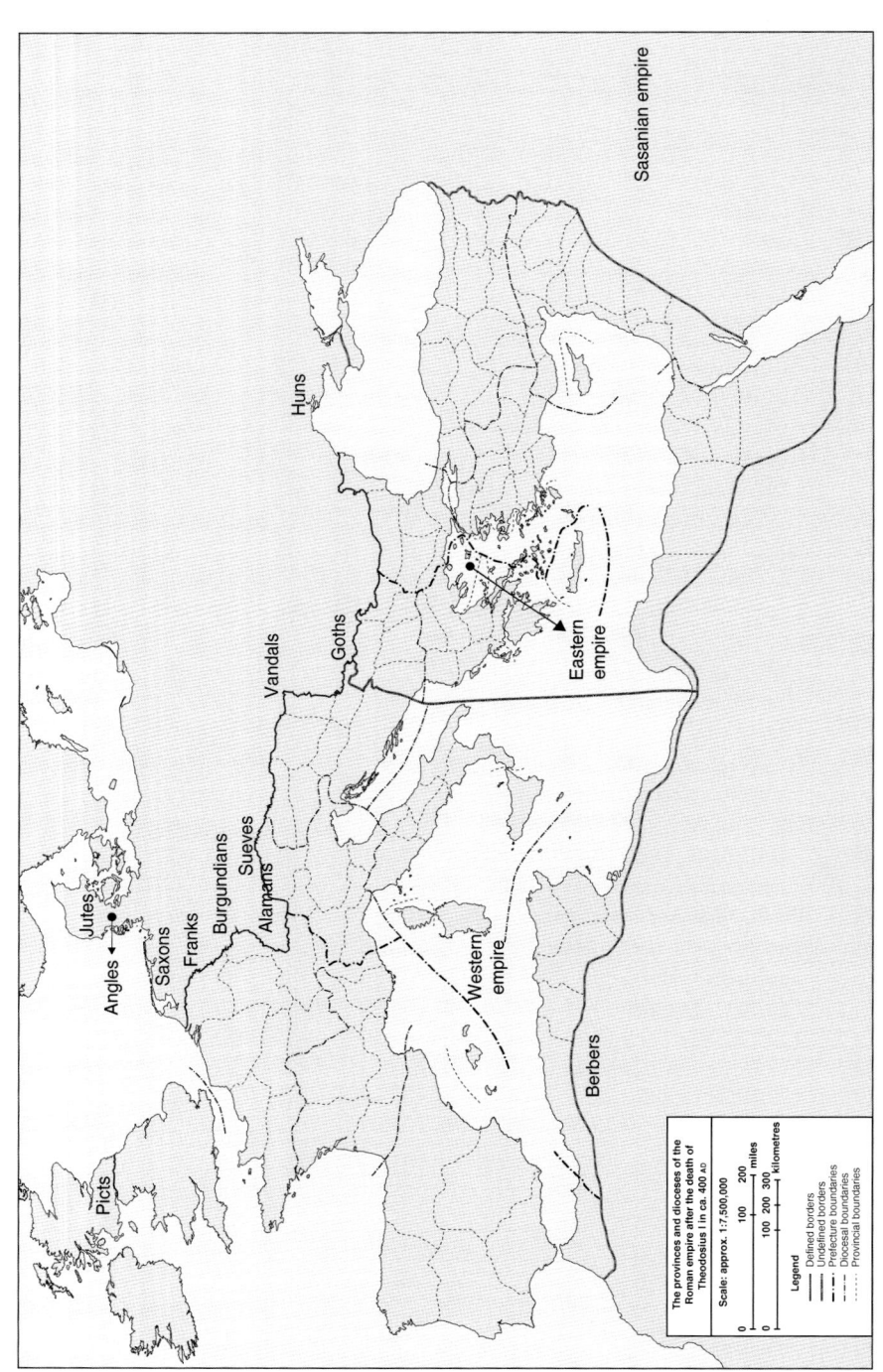

Picts

Angles →
Saxons
Franks
Burgundians
Sueves
Alamans
Jutes
Vandals
Goths
Huns
Western
empire
Eastern
empire
Berbers
Sasanian empire

The provinces and dioceses of the
Roman empire after the death of
Theodosius I in ca. 400 AD

Scale: approx. 1:7,500,000

0   100   200
                              miles
0   100   200   300
                          kilometres

Legend

———— Defined borders
——— Undefined borders
—·—·— Prefecture boundaries
—··—··— Diocesal boundaries
·········· Provincial boundaries

Map 1 The Roman empire in the early fifth century.

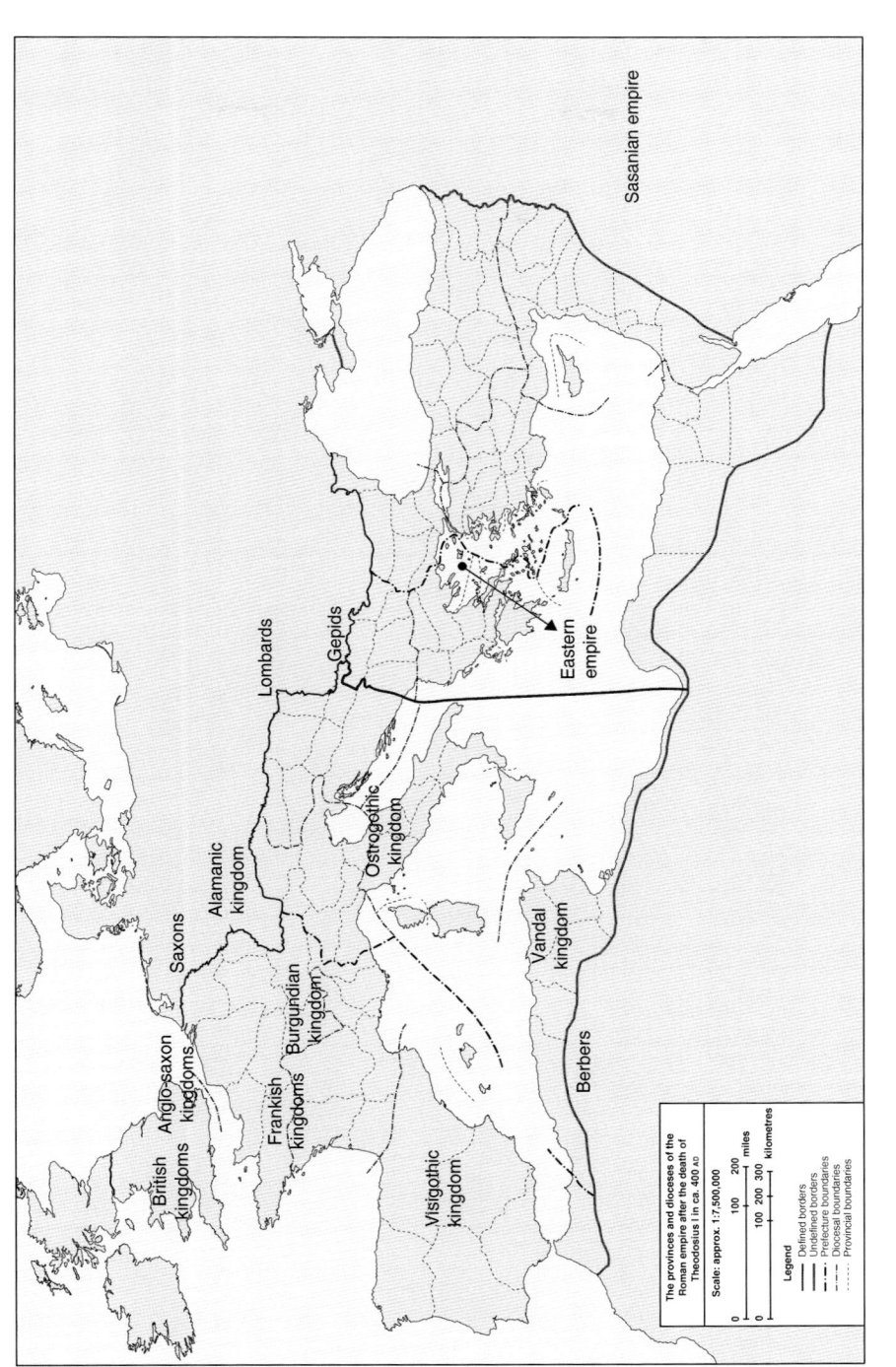

Map 2 The new political order in the early sixth century.

Introduction

Let Rome in Tiber melt and the wide arch of the ranged empire fall.

Antony and Cleopatra
William Shakespeare

This short passage from Shakespeare's tragedy implies that the failure of the Roman state was enshrined in the psyche of Renaissance literature.[1] Of course, the period that Shakespeare is referring to is the end of the Republic, but nonetheless, the notion of a fallen empire is conflated with it. Two hundred years later, in the fading years of the Enlightenment, Edward Gibbon published *History of the Decline and Fall of the Roman Empire*. In six epic volumes he chronicled the demise of the ancient superpower – its root cause, he suggested, was the erosion of civic virtue, fanned by the destructive flames of the Church; its effect, the unthinkable fall of Rome to the barbarians and the end of the civilized world.[2] The impact of this thesis ignited a debate that to a considerable extent has been fuelled by western consciousness, and fear, about its own demise. In the words of the American historian Glen Bowersock: 'From the eighteenth century onward we have been obsessed with the fall: it has been valued as an archetype for every perceived decline, and, hence, as a symbol for our own fears'.[3] This was reemphasized a little more than a decade later by Cullen Murphy, who compared the perceived decline of the US with that of Rome.[4] The fall of Rome has also found its expression in the verses of the English poet W.H. Auden[5] and the popular lyrics of the Australian musician James Michael Reyne.[6]

Historiography

This calamity has been linked to a range of factors that are as overwhelming as they are familiar, such as civil wars, according to Adrian Goldsworthy;[7] lead poisoning, as posited by Rudolph Kobert, Alfred Neuburger, Seabury Gilfillan, and Jerome Nriagu;[8] plague, as suggested by William McNeill;[9] also, military deficiency from the perspective of Arther Ferrill;[10] and multi-causal explanations as espoused by Michael Grant.[11] The German scholar

Alexander Demant listed no fewer than 210 reasons why the Roman empire declined and fell.[12]

For Gibbon, his anti-Catholic stance drove his assertion that Christianity swayed civic ambition to apathy; and the role of the Church in the fall of Rome was also an essential factor for the British historian Arnold Hugh Martin Jones.[13] This theory has crossed the Rubicon of the twenty-first century. For instance, Michael Whitby regards the rise of Christianity as a reason that contributed to the collapse of the western empire.[14] Likewise, the 'Pirenne Thesis', espoused by the Belgian scholar Henri Pirenne in the 1930s,[15] had a profound impact on subsequent thought, notably the influential Irish historian Peter Brown in the 1970s. The crux of this idea contended that the barbarians were eager to adopt Roman civilization, and they were instrumental in metamorphosing it into the early medieval Holy Roman Empire. In other words, there was not a decline or fall but a fundamental cultural and religious transformation.[16]

Some scholars do not accept the notion of a peaceful transition. The Irish historian John Bagnall Bury regarded the end of Rome as catastrophic, caused by economic decline, the influx of Germanic peoples and their enlistment in the army, and a diminished military capability.[17] More recently, Peter Heather cited external factors as the root cause of the collapse of the western empire, notably the rise of the Sasanian state and the impact on barbarian tribes caused by the arrival of the Huns in the fourth century.[18] Bryan Ward-Perkins has argued a plausible case that Germanic and Asiatic tribes precipitated the fall of the west.[19]

Some years ago I looked at the financial impact imposed on the Roman empire by the Sasanians, and the profound repercussions on imperial fortunes that stemmed from Persian military prowess.[20] My view is that conflict with the Sasanians had an indirect impact on the fortunes of the west but I think that the root cause for the fall in the fifth century is bound up with the impact of barbarian tribal confederacies on the economic infrastructure, which drastically reduced military numbers and overall capability – the Roman army was still an effective militia but not efficient enough in numerical terms. I think there is also a strong case for arguing that the Persians impacted on the plight of the east, losing its African and Syrian provinces to the Arabs in the seventh century, but it could also be argued that the pressure of the eastern Roman empire on the Sasanian state had the same effect, each power slugged it out to the bitter end, weakening their resources and making them easy prey for the Muslim invaders.[21]

Hostile takeover and collapse versus peaceful accommodation and transformation

It is reasonable to say that the influx and settlement of barbarians in the west is recognized as an historical event, and arguments are polarized: on the one hand, that Rome was wrested by barbaric aggression and harsh and chaotic rule was implemented; on the other, that they were peacefully accommodated and there followed a transition to a new world order. It should be stressed from the outset that I support the notion that the western Roman empire *did fall* as a consequence of barbarian violence in the fifth century. It is argued that there was a decline in place by the third century, but this was gradual, and accelerated in the fifth century.

Sources and the limits of inference

Primary texts and documents

The enormity of the Roman empire – from Scotland to North Africa, and western Britain to Iraq – was such that it is not possible to reconstruct anywhere near the full picture based on material and textual sources. The recovery of archaeological evidence is random at best in the urban and rural spheres, and the information that may be gleaned from them is no more than a *proxy* indication of events, and the central arguments are *propositions* rather than conclusions; it is important to emphasize this at an early stage, if not least in an attempt to stave off a fraction of the inevitable critique that this book will attract.

Primary sources, that naturally form a cornerstone of this book, and their inherent biases, have already been addressed, and as an archaeologist, rather than an historian, I am fortunate that the filtering process applied to the Roman period by many historians with such incisive skill has simplified the task of dealing with this problem. Where possible, for the sake of consistency, I have used the English translations of the original Greek and Latin works published by the Loeb Classical Library (LCL), founded by James Loeb in 1911 and published by Harvard University Press, although they do not cover every source and it has been necessary to reference other translations.

Important is the administrative study of *civitates* in Gaul, listed in the *Notitia Galliarum*, as outlined by Jill Harries;[22] and the list of bishoprics compiled for the North African provinces by Joseph Mesnage.[23] These were instrumental in helping me to attempt to gauge the loss of territorial economic units and administrative collapse as various areas were settled and conquered by barbarian tribes in those regions in the fifth century.

Archaeological data

Archaeological evidence is of course crucial but is inevitably subjective, especially in terms of the relative quality of the methodology applied in the field and its interpretation based on the theoretical standpoint of individual archaeologists, and also chronological attributions for different phases of particular sites, urban or rural. That said, the inclusion of synthetic works through the course of the study has benefitted enormously from a body of excellent scholarship. Especially informative in recent years are the *Oxford Studies on the Roman Economy*, edited by Andrew Wilson and Alan Bowman. These comprise a number of papers that analyse quantitative archaeological data.[24] I draw on other studies of this kind, for instance, Michel Ponsich and Eva Carr in the Iberian peninsula;[25] and those of Paul Van Ossel and Pierre Ouzoulias in France.[26]

Trade

The present work concentrates on the reduction of booty, agricultural product, and the extraction of precious metals in the demise of the western Roman empire, although other commodities were essentially part of an intra- and inter-regional trade. Arts and crafts were also major components of this commerce. Marble – Carrara, Island, Pentelic, Proconnesian, etc. – was in great demand, as evident in civic and private buildings across the empire, and in the visibility of sculptures in museums. This was really the product of aristocratic and imperial patronage and a conspicuous marker of economic prosperity. Other commodities were of course traded, such as bronze statuary – especially from the Greek East – but it is more difficult to quantify the trade of people, grain, lentils, beans and pulses, fruit, flowers, hides, furs, spices, papyrus, basketry, etc. simply because these items do not survive[27] – unless they are recovered in arid or anaerobic contexts. Suffice to say that the international trade of *all* products was affected by the political events that were to befall Rome from the late fourth century onwards. The crucial factor here is that the bulk of consumables were produced and extracted in the rural sphere, hence the focus on the hinterland in the chapters that follow.

Epigraphic evidence

Perhaps one of the most useful tools available is the epigraphic database of the *Epigraphische Datenbank Heidelberg*. This enables the user to interrogate it comprehensively, and it presently has 72,883 inscriptions of all categories (dedicatory/building, epitaph, honorific, etc.) and their social attribution (Augustales, emperors and members of the imperial household, *decurions*, etc.). For the purposes of my study the concentration is on imperial building inscriptions and those under the patronage of *decurions* and other officials. This has enabled me to attempt an examination of the relative number of constructions in both contexts over the entire period (27 BC – AD 476), and broadly speaking helps to paint a picture of economic conditions and how these relate to the historical picture. This should be tempered with the fact that inscriptions record repairs and refurbishments as well as new constructions, and many of the inscriptions are associated with little or none of their original structures.

Another resource is the *Corpus Inscriptionum Latinarum* (CIL), initiated by Theodor Mommsen in 1853. The corpus is administered under the auspices of the Berlin-Brandenburg Academy of Sciences and Humanities and comprises seventeen volumes of around 180,000 inscriptions. Its inclusion of Christian inscriptions is especially useful for painting a picture of ecclesiastical patronage. A selective number of inscriptions are cited to gain an impression of the sponsorship of bishops in the civic sphere, rather than an exhaustive inclusion of the quantitative data set.

Interpretative framework

Of course, the question of *why* the western empire fell cannot be tackled without clarification of *what* happened – unravelling the historical 'facts' as they are presently understood. Fundamentally, I think that the traditional 'waxing and waning' view should be refined. This begins with a critique of the so-called prosperity and relative peace of the *Pax Romana*, spanning the reigns of Augustus to Marcus Aurelius, followed by the apparent 'crisis of the third century', a return to stability under Diocletian and Constantine, a decline in the late fourth century, and a fall in the fifth. This study focuses on the pattern of conflict in the first three centuries and how serious this was for the western empire. Linked with this are the chronological and territorial movements of – and conflict with – the tribal confederacies in this period and their later developments.

It is emphasized that economic considerations are of paramount importance, the generation of agricultural product (cereals, wine, olives, and livestock) in the hinterlands of the *civitates* (city-states) in the western empire, and how this diminished to the detriment of the state – the precarious seesaw of income and expenditure and its irreversible tipping point. For the administrative structure of the *civitates*, the work of A.H.M. Jones was helpful. He defined them as the basic economic units of the Roman empire (with some exceptions), as well as the dominance of the agricultural sphere and its economic role.[28] Also, I think that the taxes and trade model of Keith Hopkins, with some necessary refinements, is important for the arguments presented.[29]

State revenue, with the exception of mineral wealth – gold and silver – and of course booty, was agricultural across the Roman empire, generated within the city-state framework of 'circumscribed' self-government. Tenant farmers (*coloni*), sold their produce in the urban market-place and paid a proportion of their revenue in tax and rent. Their landowning overlords, who were often pagan, and, later, ecclesiastical officials in turn paid parts of their tax to the state and funded public building projects (euergetism), although there were other forms of taxation in cash and kind. A substantial chunk of this rural-based taxation was consumed by maintaining the army, and what remained underpinned the lifestyle of the imperial household and the state bureaucracy, although the concentration is more on military spending to maintain the army at that level established by Augustus, and subsequently increased by Domitian, Caracalla, Diocletian, and Constantine.

Agricultural product, booty, and precious mineral extraction were the trinity of income in the Roman world. This is central to the arguments that follow, and as the Roman empire matured, these three foundation pillars began to crumble. The first of these to fall was booty, then arable and pastoral product, followed by the loss of mineral extraction and production. This is gauged in the context of economic theories, as espoused by Thomas Malthus, by others, and recently by Peter Temin; although this book does not really depend on them but rather empirical data, they are nonetheless complementary.[30]

The Roman empire was essentially a slave-society, where chattel-slavery was the norm, and slave-owners had complete mastery (*dominium*) over the physical wellbeing of slaves. They were procured chiefly as captives in war, as the victims of organized piracy and brigandage, through natural reproduction, and through trade.[31] Modern estimates put the number of slaves in Italy alone at the end of the Republic at around two million. By extension, slaves may be regarded as a component of booty and their economic importance was substantial. In the context of the arguments presented, booty incorporates precious material items (jewellery, gold, silver) as well as slaves.

This study entails an examination of some key issues, such as shifting patterns of agricultural production; the changing character of the urban and rural landscapes, including settlement and population decline; abandonment of land (*agri deserti*); the increasing burden of *decurions*; their 'metamorphosis' into ecclesiastical officials (notably bishops); reduced civic patronage; and militarization of elites. Other aspects addressed are the supply of grain to the army; how soldiers were paid; and the size and character of the army.

As the present book is about the Roman world I felt that it was appropriate to mention cities by their ancient names, although of course some names have not changed, such as Aquileia, Ostia, and Rome, but there are some exceptions where modern names are used for reasons of clarity. In a similar vein there has been a tendency to avoid the naming of modern territories and the names of Roman provinces are given. In some these encompass more than one or several modern countries. For instance, Dalmatia incorporates parts of Croatia, Serbia, and Slovenia; a large area of Bosnia and Herzegovina; and all of Montenegro. For this reason it was also less cumbersome to refer to provinces (Map 1).

Barbarian ethnicity

I have tried to avoid getting embroiled in distracting issues. A particular thorn is the attribution of ethnic identities, since archaeological evidence – burials and material culture – do not often equate with what we may associate with known tribal groupings.[32] While I draw on this material, some of which may be associated with particular tribes (Alan, Burgundian, Frankish, Gothic, Hunnic, Suevic), more emphasis is laid on coinage. This avoids the 'ethnicity problem', the concentration being more on sovereignty as expressed on pseudo-imperial issues and later coins minted in the name of individual kings.[33]

Romanization

Another contentious term is 'Romanization', its use has attracted criticism in recent decades,[34] a concept rejected by John Barrett, 1997; Greg Woolf, 1998; and David Mattingly, 2006. Others have suggested its reconsideration, such as Simon Keay and Nicola Terrenato, and Robert Hitchner. Louise Revell defines 'being Roman' as something that has 'infinite expressions generated through the varying experiences of the individual peoples of the past', and avoids the value-laden term of 'Romanitas', replacing it with 'pre-Roman', 'non-Roman', and 'Roman-ness'. I have always felt that Romanization is useful and relevant to describe the Roman cultural impact on areas that it assimilated through conquest or interaction. I think that Alan Bowman and Andrew Wilson made a sensible point when he suggested that: 'it is undeniable that the growth and development of the empire involved the spread of institutional, linguistic, cultural, economic, and religious phenomena which were in some important sense "Roman" or promulgated by Rome'.[35] This is a point of view that I embrace, and the term is used to describe this process where it occurred.

Chronological scope

Logically, the historical span of the present work is essentially the duration of the western Roman empire (27 BC – AD 476). This last date was chosen as a cutoff point because Roman sovereignty terminated with the forced abdication of Romulus Augustulus. I also consider a brief outline of political events, and their ramifications, in the late Republican period. Also, it is pertinent to explore certain aspects after 476, such as the disappearance of the villa in the former territories of the western empire, and how the eastern empire continued to prosper.

Summary

To return to Shakespeare's 'wide arch of the ranged empire', the Roman state was a virtual empire in the late Republican period, run by three oligarchs – Antony, Lepidus, and Octavian – that encompassed a vast territory expanse, accrued by Caesar, Pompey, Crassus, and their predecessors. Under Augustus this geographical block was transformed into the Roman empire and expanded. For many, his reign was the hallmark of might and culture in the history of Rome. This is understandable given the achievements of the Augustan period, foreshadowed by his victory at the Battle of Actium in 31 BC, and the great cultural programme that followed his accession in 27 BC. Beneath this veneer of greatness, there were tremors of a magnitude that I believe are symptomatic of the fate that would befall Rome. For this reason the present study begins with the so-called *Pax Romana*, or the *Pax Augusta* as it is sometimes called, after the emperor who 'initiated it'.

Notes

1 Shakespeare, *Antony and Cleopatra*, Act I, Scene I, lines 34–35.
2 Gibbon, I–VI, 1776–1789.
3 Bowersock, 1996, 31.
4 Murphy, 2007.
5 *The Fall of Rome*, 1947.
6 *Fall of Rome*, 1987, Capitol Records.
7 Goldsworthy, 2003, 214; 2009, 405–415.
8 Kobert, 1909; Neuburger, 1930, 434; Gilfillan, 1965, 53–60; 1990; Nriagu, 1983a; 1983b, 105–116; 1983c, 660–663. Lead pollution has been measured in Greenland ice cores from industrial output in the Roman empire; Hong, Candelone, Patterson, and Boutron, 1994, 1841–1843. However, the lead poisoning theory has been challenged in different ways by Scarborough, 1984, 469–475; Hodge, 2002, 308; Needleman and Needleman, 1985, 63–94; and Delile, Blichert-Toft, Goiran, Keay, and Albarède, 2014, 6594–6599.
9 McNeill, 1976. The main problem with this theory is that a combination of archaeological and historical evidence suggests that the population of the western empire increased again after the third century, as did its army (Chapters 4 and 5), and it should be expected that it would have caused the collapse of the eastern empire as well.
10 Ferrill, 1986. His arguments are refuted in Chapter 5.
11 Grant, 1976. His multifaceted approach does not hold water in the face of archaeological data and more recent historical appraisals. For instance, he cites that there was a 'credibility gap' between the people and the government and the people and the imperial circle (164–182), but this does not take account of the social cohesion provided by bishops in the late Roman period. In all, he suggested that there were eleven factors that contributed to the fall of the western empire, some plausible, others are not.
12 Demant, 1984.
13 'The clergy successfully preached the doctrines of patience and pusillanimimity; the active virtues of society were discouraged; and the last remains of the military spirit were buried in the cloister . . .' Gibbon, IV.38.120. 'Finally, the Christian Church imposed a new class of idle mouths on the resources of empire . . . and as time went on more and more monasteries acquired landed endowments which enabled their inmates to devote themselves entirely to their spiritual duties.' Jones, 1964, II, 1046–1047. These assertions simply do not hold water, since we might have expected that they applied to the eastern empire where Christianity was more deeply embedded.
14 Whitby, 2008, 71–76.
15 Pirenne, 1937; 1939.
16 Brown, 1971; 1978.
17 His assessment of the fall of the Roman empire and its root causes are logical. For instance, a combination of four contingent events were to blame for the crisis: the invasions of the Huns in Europe; the defeat and death of Valens at Adrianople;

the Visigothic settlement and death of Theodosius I; and his appointment of the inept emperor Honorius; all factors he claimed had nothing to do with the condition of the empire (Bury, 1958, II, 311–313).

18 Heather, 2005.
19 Ward-Perkins, 2005.
20 Merrony, 2002, 52–54; 2005, 33–35.
21 Howard-Johnston, 2006, 157–226.
22 Harries, 1978, 26–43.
23 Mesnage, 1912.
24 Bowman and Wilson, 2009; 2011; 2013.
25 Ponsich, 1974–1991; Carr, 1997, 2002.
26 Bowman and Wilson, 2009.
27 Wilson, 2009, 214.
28 Jones, 1964, II, 712–714.
29 Hopkins, 1980, 101–125.
30 Malthus, 1798 (1826); Temin, 2013.
31 Bradley, 2014, 736–737.
32 'Clearly, the "traditional" narrative and the identification of the ethnicity of practices and, above all, artefacts were derived from the written texts because of their chronological and intellectual primacy. Archaeology was a johny-come-lately, in its turn shaped by the pre-existing textual categories . . .' Esmonde Cleary, 2013, 387. Also, Pohl, 2015, 255–258.
33 Grierson and Blackburn, 1986.
34 Barrett, 1997; Woolf, 1998; Mattingly, 2006. Others have suggested its reconsideration, such as Keay and Terrenato, 2001; Hitchner, 2009, 655; Scott, 2010, 557.
35 Bowman and Wilson, 2009, 17.

1   The purple cloak of deceit

> Janus Quirinus, which our ancestors ordered to be closed whenever there was peace, secured by victory, throughout the whole domain of the Roman people on land and sea, and which, before my birth is recorded to have been closed but twice in all since the foundation of the city, the senate ordered to be closed thrice while I was princeps.
>
> *Res Gestae Divi Augusti*
> Augustus

Widely regarded as the symbolical 'entrée' of the *Pax Romana*, Augustus' proud statement about the Temple of Janus emphasizes a general climate of peace during his long reign.[1] This autobiographical account is pictorially supported by a multitude of coins that were minted to convey that the new Roman world was at peace under the influence of a great emperor.[2] In 9 BC the Ara Pacis Augustae, the Augustan Altar of Peace, was consecrated by the Senate.[3] Its lower register depicts an exuberant scheme of vegetal decoration, alluding to the abundance and prosperity of the Augustan age.[4] This comprehensive ideology became a feature of architectural sculpture on, and in, many public buildings in Rome and elsewhere, instilling the notion of peace in the hearts and minds of Roman citizens, a message that would have been emphatic in elite circles, whom Augustus counted on for support.

In the present chapter the military developments are examined from the Augustan period to the end of the first century, particularly the superficiality of the *Pax Romana* that was perpetuated by the successors of the princeps. This demands an appropriate historical narrative, and this is supplemented with a number of comments and observations in the primary sources, and also archaeological and dated building inscriptions in the capital, Italy, and the western provinces.

The focus here is on the extreme volume of conflict that is not normally associated with the 'golden era' of the Roman empire. In particular, how precipitous Roman security in fact was, the overextension of its militia, and how the economy benefitted from its booty income to fund monumental building projects in Rome and elsewhere in the empire. Crucial to the chapters that follow are the Augustan military reforms, which demanded persistent warfare from a massive military apparatus in order to preserve the state and its economic wellbeing; thereafter placing the reign of numerous emperors in a dangerous situation.

The Julio-Claudian period: Augustus (27 BC – AD 14)

Augustus' first, and perhaps greatest, achievement was to heal a fragmented state that had been ripped to pieces by a vicious cycle of civil wars between the leading protagonists of Rome in the late Republican period. The bitter rivalries of the Second Triumvirate were prefigured by those of Caesar, Pompey, and Crassus – the First Triumvirate. Collectively, these great men could raise massive armies with the inevitable consequence that the military were a constant threat to the political stability of Rome. For this reason, before he became emperor, Octavian drastically reduced the size of the armed forces, cutting the number of legions from around 50 to 28, but doubled the size of a legion's first cohort; they were formed from citizens of the empire. He also established the *auxilia*, regiments that were numerically comparable but comprised non-citizens (*peregrini*).[5]

In the aftermath of the Battle of Actium in 31 BC Octavian had around 700 warships at his disposal, a number far in excess of what he needed and many were scrapped. Shortly after his accession to the throne he reorganized the navy with Agrippa to create the imperial fleets. For the next 300 years they held sway over the Mediterranean, which the Romans called '*mare nostrum*' ('our sea'), comprising the Black, Red, North, and Irish Seas, the English Channel, the north-west Atlantic seaboard, and the river frontiers of the Rhine and Danube.[6]

In spite of such a large militia, the fact that Augustus closed the doors of the Temple of Janus three times of course suggests that his reign was unstable. This edifice was depicted on coinage with lofty doors, possibly bronze, and described with similar details by Plutarch, who spent much of his life in Rome and was acquainted with the building.[7] According to Dio, their first closure was after Actium in 29 BC following the suicides of Antony and Cleopatra: 'the action which pleased him more than all the decrees was the closing by the senate of the gates of Janus, implying that all their wars had entirely ceased . . .'.[8] They must have been hastily reopened since they were closed again after the successful conclusion to Augustus' military campaigns in Hispania and Gaul in 25 BC: 'After these achievements in the wars Augustus closed the precinct of Janus, which had been opened because of these wars'.[9] We lack a commentary on the third closure, and there has been considerable debate about this. It could have been in 13 BC, to commemorate Augustus' military successes in Gaul, which had recommenced in 15 BC.[10] Alternatively, 7 BC has been suggested, to celebrate the Triumph of Tiberius after his Germanic campaign.[11] In any case, these closures postdate episodes of serious conflict in the provinces of the empire.

Augustus in fact devotes a substantial part of the *Res Gestae* to his military activities and achievements. The first reference in this context is his vengeance on Brutus and Cassius for assassinating Caesar, but he does not name them: 'Those who slew my father I drove into exile, punishing their deed by due process of law and afterwards when they waged war upon the republic I twice defeated them in battle'.[12] Thereafter he is forthright: 'Wars, both civil and foreign, I undertook throughout the world, on sea and land . . .'.[13] Reference to his numerous triumphs follow: 'Twice I triumphed with an ovation, thrice I celebrated curule triumphs . . . In my triumphs there were led before my chariot nine kings or children of kings'.[14] His European campaigns, mentioned above, are also explicit, when he '. . . returned from Spain and Gaul . . . after successful operations in those provinces . . .' Augustus' immodesty reaches fever pitch in the closing paragraphs: 'I extended the boundaries of all the provinces which were bordered by races not yet subject to our empire'.[15] A favourite is: 'Egypt I added to the empire of the Roman people . . .'.[16]

Absent from the *Res Gestae*, for obvious reasons, is the catastrophe of the Teutoburg Forest in AD 9 in which *Legio XVII, XVIII,* and *XIX* were destroyed under the command of Varus by the Germanic Cherusci coalition led by Arminius. According to Suetonius, this had such a shocking impact on the emperor that 'upon hearing the news, Augustus tore his clothes, refused to cut his hair for months and, for years afterwards, was heard, upon occasion, to moan, "Quinctilius Varus, give me back my Legions!"'[17]

Suetonius mentions another defeat in Germania that he describes as 'more humiliating than serious'.[18] This alludes to the so-called 'Lollian Disaster' of 16 BC in which a raiding coalition of Tencteri and Usipetes gave *Legio V Alaudae* a bloody nose under Marcus Lollius, capturing their eagle standard. This reverse was rapidly avenged by Augustus who was in Gaul at the time.

This era was in fact fraught with major conflicts. The Bellum Batonianum (War of the Batons), also known as the Great Illyrian revolt, represented a significant struggle for the legions of the princeps. This was precipitated by territorial expansion into the region of Illyria. The uprising was instigated by Bato, chief of the Daesitiates in Dalmatia (AD 6), who gathered a coalition of tribes including the Breuci (led by another Bato). An unthinkable invasion of Italy seemed likely, and the general Velleius Paterculus, who was a participant in the subsequent counter-offensive, commented that:[19]

> Roman citizens were overpowered, traders were massacred, a considerable detachment of veterans, stationed in the region which was most remote from the commander, was exterminated to a man, Macedonia was seized by armed forces, everywhere was wholesale devastation by fire and sword. Moreover, such a panic did this war inspire that even the courage of Caesar Augustus, rendered steady and firm by experience in so many wars, was shaken with fear.

The war was protracted, and its gravity was also described by Suetonius:[20]

> When the revolt of Illyricum was reported, he [Germanicus] was trans-
> ferred to the charge of a new war, the most serious of all foreign wars
> since those with Carthage, which he carried on for three years with fifteen
> legions and a corresponding force of auxiliaries, amid great difficulties
> of every kind and the utmost scarcity of supplies.

Roman forces sustained heavy losses. The rebels are said to have numbered
800,000 but this figure is no doubt exaggerated. The revolt was quelled in
AD 9 by Tiberius, the future emperor, and his nephew Germanicus, and the
region subjugated.

The sum total of Augustus' reign was as bloody as any era in Roman history. This is perhaps not surprising when one considers that he relentlessly
murdered his enemies with a series of proscriptions and was the ruthless
victor in four civil wars before he was enthroned: the Liberators' War in
44–42 BC (against Brutus and Cassius), the Sicilian revolt, 44–36 (versus
Sextus Pompey), the Perusine War, 41–40 (against Lucius Antonius and
Fulvia), and the Final War of the Roman Republic, 32–30 (versus Antony
and Cleopatra).

By the end of the Augustan period, the Roman empire had expanded to
encompass the modern countries of western and central Europe south of the
Rhine and Danube; several countries in south-west Asia, including Turkey,
Lebanon, Syria, Israel, and the Palestinian territories; North Africa, Egypt,
Libya, Tunisia, Algeria, and Morocco. The princeps controlled the puppet
strings of several client kings to insulate the empire against trouble in
unstable regions, for instance in southern Morocco, Austria, and parts of
Slovenia, a small region of northern Germany, northern Greece, the northern
coastal area of the Black Sea, eastern Turkey, and Armenia.

Typically regarded as a 'golden age of peace', there is clearly a disparity
between this view and the harsh reality of severe military problems that
afflicted this era. This did not go unnoticed by Tacitus who commented at
the conclusion of the civil wars: 'After that there had been undoubtedly
peace, but peace with bloodshed – the disasters of Lollius and of Varus, the
execution at Rome of a Varro, an Egnatius, an Iullus'.[21]

Augustus and his peers benefitted massively from the substantial booty that
was acquired in the process of conquest (material and human). This enabled
him to maintain an effective army, which proved crucial to the survival of the
empire. It also bankrolled his substantial programme of cultural renewal,
which involved a series of major building projects, including his new forum:
'On my own ground I built the Temple of Mars Ultor and the Augustan Forum
from the spoils of war'.[22] '[He] found it [Rome] built of brick and left it in
marble' is one of the most frequently cited extracts from Suetonius.[23]

Prior to Augustus' reign, Rome had benefitted enormously from the
campaigns of its most powerful generals, especially Julius Caesar. In late

September 46 BC, Caesar organized four triumphs in Rome for his victories in Gaul, Egypt, Pontus, and Africa. The Gallic king Vercingetorix, Cleopatra's sister Arsinoe, and king Juba's young son were paraded through the streets of Rome, and the collective booty displayed was an estimated 300 million *sesterces*, which he distributed between his soldiers and the citizens of Rome.[24] Caesar also embellished the heart of the city by remodelling the Roman Forum (Forum Romanum), originally the market-place of Rome.[25] In 54 BC, construction began on the Basilica Iulia, perhaps by Aemilius Paullus, on Caesar's behalf, placed on the south side of the Forum.[26] This was a major undertaking, the basilica occupied a space 101 metres long and 49 wide, and it was not finished until early in the reign of Augustus, but it burned and was completed in an enlarged form by the princeps in AD 12.[27] It consisted of a large central court, 82 metres long and 16 wide, surrounded on all sides by two wide aisles, which were overlooked by the galleries of a second storey, and its exterior was faced with white marble.

It is certain that work under the patronage of Augustus had begun long before this completion date since an inscription with his name on was found in the Forum dating to 23–20 BC.[28] The Temple of the Dioscuri here is also commemorated with an Augustan inscription;[29] and another is known from the Lacus Iuturnae (Spring of Juturna) in the Forum.[30]

Five years before Caesar's triumphs were celebrated, he had begun his forum (the Forum Iulium). One of Augustus' first undertakings was its completion, the first of the so-called imperial fora, adjacent to the Roman Forum. It was a large rectangular precinct that was surrounded by a colonnade and dominated by the Temple of Venus Genetrix, which contained a statue of the deity, a gilded statue of Cleopatra.[31]

The Augustan period was celebrated by the construction of a host of public buildings by the emperor and his colleagues, essentially paid for by war booty from foreign campaigns (*ex manubiis*). Notable constructions include the Theatre of Marcellus (Theatrum Marcelli), built by Augustus and dedicated to the memory of its namesake in 13 BC, or perhaps 11 BC, as recorded by an inscription.[32] Marcellus was a prominent Roman consul, and the nephew and son-in-law of Augustus. The Theatre of Balbus was dedicated in the same year by the consul Lucius Balbus, a friend of Julius Caesar. Marcus Agrippa, Augustus' trusted great general, was especially active in this sphere. He built the Aqua Julia and repaired the Aqua Marcia in 33 BC.[33] The original Pantheon temple was completed in 25 BC, the Baths of Agrippa (Thermae Agrippae), the first of the great imperial bath-houses, were finished in 19 BC, and Agrippa also constructed the Aqua Virgo, one of Rome's greatest civil engineering landmarks, to supply the complex.[34]

Aside from the enormous advantage of a 'booty economy', Augustus' brilliant use of visual and literary propaganda was unprecedented (Figure 1.1). In 53 BC Crassus had suffered a major defeat by the Parthians at the Battle of Carrhae in Persia, losing the military standards as well as his life. A second invasion by Mark Antony in 36 BC had also failed, and Julius Caesar's plans

Figure 1.1 Augustus of Prima Porta, first century, Vatican Museums.
Courtesy of Till Niermann.

were terminated by his assassination. Rather than risk military revenge, although this had been long intended, the princeps brokered a deal with king Phraates, and the battle standards were returned to Rome in 20 BC. Augustus and his spin-doctors wasted no time in distorting this episode to Rome's advantage. The standards were placed in the Temple of Mars Ultor (Mars the Avenger) for all to see in the newly erected Forum of Augustus.

The second of the imperial fora, it was originally built by the emperor to provide additional room for the courts and other needs of an expanding population. It consisted of a large rectangular precinct paved with marble and flanked by impressive marble colonnades with semicircular niches. This grandiose complex expressed the aspirations in the Augustan period perhaps more so than any other construction, with its powerful visual programme of ideology. Augustus placed bronze statues of all the Roman *triumphatores* from Aeneas down to his own era and later statues of other personages of varying distinction.[35] The impressive spirit of the age, its propaganda, and impact, is aptly summed up by Ovid:[36]

> The god is huge, and so is the structure: no otherwise ought Mars to dwell in his son's city. That shrine is worthy of trophies won from giants; from its might the Marching God fitly open his fierce campaigns, whether an impious foe shall assail us from the eastern world or whether another will have to be vanquished where the sun goes down. The god of arms surveys the pinnacles of the lofty edifice, and approves that the highest places should be filled by the unconquered gods. He surveys on the doors weapons of diverse shapes, and arms of lands subdued by his soldiery. On this side he sees Aeneas laden with his dear burden, and many an ancestor of the noble Julian line. On the other side he sees Romulus carrying on his shoulders the arms of the conquered leader, and their famous deeds inscribed beneath the statues arranged in order. He beholds, too, the name of Augustus on the front of the temple; and the building seems to him still greater, when he reads the name of Caesar.

Issues of *cistophoroi* were minted depicting the standards in this temple, and *denarii* show the cult statues of Mars Ultor and a kneeling Parthian with the standards. Later, in the *Res Gestae*, Augustus claimed that:[37]

> The Parthians I compelled to restore to me the spoils and standards of three Roman armies, and to seek as suppliants the friendship of the Roman people. These standards I deposited in the inner shrine which is in the Temple of Mars Ultor.

His policy here is unusually at odds with his expanding empire but was probably tempered with the reality that even his huge military resource was finite, and stretched to its maximum potential. Subsequent conflicts outlined above and below underline this. Quelling the Illyrian revolt was one thing, but taking on an empire with a proven track record against the Roman state was another matter. Conversely, from the perspective of the Parthians, a diplomatic solution would have been favourable, since they would be reluctant to tackle a newly centralized Roman state. The reality of this situation through imperial eyes is corroborated by Augustus' recommendations to Tiberius, his successor, and this is especially portentous:[38]

> They were stretching their hands to heaven, to the effigy of Augustus, to his own knees, when he gave orders for a document to be produced and read. It contained a statement of the national resources – the strength of the burghers and allies under arms; the number of the fleets, protectorates, and provinces; the taxes direct and indirect; the needful

disbursements and customary bounties catalogued by Augustus in his own hand, with a final clause (due to fear or jealousy?) advising the restriction of the empire within its present frontiers.

Constructions

It is logical that Augustus sought to project his ideology outside of Rome in regional Italy and in the provinces by erecting public monuments. Epigraphy is an especially useful medium to gauge this output and in most cases is rather accurate. One of the pitfalls, however, is that inscriptions are accidents of survival and for this reason they do not provide a comprehensive index of the princeps' achievements in this sphere. The same is true of course in successive reigns, but they do certainly give a proxy of expenditure. Another problem is that many inscriptions do not tell us the identity of individual buildings. However, their dedicatory nature at least records that they referred to public monuments in many cases. The emphasis throughout is on dedicated building inscriptions rather than honorific inscriptions. The latter were mainly carved on statue bases, and less frequently on columns, monumental arches, and building plaques, the main elements were the name of the person honoured, the outline of the *honores* achieved, and usually the name of the dedicator, allowing the latter to be associated with the act commemorated. Building inscriptions relate to the construction, repair, and embellishment of public buildings (although some are military), and are regarded as a sub-category of honorific inscriptions, and for the purposes of the arguments presented, are the most instructive.[39]

A group of survivals indicate that Augustus commissioned public buildings across the Roman empire; however, it is appropriate to confine this outline to the western empire and the same practice is followed in the reigns of other emperors, with rare necessary exceptions. This information is provided by the Heidelberg database, and the inscriptions for the period are presented below and discussed towards the end of the present chapter, in all cases referenced by their number, prefixed with HD. All are single examples unless otherwise stated. Ancient names are used for each location and province.

In the Italian regions, five public building inscriptions are dedicated to Augustus,[40] as are nine in the western provinces.[41]

Legacy

On his death the princeps was interred in his mausoleum near the Ara Pacis and he was deified. Augustus' military policies had, it is contended, set a dangerous precedent. Rome was far more vulnerable during the age of Augustus than is generally perceived. I believe that this period cemented the future and sealed the fate of the western Roman empire, placing the army as a burden on the finances of the state that would eventually prove unsustainable. This was due to the high proportion of state expenditure needed to preserve the military status quo, a factor that demanded the lion's share of tax revenue, which depended on booty, agricultural output, and mineral extraction across the empire.

Taking the arguments of Richard Duncan-Jones, Ramsay MacMullen, and David Potter into careful consideration, it is argued in subsequent chapters that the military spend on the militia was around 60 to 70 per cent of the state budget.[42] At its core the production base revolved around the cultivation of cereals, olives, and wine, as well as other products such as *garum* (fish sauce), but also animal husbandry (cattle, sheep, chickens, geese, etc.). This is supported by a substantial corpus of archaeological data from the rural sphere from a range of settlements where grain mills, olive oil- and wine-presses have been surveyed and excavated throughout the territories of the Roman empire, and this output appears to have peaked in the first and second centuries AD.[43]

This fragility was to continue for the duration of the first and second centuries, and into the so-called crisis of the third century, and beyond. Also it should be considered that the Roman state was eager to exploit the precious mineral resources (gold and silver) of conquered provinces for the purposes of extracting bullion to mint coinage. The implications of all this are touched on in more detail below and my ideas pertaining to this phenomenon are developed in subsequent chapters. For this reason, it is argued that successive emperors also sought to prosecute campaigns in order to extract booty and tribute whenever possible. It is no coincidence, it is argued, that there was a direct correspondence between monumental building programmes and the acquisition of booty. Furthermore, it is contended that those emperors who prosecuted foreign expansions funded by the spoils of war were able to stamp their mark in the provinces with public building works, and this is attested by a number of preserved building inscriptions, an aspect that is discussed below.

It is curious that the end of the Augustan era is often regarded as a seamless transition between the end of the *Pax Augusta* and the continuity of the *Pax Romana*, the latter being an umbrella term for the former. The concept of the *Pax Romana* has its roots in Roman literature, perhaps the most influential of which are the writings of Seneca in the middle of the first century AD: 'Consider all the tribes whom Roman civilization does not reach – I mean the Germans and all the nomad tribes that assail us along the Danube'.[44] In modern reckoning, this period of 'Roman peace' is typically seen to extend until the death of Marcus Aurelius (161–180).[45] The reality is a continuum of extreme violence and bloodshed and it is difficult to reconcile this with interpretations that state otherwise.

Tiberius (14–37)

Shortly after the death of Augustus, Tiberius sought to avenge the Battle of the Teutoburg Forest. Germanicus had been campaigning in the region since the year of the princeps' death. In 15 he had made inroads against the

Chatti and the Cherusci, and he also interred the bones of his fallen comrades in the Teutoburg Forest, and a legionary standard was recovered. He took no chances, wielding a massive force under his command, including *Legio I Germanica*, *II Augusta*, *V Alaudae*, and four additional legions, with the support of the Praetorian Guard. The site of the catastrophe is recorded by Tacitus:[46]

> . . . hideous to sight and memory. Varus' first camp, with its broad sweep and measured spaces for officers and eagles, advertised the labours of three legions: then a half-ruined wall and shallow ditch showed that there the now broken remnant had taken cover. In the plain between were bleaching bones, scattered or in little heaps, as the men had fallen, fleeing or standing fast. Hard by lay splintered spears and limbs of horses, while human skulls were nailed prominently on the tree-trunks. In the neighbouring groves stood the savage altars at which they had slaughtered the tribunes and chief centurions. Survivors of the disaster, who had escaped the battle or their chains, told how here the legates fell, there the eagles were taken . . .

Also with the assistance of a sizeable contingent of Batavian allies, he took the fight to the Cherusci on German soil with emphatic Roman victories at the Battle of the Long Bridges in 15 and Idistavius in 16, of which Tacitus remarked: 'It was a brilliant, and to us not a bloody'.[47] This was followed by another success at the Battle of the Angrivar Barrier, about which Tacitus recorded that: '. . . there was no hope but in courage, no salvation but from victory'.[48] The matter was settled in the region for the time being and Germanicus was recalled to Rome where he celebrated a triumph.[49]

Meanwhile in North Africa a serious revolt broke out in 17 under the leadership of Tacfarinas, a native of Numidia. He had deserted the Roman army and ran amuck with his Moorish allies (from Mauretania). This was a protracted campaign involving *Legio III Augusta* and *IX Hispana*; Publius Dolabella eventually crushed the rebels in 23.[50]

Later on in the reign of Tiberius, Germanicus' forces were obliged to quell a revolt by the Frissi in the Netherlands in 28. According to Tacitus:[51]

> The men of the fifth dashed forward in advance of the others, drove back the enemy in a sharp engagement, and brought off the cohorts and cavalry squadrons in a state of exhaustion from their wounds. The Roman general made no attempt at revenge; nor did he bury his dead, though a considerable number of tribunes, prefects, and centurions of mark had fallen.

Constructions

Tiberius is not widely regarded as a prolific builder but during his tenure the state had sufficient funds to enable him to erect a substantial number of public monuments in Rome, the Italian peninsula, and the provinces. Three public building inscriptions are known from Rome and its environs; the first names Germanicus, but this is posthumous, since he was assassinated in 19; Tiberius is also recorded, and this was clearly under his patronage.[52] Several public building inscriptions have been found in the Italian regions;[53] and he was a reasonably active builder in the western provinces.[54]

Legacy

Tiberius was not a popular emperor, especially with the Senate, who he relentlessly persecuted and placed on trial for *lèse-majesté* (injured majesty) or treason, which encompassed a wide range of charges. Something of the 'flavour' of his rule can be gauged by Tacitus, although it should be borne in mind that he was especially biased against him:[55]

> His character, again, has its separate epochs. There was a noble season in his life and fame while he lived a private citizen or a great official under Augustus; an inscrutable and disingenuous period of hypocritical virtues while Germanicus and Drusus remained: with his mother alive, he was still an amalgam of good and evil; so long as he loved, or feared, Sejanus, he was loathed for his cruelty, but his lust was veiled; finally, when the restraints of shame and fear were gone, and nothing remained but to follow his own bent, he plunged impartially into crime and into ignominy.

He apparently suffered from depression and became increasingly introverted, retreating to his villa on Capri in 26. En route to Rome for a final visit in the spring of 37 he apparently died of natural causes at a villa in Misenum in the Bay of Naples in March. Despite his suggested lack of popularity, he was interred in the Mausoleum of Augustus, although he was not deified like his predecessor.[56]

Caligula (37–41)

It appears that the imperial treasury was still in good shape during the reign of Tiberius, who seems to have been quite frugal, therefore enabling his successor, the infamous Gaius, more commonly known as Caligula, to make some massive hand-outs on his accession. His nickname derives from his military service, and translates to 'little boots', after the character of his footwear. He gave each member of the Praetorian Guard 1,000 *sesterces*; 45 million were paid out to the people of Rome; urban cohorts (police) and firemen each received 500, and every soldier in the Roman empire was given 300 *sesterces*; he also doubled the pay of the Praetorian Guard.[57]

His reign appears to have been tainted by a grave illness in the eighth month of his reign; although the nature of this malady is not recorded, it is possible that he was poisoned. He subsequently recovered and this event appears to have motivated him to murder a number of people who were accused of behaving inappropriately pertaining to his succession. His brutality was attested before this while he lived under the guardianship of Tiberius on Capri. According to Suetonius:[58]

> ... he could not control his natural cruelty and viciousness, but he was a most eager witness of the tortures and executions of those who suffered punishment, revelling at night in gluttony and adultery, disguised in a wig and a long robe ...

In Judaea he prosecuted an aggressive policy towards the Jews who he resented for their worship of *one* God, rather than a pantheon of deities, and this also contradicted his own belief that he was divine.[59] Preparations began in 39 for a large-scale campaign in Germania but this was abandoned in favour of an expedition to invade Britain.

In the following year Caligula apparently launched a virtual invasion, but it is difficult to unravel what actually occurred. One version of events holds that Adminius, son of the British king, Cunobelinus, ruler of the Catuvellauni, surrendered to the emperor with a small force on the Gallic shore (presumably in Normandy). Caligula then wrote a boastful letter to the Senate claiming that the whole island had been surrendered to him. Another account says that he ordered his troops in battle formation on the beach before he set sail in person for a brief time, and on his return he ordered his troops to gather seashells from the beach and take them back to Rome as booty. He paid them 400 *sesterces* each before addressing his men, saying 'Go your way happy; go your way rich'.[60] Aloys Winterling has suggested that insubordination lay at the root of this:[61]

> It seems, then, that the campaign against the Britons may have failed because of a mutiny in which *Legio I* and *XX* took part; both had refused to fight in 14 and had now joined Caligula's forces from their original station on the Rhine.

This is a plausible explanation, but an especially fascinating idea has been proposed by John Creighton. Drawing attention to an ambiguous phrase in Dio he suggests that a contingent of Caligula's army may have in fact campaigned in Britain:[62]

> ... as soon as he had proceeded a short distance from the Rhine, he returned, and then set out as if to conduct a campaign against Britain, but turned back from the ocean's edge, showing no little vexation at his lieutenants who won some slight success – but upon the subject peoples, the allies, and the citizens he inflicted vast and innumerable ills.

Constructions

Caligula also presided over some important building projects, including substantial improvements to the harbours at Rhegium and Sicily for the increased provision of grain, as mentioned by Josephus;[63] the completion of the Temple of the Divine Augustus between the Capitoline and Palatine Hills; an amphitheatre on the Campus Martius; the expansion of the imperial palace on the Palatine; and he began the construction of the Aqua Claudia and Anio Novus, regarded by Pliny the Elder as marvels of civil engineering.[64]

There are no building inscriptions recording Caligula's building achievements in Rome and this is perhaps best explained by his short reign and also suggests that his contribution to the urban landscape in the capital was modest in relative terms to both his predecessors and successors (with the exception of Nero), and, of course, by the random nature of archaeological discovery. However, in the regions an inscription is known from Bononia in Aemilia (Regio VIII),[65] but it is significant that no inscriptions are preserved in the western or eastern provinces.

Legacy

After Caligula's extravagances there followed desperate attempts to obtain funds, so while his reign began with a large surplus it ended with a deficit.[66] It is widely held that he was insane, an opinion that is informed by several Roman sources, including: Seneca, Philo, Pliny the Elder, Josephus, Tacitus, Suetonius, and Dio.[67] This has understandably coloured modern literature, notably since the writings of Ludwig Quidde in the nineteenth century,[68] and subsequent references to the emperor usually touch on his insanity.[69] However, Winterling has recently presented an interesting critique of the primary and secondary sources in this context.[70] All writers, ancient and modern, would perhaps agree that Caligula's sexual excesses and violence made his reign untenable, and he was assassinated by the Praetorian Guard in January 41.[71]

Claudius (41–54)

Notwithstanding the difficulties of Caligula's reign, in the interim, Rome's iron fist policy had settled the empire down, but this was short-lived. The new emperor, the politically weak Claudius, needed a rapid solution to his vulnerable position. Julius Caesar had invaded Britain in 55 and 54 BC, but not conquered the island, but is thought to have established diplomatic links with various Celtic tribal leaders; and the aborted 'mission' of Caligula provided Claudius with the perfect opportunity to break new ground and cement his political reputation as a leader who meant business.

In order to enlist the support of the Praetorian Guard, and the goodwill of the army in general, Claudius acted swiftly with financial incentives. In 41 he gave 15,000 *sesterces* to each Praetorian,[72] substantially more than the 2,000 per head that they had received from Caligula. Each cohort of five hundred men received 100 *sesterces*,[73] which totalled 450,000 *sesterces*. In addition, the emperor gave other troops a *donativum*, expending a total of 747 million *sesterces*, which by some estimates amounted to around 90 per cent of the tax revenue for that year.[74]

This demands the obvious question of how these expenditures were subsidized. The simple answer is yet more military expansion, annexing Mauretania, Lycia, Thrace, and Noricum, the latter being especially prosperous, and he had at his disposal the productive gold mines of north-western Spain.[75] In fact Claudius boasted about the combined gold wealth from the three Gallic provinces and Tarraconensian Spain, which amounted to an output of 16,000 pounds of gold or 67 million *sesterces*.[76]

The conquest of Britain

A key motivation for the conquest of Britain is thought to have been its rich mineral wealth, notably gold in mid-Wales, argentiferous lead in the Mendips and elsewhere, and Cornish tin, commodities listed by Strabo.[77] In the words of Tacitus: 'Britain contains gold and silver and other metals, as the prize of conquest'.[78] Realistically, in the short term, Claudius was reliant on his financial reserves to support his expeditionary force before Britain became a financially viable province, perhaps within a decade, with its rich potential of booty and tribute.[79]

The conquest began in 43, exploiting the political turmoil of the Celtic tribes, several of whom had sustained relations with Rome since the time of Caesar's invasions. In this case, he re-instated Verica, the exiled king of the Atrebates. The task force consisted of four legions and an equivalent number of *auxilia* under the command of Aulus Plautius, later a governor of Britain. Also involved in the invasion were the future emperors Vespasian, who led *Legio II Augusta*, and his son Titus, who served under him. The other legions enlisted were: *Legio IX Hispana*, *XIV Gemina*, and *XX Valeria Victrix*.[80]

Claudius was quick to exploit the new province's mineral resources where available. In the Mendips, the earliest lead pigs date to 49.[81] Britain's gold resources in Wales were in the territory of the Demetae, who were apparently 'pro-Roman', blocked by the hostile Silures to the east, and it was not possible to subjugate them until the Flavian period.

Constructions

Claudius was the most active of the Julio-Claudian emperors in the sphere of public building in Rome, the Italian regions, and the provinces, most likely for ideological reasons, seeking to align himself with Augustus and Tiberius and shake off the spectre of his predecessor.[82] The issue of the random nature of surviving inscriptions is especially relevant in Britannia, since no inscription has been recovered from the Temple of Claudius in

Camulodunum, the largest Roman temple in the province, built between 49 and 60. This is probably due to the fact that the edifice was burned down in the Boudiccan revolt early in the reign of Nero.

Legacy

Claudius did not outlive the invasion for long. Some scholars think that he died of natural causes, but it is likely that he was murdered by his wife Agripinna.[83] His reign is symptomatic of the Roman state's need for territorial expansion to satisfy military expenditure in the face of massive increases through the acquisition of tribute and booty, and this would prove to be a recurring theme in the centuries that followed. Also, it is contended that public building tends to be a corollary of the 'booty economy', the reign of Claudius being a case in point, as attested by the number of inscriptions, especially in the provinces.

Nero (54–68)

In Nero's reign Rome fell for the first time in a physical sense since a large part of the city was burned down. Also, the First Jewish War proved to be a virtual Armageddon. The protracted campaign to conquer Britain had witnessed countless successful yet bloody battles. However, in 60 under Nero, whose behavioural tendencies are said to have echoed those of Caligula, the level of violence rose to a new and terrible high, culminating in the extermination of the Welsh Druids on Anglesey, whose trace was wiped from the historical record:[84]

> On the beach stood the adverse array, a serried mass of arms and men, with women flitting between the ranks. In the style of Furies, in robes of deathly black and with dishevelled hair, they brandished their torches; while a circle of Druids, lifting their hands to heaven and showering imprecations, struck the troops with such an awe at the extraordinary spectacle that, as though their limbs were paralyzed, they exposed their bodies to wounds without an attempt at movement. Then, reassured by their general, and inciting each other never to flinch before a band of females and fanatics, they charged behind the standards, cut down all who met them, and enveloped the enemy in his own flames.

In the same year, the revolt of Boudicca, queen of the Iceni, saw the capitals of Camulodunum and Londinium razed by fire, as was Verulamium, and tens of thousands of colonists were slaughtered. Such was the gravity of the event that it nearly forced a tactical withdrawal from the province under governor Suetonius Paulinus.[85] Subsequently, according to Tacitus, matters were brought to a ruthless conclusion:[86]

> At first, the legionaries stood motionless, keeping to the defile as a natural protection: then, when the closer advance of the enemy had enabled

them to exhaust their missiles with certitude of aim, they dashed forward in a wedge-like formation. The auxiliaries charged in the same style; and the cavalry, with lances extended, broke a way through any parties of resolute men whom they encountered. The remainder took to flight, although escape was difficult, as the cordon of wagons had blocked the outlets. The troops gave no quarter even to the women: the baggage animals themselves had been speared and added to the pile of bodies. The glory won in the course of the day was remarkable, and equal to that of our older victories: for, by some accounts, little less than eighty thousand Britons fell, at a cost of some four hundred Romans killed.

Events elsewhere in the empire were to prove that Rome had overstretched its military resource by conquering Britain. The Boudiccan revolt had clearly shocked Rome to the core, but there was worse to come. In Judaea, yet another revolt broke out in 66, the First Jewish–Roman War. The root of this was tension between the Greek and Jewish population, but it ignited properly as a protest against the high taxation imposed by Gessius Florus, the Roman *procurator*:[87]

> Gessius Florus . . . ostentatiously paraded his outrages upon the nation, and as though he had been sent as hangman of condemned criminals, abstained from no form of robbery or violence. Was there a call for compassion, he was the most cruel of men; for shame, none more shameless than he. No man ever poured greater contempt on truth; none invented more craftly methods of crime. To make gain out of individuals seemed beneath him: he stripped whole cities, ruined entire populations, and almost went the length of proclaiming throughout the country that all were at liberty to practice brigandage, on condition that he received his share of the spoils. Certainly his avarice brought desolation upon all the cities, and caused many to desert their ancestral haunts and seek refuge in foreign provinces.

In response, Nero appointed Vespasian, with Titus under his command once more. Roman fortunes were somewhat aided by bitter infighting between Jewish factions. The tide turned in 67 after the protracted siege of Jotapa in the Galilee: the Jews were led here by Josephus, who later changed sides and subsequently became our prime source for this conflict. *Jewish War*, his earliest work, was written in Rome with the advantages of an ex-combatant and eyewitness.

Constructions

Perhaps the best-known building in Rome is the Domus Aurea, built by Nero after the great fire in 64, as referenced by Tacitus:[88]

> However, Nero turned to account the ruins of his fatherland by building a palace, the marvels of which were to consist not so much in gems and

gold, materials long familiar and vulgarized by luxury, as in fields and lakes and the air of solitude given by wooded ground alternating with clear tracts and open landscapes.

Archaeological evidence for the complex is understandably sketchy in light of the fact that it was built over repeatedly in the long urban history of the city, but perhaps the best-known remains are situated on the Quirinal Hill, the main palace covering parts of the Caelian, Esquiline, and Palatine Hills.[89] A substantial preserved section is sited under the Baths of Trajan. Tacitus' description of its scale is perhaps not an exaggeration, since estimates place its surface area ranging from 100 to 300 acres (40 to 120 hectares).[90] Elements of the Domus Aurea, such as its domed room with an oculus, is an extraordinary innovation, and prefigures the Pantheon, and for this reason it occupies a special place in architectural history.[91]

Tacitus also records that Nero commissioned a number of theatres in the capital: 'In the consulate of Nero – his fourth term – and of Cornelius Cossus, a quinquennial competition on the stage, in the style of a Greek contest, was introduced at Rome. Like almost all innovations it was variously canvassed'.[92] However, his avid construction in the sphere of public entertainments was not matched elsewhere, and this should be seen as a projection of his obvious megalomania, since public building inscriptions in Rome, Italy, and the western and eastern provinces are scant.[93]

Legacy

The reign of Nero was especially tarnished by the destruction of large parts of the capital. In July 64, the great fire destroyed an estimated 70 per cent of Rome, and it is rumoured that Nero started it, or more likely ordered its incendiary, although he was in his villa at Antium about 60 kilometres south-west of Rome at the time, and returned to the city to apparently assist in extinguishing the fire. According to Dio: 'Nero ascended to the roof of the palace, from which there was the best general view of the greater part of the conflagration, and assuming the lyre-player's garb, he sang the "Capture of Troy". . .'.[94] This last reference is the root of the idiom 'Nero fiddled while Rome burned'; however, the allusion to the 'lyre-player's garb' implies that Nero may have been playing a *cithara*, an instrument of the lyre family that gives its name to the modern guitar.[95] Tacitus says that Nero blamed the Christians for the calamity:[96]

> . . . to scotch the rumour, Nero substituted as culprits, and punished with the utmost refinements of cruelty, a class of men, loathed for their vices, whom the crowd styled Christians. Christus, the founder of the name, had undergone the death penalty in the reign of Tiberius, by sentence of the *procurator* Pontius Pilatus.

Unsurprisingly, Nero was forced to commit suicide in June 68.[97] According to Dio, his last words were: 'Jupiter, what an artist perishes in me!'[98]

The Year of the Four Emperors (68–69)

After the death of Nero, Rome was thrown into chaos with a bitter dispute between four contenders to the throne and civil war raged once more, with legion pitted against legion. The so-called Year of the Four Emperors witnessed the rise of Galba in June 68 and his murder in the Roman Forum by the Praetorian Guard in January 69; the accession of Otho and his suicide three months later; and the rise of Vitellius and his assassination by the colleagues of Vespasian in the imperial palace in December. The gravity of these events is summed up by Tacitus:[99]

> This was the condition of the Roman state when Servius Galba, chosen consul for the second time, and his colleague Titus Vinius entered upon the year that was to be for Galba his last and for the state almost the end.

Also, this calamitous 'year' had grave consequences for the stability of the empire with a serious uprising in Moesia by the Sarmatians, but this was crushed by *Legio VIII Augusta* and a rejuvenated *Legio III Gallica*.[100] There was further trouble with the revolt of the Batavi in the area of the southern Netherlands and northern Rhineland of Germany in 69 and 70, in which *Legio V Alaudae* and *XV Primigenia* were destroyed. The uprising was crushed by Cerialis who marshalled several legions, including *XIV Gemina*, who had been recalled from Britain.[101]

The Flavian period: Vespasian and Titus (69–81)

Vespasian was compelled to leave Judaea in 68 due to the internecine troubles that were tearing the Roman empire apart, entrusting Titus to finish the task. The culmination of this was bloody: the Romans stormed and torched the Second Temple in Jerusalem and butchered 6,000 Jews, looted the sacred gold treasures and destroyed the edifice:[102]

> Caesar, finding himself unable to restrain the impetuosity of his frenzied soldiers and the fire gaining the mastery, passed with his generals within the building and beheld the holy place of the sanctuary and all that it contained – things far exceeding the reports current among foreigners and not inferior to their proud reputation among ourselves ... While the temple blazed, the victors plundered everything that fell in their way and slaughtered wholesale all who were caught.

The furore caused by this sacrilegious act resulted in further Roman blood-shed, but they broke the siege of Jerusalem in 70,[103] and concluded affairs by destroying the zealot citadel in what was probably the greatest siege of the Roman period, at Masada on the Dead Sea in 73–74.[104]

Rome's ability to wield such large numbers of soldiers, especially after the heavy casualties or destruction of individual legions, of course depended on continued financial input. As suggested above, while a substantial propor-tion of this was levied in tax, especially in agricultural product, notably cereals, olive oil, and wine, booty continued to be a major factor. Titus had eagerly plundered the treasures of the Second Temple and those spoils enabled Vespasian to build the Colosseum (Amphitheatrum Flavium).[105]

Constructions

The letters of an inscription mentioning that the Colosseum was built from the spoils of war were originally on a marble block on the building, once placed below an architrave. This is translated by Géza Alfödy as follows:[106]

IMP CAES VESPASIANUS AVG
AMPHITHEATRUM NOVVUM
EX MANVBIIS FIERI IVSSIT

The emperor Caesar Vespasian Augustus
ordered that a new amphitheatre be constructed
from the spoils of [the Jewish War].[107]

In its general design it was modelled on the Theatre of Marcellus, espe-cially its arcades. The vital statistics of the building are extraordinary, mea-suring 186 metres in length and 156 along its minor axis, the outer wall is 58.50 metres in height and faced with travertine at an estimated 100,000 tonnes (Figure 1.2). Modern estimates suggest its capacity to have been around 50,000 people.

Vast sums of gold *aurei* were minted and circulated to celebrate Vespasian's military successes in Judaea – the so-called 'Judaea Capta' series. Roman propaganda continued unrelenting in this sense on other issues of *orichal-cum sestertii* under Titus depicting the Colosseum. These are important in a pictorial sense, since they of course show the monument as it would have originally appeared, rather than the monument as we know it today, with extensive damage to the outer south wall caused by the great earthquake of 1349.[108] A brief description of the Colosseum is provided by Ammianus Marcellinus in the fourth century, who recorded: 'the huge bulk of the amphitheatre, strengthened by its framework of Tiburtine stone, to whose top human eyesight barely ascends . . .'.[109]

As for the Temple Treasure, it is known that it was placed, ironically, on display in a library alongside famous Greek artistic works, known as the

Figure 1.2 Aqueduct in Segovia, built by Domitian in the later first century.
Courtesy of Jebulon.

Bibliotheca Pacis (Library of Peace) within the Templum Pacis (Temple of Peace) in the newly constructed forum, also the Forum Pacis (Forum of Peace).[110] This was the third of the great imperial fora, befittingly grandiose, flanked by colonnades with the temple characteristically on a long axis. Unlike its predecessors it is thought that it was a garden precinct rather than a paved meeting area in the conventional sense of a forum. It was constructed from the spoils of this campaign, and described by Pliny the Elder, a contemporary, who was an admirer of the construction, as: 'the largest and most beautiful of all the buildings in the city', although the observation is no doubt coloured by his pro-Flavian bias.[111] A fuller, and understandably favourable, account of the complex is provided by Josephus after the conclusion of the First Jewish War:[112]

The triumphal ceremonies being concluded and the empire of the Romans established on the firmest foundation, Vespasian decided to erect a temple of Peace. This was very speedily completed and in a style surpassing all human conception. For, having prodigious resources of wealth on which to draw, he embellished it with ancient masterpieces of painting and sculpture; indeed, into that shrine were accumulated and stored all objects for the sight of which men had once wandered over the whole world, eager to see them severally while they lay in various countries. Here too he laid up the vessels of gold from the temple of Jews on which he prided himself; but their Law and the purple hangings of the sanctuary he ordered to be deposited and kept in the palace.

Our best understanding of the treasure's appearance is the fine relief carved on the wall of the Arch of Titus in Rome, built in honour of the emperor to commemorate the siege of Jerusalem in 71.[113] The connection between a 'booty economy' and the building of monuments appears to be confirmed by Vespasian's build-spend in the provinces. In this period the gold mines at Dolocothi in mid-Wales would have come on stream and, by inference, this would have filtered into the treasury. In Rome, the Italian regions, and the western provinces a number of building inscriptions under Vespasian are recorded.[114]

Legacy

In the summer of 79 Vespasian fell ill and retired to his villa near Rieti in Lazio.[115] Titus succeeded his father in 79 but was probably poisoned by Domitian.[116] This occurred in his father's house in 81, on his death uttering: 'I have made but one mistake'. Looting the temple may have been that miscalculation, trusting his younger brother was another.

The Antonine period: Domitian and Nerva (81–96)

Domitian's notorious reign was characterized by the ruthless persecution of the senatorial classes and an ambitious programme of public building, bankrolled, by extension, from the wealth accumulated during the reign of Vespasian.[117]

His military policy appears to have been ill judged, since he was castigated for prosecuting an 'uncalled for' and 'unprovoked' war against the Chatti, who were allied with Rome, in 83.[118] The wealth accrued from his predecessor must have been substantial, since aside from his spree of public and private building he was able to give the army a large pay rise in the same year as the conflict with the Chatti, the first since Augustus, presumably because he keenly felt the precariousness of his own position; however, it appears that this proved to be unsustainable, according to Dio:[119]

> After this [his execution of Vestal Virgins] he set out for Gaul and plundered some of the tribes beyond the Rhine that enjoyed treaty rights – a performance which filled him with conceit as if he had achieved some great success; and he increased the soldiers' pay, perhaps on account of this victory, commanding that four hundred sesterces should be given to each man in place of the three hundred that he had been receiving. Later he thought better of it, but, instead of diminishing the amount of their pay, he reduced the number of soldiers. Both changes entailed great injury to the State; for he made its defenders too few in number and yet at the same time very expensive to maintain.

In fact his generosity extended to the citizens of Rome, his *congiaria* and *donativa* on a per-reign-years basis totalled eighteen million *sesterces* compared with ten million under Vespasian.[120]

After Domitian's assassination, Nerva faced the perennial problem of currying favour with the Praetorian Guard. They were given a *donativum* which may have been as much as 5,000 *denarii* per head. The citizens of

Rome were also financial beneficiaries, each receiving a *congiarium* of 75 *denarii*.[121] This was to prove financially unsustainable.

Constructions

Constructions included the Flavian Palace on the Palatine Hill, the Temple of Jupiter on the Capitoline Hill, and a new forum that was finished after his death and dedicated by Nerva in 97. This was the fourth and smallest of the imperial fora, and occupied the space between the Forum Augustum and the Forum Pacis, transforming the narrow via Argiletum between the two fora into a long and narrow forum, known also as the Forum Transitorium (the Transitory Forum). The periphery consisted of a colonnade and the Temple of Minerva on the long axis.[122] This is commemorated by an inscription.[123]

A further inscription in the capital was found on the site of the later Baths of Caracalla, and this is assigned either to the reign of Domitian or Nerva. A number of other inscriptions are recorded in Rome, the Italian regions, and the western provinces.[124]

Legacy

Governor Julius Agricola furthered the conquest of Britain at Mons Graupius in 84 with an emphatic defeat against the Caledonian tribes in Scotland.[125] In 89 Domitian faced a serious problem with the revolt of Lucius Saturnus, governor of upper Germany, but this was quelled, according to Dio: 'Lucius Maximus overcame him [Saturnus] and destroyed him'.[126] In 86, catastrophe struck once more against the Dacians in Pannonia, and it is thought that *Legio V Alaudae* was wiped out at Tapae, although Suetonius mentions that the Sarmatians were responsible.[127] Domitian was assassinated by the Praetorian Guard in September in 96.[128] The reign of Nerva, the first of the so-called Five Good Emperors, was short-lived; he passed away in January 98. His weak and ineffectual rule made it necessary for him to nominate a successor. His preferred choice was Trajan. According to Dio:[129]

> Thus Trajan became Caesar and later emperor, although there were relatives of Nerva living. But Nerva did not esteem family relationship above the safety of the State, nor was he less inclined to adopt Trajan because the latter was a Spaniard instead of an Italian or Italot, inasmuch as no foreigner had previously held the Roman sovereignty; for he believed in looking at a man's ability rather than at his nationality.

The suggested correspondence between foreign wars and public building

Building inscriptions, as summarized below, are informative in Rome, Italy, and the western provinces for several reasons, the focus here is only on those inscriptions that can be assigned to individual reigns with 'precision' rather than those that overlap the tenure of one or more emperors. First, they appear to support the historical picture pertaining to the character of particular emperors. The absence of any dated monumental inscriptions in the reign of Caligula is curious, and although he was active in this sphere in a relatively limited capacity, the pausity of inscriptions in his short time on the throne across the empire supports the notion of a deranged self-interested emperor, although had his reign been longer then perhaps the epigraphic record would have told a different story, but this of course is conjecture. While Nero's reign was considerably longer, the relatively scant number of inscriptions suggests that his megalomanic tendencies directed him to focus more on the beautification of his palace than adorning the empire with monumental edifices. As for Nerva, the modest number of inscriptions that correspond to his short reign support the notion that the imperial treasury was struggling with its finances in the face of substantial military handouts. The epigraphic record for the reigns of Augustus, Tiberius, Claudius, Vespasian, and Titus speak for themselves. All, with the exception of Titus, had relatively long reigns, with some differential, and exercised aggressive foreign policies to obtain booty and tribute, and the latter benefitted enormously from his own looting. Domitian appears to be an exception, with fewer inscriptions, and this would seem to square with his martial failures and exorbitant spending on military and civilian hand-outs. Nerva was obligated in a similar manner, and this, in combination with his short reign, best explains the relatively low number of dated buildings.

The total number of inscriptions in the western empire by reign in the first century is as follows: Augustus, 14, Tiberius, 23, Claudius, 19, Nero, 7, Vespasian, 21, Titus, 9, Domitian, 10, and Nerva, 9.

Building under *decurions* and other local officials

Imperial edifices were of course only a part of the story, since patronage in the sphere of elites, notably *decurions* and other local officials, played a key role in the civic sphere, erecting a substantial number of public monuments. It is logical that this social order was more 'insulated' from the 'booty economy' in the sense that they were essentially the landowners, who marshalled agricultural product to their benefit from tenants, the net result being the generation of essential state tax revenue, but also accruing wealth as manifest in euergetism. The financial mechanisms of state will be examined in more detail in the chapters that follow. Suffice to say that a significant number of recorded inscriptions in the first century (and subsequently) are from civic monuments.

In the western empire during the first century, 28 inscriptions are known from this social order and those that are associated with identifiable civic buildings include: an aqueduct at Segovia, Hispania Citerior; inscriptions record a basilica and forum at Lucus Feroniae, and fora at Rusellae, Etruria

(Regio VII), Emporiae, Hispania Citerior, and at Asseria, Dalmatia; two theatre inscriptions at Italica, Baetica; and a theatre at Ostia, Latium et Campania (Regio I).[130]

The sum total of booty and bloodshed

This is a convenient juncture to reflect on the first century and a quarter of the '*Pax Romana*'. It had proven to be both bloody and costly. The '*Pax Augusta*' was a façade; in fact the princeps had been elevated to power as the ruthless victor of four major civil wars. Thereafter, his reign was marred by slaughter in the Lollian and Teutoburg disasters, and the Bellum Batonianum in Illyria. The bloodshed continued under Tiberius in Germania and he was forced to intervene in the Low Countries, and also to quell the serious revolt of Tacfarinas in North Africa. The reign of Claudius saw the invasion of Britain, which was subsequently characterized by genocide, revolt, and warfare. In Nero's tenure, the First Jewish War was afflicted by much of the same. There followed the bloody civil war in the Year of the Four Emperors, the Sarmatian uprising in Moesia, the grave Batavian revolt, and the ruthless conclusion to matters in Judaea in the reign of Vespasian. Finally, Domitian prosecuted a mock war against the Chatti, dealt with the revolt of Saturnus, and suffered catastrophic defeats against the Dacians and Sarmatians.

The sum total of the first century as far as Roman military resources were concerned was a series of heavy casualties and destruction of seven legions, and *auxilia* losses were probably broadly commensurate. In the first era of the Principate it is clear that the Roman army was overstretched, having to deal with one crisis after another. The great building projects from the end of the first century BC onwards, such as the imperial fora, and the Colosseum, were only made possible by the proceeds of war and tribute, or when such sums where frugally administered for the fortune of future emperors; as in the case of Tiberius' financial administration benefitting Caligula's build-spend and extravagant hand-outs, the same is true for Domitian, gaining from the rich legacy of Vespasian and Titus. Also, building in the Italian regions and the provinces was boosted by booty – slaves and precious items – and tribute. However, elites, such as *decurions* and other officials were, it is contended, 'independent of' the booty and tribute dynamic, generating their wealth through the extraction of economic products, as expressed in civic munificence.

With some justification the first century of the Principate has been hailed as a golden era. This is indeed true when the achievements in administration, the arts, and civil engineering are taken into account (Figure 1.3). This needs to be tempered with the loss of tens of thousands of lives in the Augustan period alone, and many more thereafter between belligerents. In fact, the scale of conflict was so great in the first century that it is not practical to mention all of the battles that occurred in this time frame and the centuries

Figure 1.3 The Colosseum, built by Vespasian in the later first century.
Courtesy of David Iliff.

that followed, and further comment about this is made towards the end of Chapter 2. Perhaps the most appropriate way to view this period is much in the same way as the former US President Richard Nixon regarded the twentieth century – 'the bloodiest and the best in the history of man'.[131]

Aside from the fiscal advantages of booty, the massive cost of the army demanded a concordant extraction of taxation. This, in turn, drove a phenomenal agricultural output in order to meet its obligation; although the imperial authorities could mint vast sums of gold and silver coinage to pay the troops, there was of course an imperative to keep mines operational across the empire and, in many cases, as we will see, mines had a limited lifespan, especially when individual provinces were relinquished or were eventually overrun in the fifth century.

Agricultural productivity is attested by archaeological data from villas and farms, and this demonstrates a massive output of cereals, olive oil, and wine in the first two centuries BC, reaching a peak in the course of the second century AD.[132] Tenant farmers sold their arable and pastoral produce in the cities in order to pay tax, and their landlords, mostly the ruling elites of the urban sphere, paid a proportion of this income to the central government. Tax was also requisitioned in kind from rural producers. In this period the economy benefitted enormously from substantial injections of booty. However, somewhat ominously, this would diminish through the course of the second century until the reign of Septimius Severus, falling off again after Caracalla, with a resurgence under Diocletian and Constantine in the late third/early fourth centuries, and Constantine, but tailing off thereafter.

Agricultural productivity is a factor that becomes increasingly germane to my central proposition pertaining to the collapse of the western Roman empire. The fundamental question is the extent to which agricultural output and precious mineral production could be maintained in the third through the fifth centuries. This factor will be closely scrutinized in the chapters that follow.

Notes

1 Augustus, *Res Gestae Divi Augusti* (13). 1924. Translated by F.W. Shipley. Loeb Classical Library 152. Cambridge, MA: Harvard University Press. Hereafter, LCL.
2 One such issue, minted in Ephesus in 28 BC, was a series of silver *cistophori* depicting Augustus on the obverse and a female personified as *Pax* on the reverse. For Augustan coinage and its propaganda, Sear, 2000, 312–340.
3 Rossini, 2007.
4 Zanker, 1988, 167–238.
5 Haynes, 2013, 95–102.
6 Pitassi, 2012, 13.
7 Plutarch, *Lives*, vol. I, *Numa* (XX.1–2). 1914. Translated by B. Perrin. LCL 46. For a biography, xi–xix.
8 Dio, *Roman History* (L.20.4). Books, 1–11, 46–50, 51–55, 56–60, 61–70, 71–80. 1914. Translated by E. Cary. (with E. Foster), 1914, 1917, 1917, 1924, 1925, 1927. LCL 32, 82, 83, 175, 176, 177. For the biography, 1914, vii–xxiv.
9 *DRH*, LIII.26.
10 Ryberg, 1949, 93.
11 Syme, 1979, 188–212.
12 *ARG*, II.
13 *ARG*, III.
14 *ARG*, IV.
15 *ARG*, XXVI.
16 *ARG*, XXVII.
17 Suetonius, *Lives of the Twelve Caesars* (II.23). 1913, 1914. Translated by J.C. Rolfe. LCL 31, 38. For the biography, Bradley, 1913, 1–29. *DRH*, LVI.23.1.
18 *SL*, II.23.
19 Velleius Paterculus, *Compendium of Roman History* (CX.6). 1924. Translated by F.W. Shipley. LCL 152. For a biography, viii–xvii.
20 *SL*, III.16.
21 Tacitus, *Annals* (I.10). Tacitus. *Agricola*. 1914. Translated by M. Hutton, W. Peterson. Revised by R.M. Ogilvie, E. H. Warmington, M. Winterbottom. LCL 35. *Histories*. Books 1–3. 1925. Translated by C.H. Moore. LCL 111. *Histories*. Books 4–5. *Annals*. Books 1–3. 1931. Translated by C.H. Moore, J. Jackson. LCL 249. *Annals*. Books 4–6, 11–12, 13–16. 1937. Translated by J. Jackson. LCL 312, 322. For a biography, Moore, 1925, vii–xiii.
22 *ARG*, XXI.
23 *SL*, II.28.
24 Paterculus (II.56.2); Appian (II.15.101, 102), *Roman History: the civil wars*. Books 1–3.26. 1913. Translated by Horace White. LCL 4. For a biography of Appian, *Roman History*. 1912. Edited by Horace White. LCL 2, vii–xii.
25 Platner and Ashby, 1926, 230–236.
26 Platner and Ashby, 1926, 78–80; Gros, 2011, 212–214.

27 D*RH*, LVI.27; *SL*, II.29.
28 HD024920 (AD 6).
29 HD024920 (AD 6).
30 HD043931 (AD 12).
31 D*RH*, LI.22; Appian, II.15.102; Platner and Ashby, 1926, 225–227.
32 HD024872 (11 BC).
33 A definitive study of aqueducts, and those feeding Rome, is presented by Hodge, 2002.
34 Platner and Ashby, 1926, 518–520.
35 *SL*, II.31; T*An*, IV.15; XIII.8; Platner and Ashby, 1926, 221–223; Gros, 2011, 216.
36 Ovid, *Fasti* (V.545–569). 1931. Translated by J.G. Frazer. LCL 253. For a biography, xi–xxviii.
37 A*RG*, XXIX. For Augustan coinage and its propaganda, Sear, 2000, 312–340.
38 T*An*, I.11.
39 Beltrán Lloris, 2015, 91–94.
40 HD032599 (2 BC – AD 14), HD032629 (12–2 BC), HD032644 (AD 14), HD032653 (27 BC – AD 14), HD032479 (23–22 BC).
41 HD032941 (AD 4–14), HD057998 (11–10 BC), HD060134 (27 BC – AD 14), HD004825 (27 BC – AD 14), HD019680 (AD 11–12), HD059268 (AD 1–2), HD021415 (8 BC), HD021909 (AD 1–2), HD059267 (AD 1–2).
42 Duncan-Jones, 1994, 45–46; MacMullen, 1984, 571–580; Potter, 2015, 32.
43 Bowman and Wilson, 2009, 2011, 2013.
44 Seneca, *Moral Essays* (IV.33). 1928. Translated by J.W. Basore. LCL 214. For a biography, vii–xiv.
45 Heather, 2005, 1–143; Goldsworthy, 2016.
46 T*An*, I.61.
47 T*An*, II.18.
48 T*An*, II.20.
49 T*An*, II.26.
50 T*An*, II.52, 3.73–3.74.
51 T*An*, IV.73.
52 HD024929 (23), HD025499 (22), HD065408 (14–37).
53 HD032587 (14–37), HD032434 (27–28), HD032437 (29–37), HD032470 (14–37), HD032476 (15), HD031156 (19–23), HD001966 (14–37).
54 HD019729 (30–37), HD035676 (34–35), HD057945 (14–37), HD032704 (18–19), HD025111 (33), HD018010 (16–17), HD018013 (19–20), HD050133 (16–20), HD004274 (14–37), HD025362 (29–30).
55 T*An*, VI.51.
56 T*An*, VI.50; *SL*, III.73; D*RH*, LVIII.28.
57 D*RH*, LIX.
58 *SL*, IV.11.
59 Josephus, *Jewish Antiquities* (XIX.1–4). Books 18–19. 1965. Translated by Louis H. Feldman. LCL 433. Philo, *On the Embassy to Gaius* (XXX.203, XVI.115). 1962. Translated by F.H. Colson. LCL 379. For a biography, ix–xxxi.
60 *SL*, IV.46.
61 For this bizarre episode, Winterling, 2011, 117–120.
62 D*RH*, LIX.21; Creighton, 2006, 52.
63 *JJA*, XIX.5–6.
64 *SL*, IV.21; Pliny the Elder, *Natural History* (XXXVI.22.). Books XXXVI–XXXVII. 1962. Translated by D.E. Eicholz. LCL 419. Reference hereafter is also made to Books I–II; Books XXXIII–XXXV. 1938, 1952. Translated by H. Rackham. LCL 330, 394.
65 HD032449 (37–41).

66 Duncan-Jones, 1994, 11; Bodei Giglioni, 1974, 157–160.
67 Seneca, *Moral Essays* (I.20.9, III.19.3, III.21.5). 1928. Translated by J.W. Basore. LCL 214. P*NH*, XXXVI.113; J*JA*, XVIII.277, XIX.1–5, XIX.193; T*An*, XIII.3; S*L*, IV.50, 51; D*RH*, LIX.26.
68 Quidde, 1894, 67.
69 These are numerous and a small number are cited here: Yavetz, 1996, 105.
70 This suggests that Caligula's insanity should be redefined in light of fundamental biases in primary sources that have impacted on modern literature, Winterling, 2011, 1–7.
71 J*JA*, XIX.110–114; S*L*, IV.58; D*RH*, LIX.29.
72 S*L*, V.10.
73 D*RH*, LX.12.
74 Levick, 2015, 153.
75 Wilson, 2012, 134.
76 P*NH*, XXXIII.16.54; Levick, 2015, 157.
77 Strabo, *Geography* (IV.5.2). Books I–II, III–V. 1917, 1923. Translated by H.L. Jones. LCL 49, 50. For a biography, 1917, xiii–xxx.
78 T*Ag*, 12.
79 Levick, 2015, 156.
80 S*L*, V.17; T*Ag*, 13. For the conquest of Roman Britain, Salway, 1993, 55–90.
81 Elkington, 1976, 183–197.
82 HD002737 (44–45), HD004466 (43), HD014574 (46), HD019450 (51–52), HD023732 (42), HD025490 (51–54), HD026605 (47), HD032425 (41–54), HD032461 (42), HD035391 (50), HD035395 (51–52), HD061818 (50–51), HD062197 (47), HD062198 (47), HD073418 (52–53).
83 T*An*, XII.66–67; D*RH*, LXI.34.
84 T*An*, XIV.30.
85 T*An*, XIV.31–38; T*Ag*, I.5; D*RH*, LXII.1–12.
86 T*An*, XIV.37.
87 Josephus, *Jewish War* (II.14). Books I–II, III–IV, V–VII. 1927 [a], 1927 [b], 1928. Translated by H. St. J. Thackeray. LCL 203, 487, 210. For a biography, 1927 [a], vi–x.
88 T*An*, XV.42.
89 Platner and Ashby, 1926, 166–172.
90 Warden, 1981, prefers the first estimate; Roth, 1994, 227, the second.
91 See especially the study presented by Ball, 2003.
92 T*An*, XIV.20.
93 HD025493 (55–56), HD025502 (57), HD032668 (54–66), HD059275 (61–62) HD064272 (67).
94 D*RH*, LXII.18.
95 Mary Francis Gyles (1947, 211–217) has unravelled the thread of this common saying. A ninth-century distortion incorrectly identifies *fidicula* with harp (*harperi*). Also, an eleventh-century misinterpretation defines harp as *cithara*. In fact, not until Shakespeare's *Henry VI* did Nero hold an instrument (in this case a flute) and subsequently in *Taming of the Shrew* he regarded the emperor as 'a fiddler'. 'Nero fiddled while Rome burned', it seems, came from the Bard.
96 T*An*, XV.44.
97 S*L*, VI.49.
98 D*RH*, LXIII.29.
99 T*H*, I.11.
100 T*H*, I.79.
101 T*H*, V.14–26.
102 For a full account of the episode, J*JW*, VI.260–274.
103 J*JW*, VI.403.

104 *JJW*, VII.252, 275, 304–406.
105 For a study of the Colosseum, Platner and Ashby, 1926, 6–11.
106 Alfödy, 1995, 195–226.
107 HD025559 (79–81).
108 For the coinage of Vespasian, Titus, and its propaganda, Sear, 2000, 428–470.
109 Ammianus Marcellinus, *History* (I.16.10.14). Books 14–19, 20–26, 27–31. 1939. Translated by J.C. Rolfe. LCL 300, 315, 331. For a biography, ix–xlvii.
110 For a detailed account of the Temple treasure and its subsequent fate, Kingsley, 2006.
111 Platner and Ashby, 1926, 386–388; Gros, 2011, 216–217. For the description of Pliny the Elder, P*NH*, XXXVI.102.
112 *JJW*, VII.158–162.
113 Platner and Ashby, 1926, 45-47; Holloway, 1987, 183-191; Gros, 2011, 70-72.
114 HD006225 (75–76), HD022983 (73), HD025535 (69–79), HD026974 (72–73), HD029160 (77–78), HD031114 (76), HD032156 (79), HD032422 (79), HD032473 (73), HD032530 (69–79), HD032557 (73–79), HD032590 (76), HD032665 (78–79), HD035262 (75–78), HD059971 (76–77), HD068237 (73), HD068238 (73), HD069737 (79), HD073419 (69–79), HD073420 (76).
115 *SL*, VIII(I).24.
116 *SL*, VIII(II).10–11.
117 Duncan-Jones, 1994, 46.
118 *SL*, VIII(III).6.
119 D*RH*, LXVII.7. Although not stated this probably represented an annual pay rise from 300 to 400.
120 Duncan-Jones, 1994, 41.
121 *SL*, VIII(III).4; Syme, 1930, 55–70.
122 Platner and Ashby, 1926, 227–229; Gros, 2011, 216–218.
123 HD065460 (96–98).
124 HD001920 (95–96), HD005576 (81–83), HD025565 (81–96), HD027371 (83–96), HD031126 (85–86), HD031165 (84), HD03244 (92–93), HD032524 (81–96), HD032581 (81), HD032584 (82), HD039970 (82), HD039972 (82), HD040001 (85–96), HD045894 (83–96), HD050948 (83–96), HD057403 (85–96), HD059494 (89–96), HD062201 (85–96), HD067664 (81–96).
125 T*Ag*, 11, 27, 29, 36–38.
126 D*RH*, LXVII.11.
127 *SL*, VIII(III).6.
128 *SL*, VIII(III).17.
129 D*RH*, LXVIII.4.
130 HD045267 (98), HD003950 (1–100), HD004691 (1–100), HD003225 (1–100), HD003975 (27–20 BC), HD020756 (54–69), HD000112 (27 BC – AD 14), HD004825 (27 BC – AD 14), HD004268 (1–100).
131 Nixon, 1998, 4.
132 Bowman and Wilson, 2009, 5.

2   The bloody peace

Efface imagination! Cease to be pulled as a puppet by thy passions. Isolate
the present. Recognize what befalls either thee or another. Dissect and analyze
all that comes under thy ken into the Casual and the Material. Meditate on
thy last hour. Let the wrong thy neighbor does thee rest with him that did the
wrong. Do thy utmost to keep up with what is said. Let thy mind enter into
the things that are done and the things that are doing them. Make thy face to
shine with simplicity and modesty and disregard all that lies between virtue
and vice. Love human-kind. Follow God.[1]

Meditations
Marcus Aurelius

It is extraordinary to think that this instruction of tolerance, peace, and
good will to humanity, couched in philosophical Stoicism, was written by an
emperor whose reign was consumed with the prosecution of a vicious war
against Germanic tribes on the Danube frontier. In fact, the second century
of the '*Pax Romana*' differed little from the first in terms of imperial aggression, culminating in foreign campaigns, active genocide, and defensive
responses to dangerous situations. The observations made in the present
chapter relate once more to a 'booty economy' and how it enabled successive emperors to sponsor impressive public monuments, somewhat devolved
from civic patronage. Conversely, it is contended, when booty was no longer
available, the expenditure on public buildings tended to cease, and the
burden of the army on the state depended on ever increasingly high agricultural productivity and mineral wealth.

The Antonine period: Trajan (98–117)

After the short-lived reign of Nerva (who abdicated in favour of his adopted
heir), Trajan, the second of the 'Five Good Emperors', pursued a decidedly
bellicose policy. His first course of action was to avenge the crushing defeat
of V Alaudae. In 101–102 and 105–106 the new emperor prosecuted successive campaigns in Dacia, and Arabia was annexed in 106.[2] A major factor in
previous Dacian successes was the *falx*, a weapon comprising a long handle

with a hook, resembling a sickle, and effective in close combat – a vertical blow inflicted gruesome damage to the back of the head or crown.[3] For this reason, combat helmets were developed with a wider neck-guard from the reign of Trajan onwards. In their final campaign, the forces of the emperor took the stronghold of Decebalus at Sarmizegetusa and subsequently conquered Dacia. Pliny the Younger called it: 'a great and glorious victory ... agreeable to the heroism of Rome'.[4]

Constructions

The Forum of Trajan (Forum Traiani) was the last of the imperial fora to be built, and not wishing to be upstaged by his predecessors, it was the largest and most magnificent complex of its kind, constructed with the assistance of the Greek architect Apollodorus and dedicated in 113, although it is possible that it was begun by Domitian. Its totality comprised the forum *per se*, the basilica Ulpia, the bibliotheca (its library), and the column of Trajan. Unusually, it did not have a temple, unlike its forerunners. The forum consisted of a large rectangular court flanked by hemicycles, with marble colonnades on three sides and the basilica on the long axis. Within the porticoes, Trajan set up statues of distinguished statesmen and generals, thereby promoting his own greatness in the manner of the propaganda in the Forum of Augustus. It was apparently intended as a setting where officials conducted their duties of the state. The great basilica had a façade of marble columns and an apse at each end. Its hall was surrounded by a double row of columns and its walls faced with marble.[5]

Part of the complex is depicted on issues of gold *aurei* minted in Rome around 112–115. On the reverse the Arcus Traiani (Arch of Trajan) is shown as a hexastyle building façade surmounted by a chariot drawn by six horses. Three figures stand to the left and right, while four statues occupy niches in the arches below. The reverse legend reads: FORVM TRAIANA.

Something of its appearance, and funding, may be gleaned from the historian Aulus Gellius, who was thought to have been born in Rome at the time of its construction or in the years that followed, and subsequently resided there: 'All along the roof of the colonnades of the forum of Trajan gilded statues of horses and representations of military standards are placed, and underneath is written *Ex manubiis* [from the spoils of war] ...'.[6]

Arguably the most famous victory monument was erected adjacent to the great edifice – Trajan's column – a graphic narrative of yet another bloody campaign, and a great tourist attraction in the modern era. This was recorded by Dio:[7]

> He also built libraries [in the forum]. And he set up in the Forum an enormous column, to serve at once as a monument to himself and as a memorial of the work in the Forum. For that entire section had been hilly and he had cut it down for a distance equal to the height of the column, thus making the Forum level.

It was constructed from Parian marble, the shaft, bases, and capital are composed of nineteen blocks, and it is nearly 30 metres in height. Aside from its monumentality, its greatest achievement is artistic, the entire surface of the shaft being covered with reliefs arranged on a spiral band, representing the main events in Trajan's Dacian campaigns, some of which are decidedly gory, depicting the severing of barbarian heads, held aloft by victorious Roman soldiers. The scenes are carved in such detail that they have provided a comprehensive body of information on Roman military equipment in this era, including helmets, armour, shields, and weapons along with a wealth of other information. On his death the emperor's ashes were interred in the base of the column.[8]

Commenting on the visit of Constantius II to Rome in the fourth century, Ammianus Marcellinus commented that:[9]

> ... when he came to the Forum of Trajan, a construction unique under the heavens, as we believe, and admirable even in the unanimous opinion of the god, he stood fast in amazement, turning his attention to the gigantic complex about him, beggaring description and never again to be imitated by mortal men.

The latest in a series of monuments built from the spoils of war, an interesting approximation of its scale is provided on the authority of Statilius Crito, Trajan's physician. The sixth-century writer Ioannes Lydus estimated the booty to be five million *litra* of gold and ten million in silver with additional plunder and half a million slaves. This equates to 1,637,500 and 3,275,000 kilogrammes, which is probably exaggerated but gives a general indication of a substantial sum.[10]

In the same period, the architect of Trajan's forum, Apollodorus, built the Thermae Traiani (the Baths of Trajan) on the Esquiline Hill, partly over the Domus Aurea (Nero's Golden House). In keeping with his massive forum, these were grandiose, 240 metres in width and 330 in depth, and consisted of a large court flanked by a wall (peribolus), which contained reading rooms, gymnasia, and a theatre. The complex had the additional trappings of a monumental Roman bath-house: *apodyteria* (changing rooms), a large *natatio* (swimming pool), *frigidaria* (cold pools), *tepidaria* (tepid pools), *caldaria* (hot pools), and *palaestrae* (exercise courts), surrounded with colonnades. There is no textual or epigraphical evidence that the baths were built from the spoils of war; however, the timing of their construction suggests that they were: dedicated in 109, after the Dacian campaigns.[11]

Trajan also embellished the Forum of Caesar, since a building inscription is recorded there.[12] Several individual inscriptions have been recovered from parts of Rome, including two thought to be from the Forum of Trajan.[13] In the Italian regions and Sicily his constructions are also attested.[14] In the western provinces, Trajan's public building is attested by a number of inscriptions.[15]

Excluding those inscriptions that adorn buildings constructed by Nerva and completed by Trajan in the previous chapter, the total number of building inscriptions in the western empire on buildings under Trajan is 33.

Flawed foreign policy

In 113, thirsty for military glory, Trajan launched an ambitious and successful campaign in Persia, and made his nephew Hadrian governor of Syria. The following year he annexed Armenia, overthrowing Osroes I, and placed his own puppet king, Parthamaspates, on the throne. Parthia was severely weakened by its own civil war and this enabled the emperor to sweep the board, capturing a number of cities in Mesopotamia, including the capital Ctesiphon in 116. Rather than annexing Parthia, he made Parthamaspates a client king and formed two new provinces – Assyria and Mesopotamia. The empire was now at its greatest extent, including large parts of modern Iraq and northern Iran. However, there followed a series of revolts in Armenia and Parthia, and the situation elsewhere was calamitous.[16]

A serious revolt in 115–117 exposed the empire's overextension under Trajan.[17] This was a critical situation ignited and fuelled by ethnic tension between Jews and Greeks in the provinces of Judaea, Proconsularis, Cyrene, Egypt, and Cyprus. Under the rebel leadership of Lukuas, Artemio, Julian, and Pappus, hundreds of thousands of gentiles were slaughtered along with heavy Jewish losses. The rebellion was ruthlessly crushed by legionary contingents under the command of Lusius Quietus.[18] For this reason the conflict is sometimes referred to as the 'war of Quietus'.[19]

Unfortunately, no contemporary account survives of Trajan's Parthian campaigns and we are therefore reliant on Dio's *History* and excerpts from Arrian's *Parthica*, and it is difficult to piece together the motivations for his invasion.[20] The sources are absent on the subject of booty and there are no monuments recording his exploits. However, when Septimius Severus invaded Parthia in 197 and 198, he plundered a massive quantity of war spoils from the empire and this is depicted on the Arch of Severus in Rome, and also mentioned in the *Historia Augusta*. By inference, therefore, we should consider that Trajan's campaigns in Parthia would have yielded rich pickings.

Legacy

Trajan suffered a stroke at Antioch in 117 while planning a new campaign against the Parthians, and died in the summer of that year on his way back to Rome.[21] The net result of his Parthian campaigns proved fruitless in terms of territorial gain and Roman losses ran into the thousands. Hadrian, his successor, had the foresight to terminate the Parthian campaign, and the provinces of Assyria and Mesopotamia were relinquished. The conflicts that ensued in the wake of Trajan's expedition makes it clear that Rome had overextended its limits and this was unsustainable in terms of military and financial resources. This is borne out by a passage in the *Historia Augusta*:[22]

> For the nations which Trajan had conquered began to revolt; the Moors, moreover, began to make attacks, and the Sarmatians to wage war, the Britons could not be kept under Roman sway, Egypt was thrown into disorder by riots, and finally Libya and Palestine showed the spirit of rebellion.

Hadrian (117–138)

Hadrian, the third of the 'Five Good Emperors', was not an imperator that rested on his laurels, spending much of his tenure travelling around the empire to oversee its security needs, and his legacy is often seen through his impressive building achievements, especially Hadrian's Wall and the Pantheon;[23] and he must have inherited the substantial spoils of war that his predecessor had acquired in Parthia a short time before his accession.

Constructions

The original Pantheon was built by Agrippa in 27 BC and is thought to have been a temple intended for the deification of the gens Iulia, dedicated in particular to Mars and Venus, the most prominent ancestral deities of that family. It is possible that the temple had seven niches occupied by the planetary deities. In the *pronaos* (porch) were statues of the patron and Augustus and caryatides were installed in this part of the building. The Pantheon was burned in 80 and was restored by Domitian, and struck by lightning and burned in the reign of Trajan. Hadrian restored the Pantheon after 126 and the inscription visible today (Figure 2.1), refers to the original construction by Agrippa:

> M AGRIPPA LF COS TERTIVM FECIT
> Marcus Agrippa, son of Lucius, made [this building]
> when consul for the third time.

The building consists of a large pedimented *pronaos* connected to a drum of brick-faced concrete with seven niches at ground level in the interior, possibly housing the deities mentioned above. The walls and floor are of marble and the walls consist of a complex series of relieving arches that bear the thrust of the dome, which is pierced by its famous oculus (9 metres in diameter). Perhaps the most extraordinary feature of this incredible building are its internal statistics – the height from the floor to the oculus being 43.20 metres, the same as the inside diameter of the drum, allowing us to imagine the insertion of a giant sphere.

Many of the brick-stamps examined from the Pantheon are Hadrianic and it is tempting to regard the monument as a rare example of an edifice

Figure 2.1 Das Pantheon und die Piazza della Rotunda in Rom.
Jacob Alt (1836), watercolour. Albertina, Vienna.

not built from the spoils of war. However, Lise Hetland has plausibly argued that the present construction commenced in the reign of Trajan, four years after it burned (in 114), on the basis of Trajanic era brick-stamps.[24] If this is correct then we should consider that the initial phase of construction was bankrolled by the booty from Trajan's Dacian campaigns.

The Temple of Venus and Rome was another important construction, thought to have been the largest temple ever built in the city.[25] It was a double temple on the Velia dedicated to Venus Felix, the ancestress of the Roman people, and to Roma aeterna, the genius of the city, dedicated in 135. The plans were drawn by Hadrian and their design criticized by Apollodorus, Trajan's architect, who Dio says was executed: '. . . he first banished and later put to death Apollodorus, the architect, who had built the various creations of Trajan in Rome – the forum, the odeum and the gymnasium'.[26] Unusually, each *cella* for the goddess was placed back to back rather than side by side (as in the Temple of the Capitoline Triad), with Venus facing east and Roma west. The temple was of the Corinthian Order, built on a large podium of concrete faced with travertine, 145 metres long and 100 wide. The apse and part of the east *cella* are visible today. Four Hadrianic building inscriptions are known in Rome. Perhaps the most important of these is from the Temple of the Dioscuri in the Roman Forum.[27]

Hadrian's villa (the Villa Adriana), located some 30 kilometres east of Rome at Tivoli, constitutes the most extraordinary series of architectural innovations in the history of the Roman empire.[28] The complex is laid out on a massive scale, occupying an area of 100 hectares, and provided a welcome alternative to the Palatine Hill for Hadrian, who governed the empire here from 128. The choice of this location was influenced by its close proximity to the source of the great aqueducts that fed Rome, since an abundant supply of water was required to feed the bath-houses, fountains, and pools within the villa complex. Some of the innovations preserved today include a pool and grotto named respectively as Canopus and Serapeum, deriving from the Egyptian city of Canopus and its Serapeum, although the columns that are integral to this structure are of the Corinthian Order and typically Roman. The famous 'half-dome', a prominent feature of this monument, also attracted the criticism of Apollodorus, who likened it to a pumpkin, according to Dio, he said: 'Be off, and draw your gourds. You don't understand any of these matters . . .'.[29]

One of the most interesting features of the villa is the Maritime Theatre, comprising a circular barrel-vaulted portico, this building incorporated a lounge, library, heated baths and suites, an art gallery, and a large fountain. Within this structure is a circular pool, demarcating an island enclosure some 40 metres in diameter. The island was equipped with its own luxurious house, perhaps the emperor's private retreat. The footprints of these structures are visible, taking the form of curves and recurves, hitherto unprecedented in the history of architecture.

A number of inscriptions are recorded in other parts of Italy.[30] Hadrian's contemporary, Cornelius Fronto, wrote that one might 'see memorials of his journeys in most cities of Europe and Asia'. The *Historia Augusta* records that 'He built something in almost every city'.[31] These sources are attested by extant remains and building inscriptions, especially in the Greek east, which expressed his love of all things Hellenic, but also at Italica in Spain, the city of his birth. Some of the most important buildings included the colossal Temple of Zeus at Kyzikos in Asia Minor and the Temple of Zeus Olympios in Athens. Hadrian restored a number of buildings in Cyrene that had been destroyed during the 'war of Quietus' in 115.[32] At Italica he enlarged the city laying it out on an orthogonal grid with porticoed streets and impressive bath-houses, and a new aqueduct. He also constructed a large amphitheatre, and elevated the legal status of the city to a *colonia*, renaming it Colonia Aelia Augusta Italica – Aelius was part of his family name.[33]

A number of dated building inscriptions have been found in the provinces, although, curiously, none are known from Italica; also, there are fewer in the western provinces than perhaps should be expected (albeit fractionally), and this could reflect his focus on the Greek east; however, only 24 building inscriptions are recorded in the eastern empire, compared with 25 in the western empire. Some examples in Britannia are from Hadrian's Wall and their date may relate to his visit to the province in 122.[34]

Hadrian's Wall

Turning to military architecture, Hadrian fully considered the vulnerability of Rome's welfare in strategic areas. His reign has been generally regarded as peaceful, when in fact there were episodes of severe conflict. Shortly after 120, *Legio IX Hispana* disappeared from the historical record. Since their last posting was northern Britain, a number of scholars have suggested that they were wiped out by the Caledonians on their way to build Hadrian's Wall (Figure 2.2). Others have contended that the legion was destroyed in the Second Jewish revolt based on a supposed inference from Dio.[35] An additional suggestion places their destruction in Armenia in 161. However, there is no evidence to support either claim, and those legions that perished were almost certainly not the IX Hispana; therefore the first scenario seems more likely.[36]

Hadrian's Wall ran from the River Tyne on the North Sea to the Solway Firth on the Irish Sea (117.5 kilometres), and was completed around 130. It comprised a stone wall and foundation base, fortified with mile-castles and two turrets in between, and a fort every five Roman miles (7.5 kilometres). From north to south the wall consisted of a ditch, wall, and military road, and a ditch and bank on either side (*vallum*). The construction of the wall is recorded in the *Historia Augusta*:[37]

> And so, having reformed the army quite in the manner of a monarch, he set out for Britain, and there he corrected many abuses and was the first to construct a wall, eighty miles in length, which was to separate the barbarians from the Romans.

Two of the best-preserved forts are at Housesteads and Vindolanda. The former affords the most iconic view of the wall as it winds east; the latter

Figure 2.2 Hadrian's Wall, near Housesteads fort, looking east.
Courtesy of Ian Robertson.

has yielded many wooden tablets that are informative about everyday life on the wall. As for its function, it is thought that its gates served as customs posts; however, it was mainly defensive and this indicates that the region was hostile,[38] a factor borne out by later historically documented accounts.[39]

In terms of its financial outlay, it was constructed by the soldiers of *Legio II Augusta*, *VI Victrix*, and XX Valeria Victrix, so the actual cost of building the wall may have been relatively minimal. *Legio VI* was later based at York and *XX* at Chester. The forts along the wall were garrisoned by auxiliary regiments recruited from across the empire, including the Iberian peninsula, Dacia, northern Gaul, Syria, and North Africa. These were estimated to be around 600 strong comprising around 480 infantry and 120 cavalry. The Roman military garrison there has been estimated at around 9,000. Some 15 per cent of the Roman army was stationed in Britain, mainly in the north of the province: on the wall, along the Cumbrian coast, and along the roads leading to the frontier from the legionary fortresses at York and Chester. *Legio II* was based at Caerleon in south-east Wales. As for overall military spend, the presence of three legions and their *auxilia* in Britain would have constituted a massive financial burden, and soldiers were often drafted from the province to assist in conflicts elsewhere. Ultimately, this would prove unsustainable, and Britain was abandoned early in the fifth century.[40]

The Third Good Emperor?

In Judaea, the First Jewish revolt and Kitos War had demonstrated the problematic character of the province as far as major uprisings were concerned. In 132–135, the Second Jewish revolt would prove to be especially terrible. The catalyst for this was the unusually poor judgement of Hadrian. Jerusalem was a city of rubble after Titus' exploits. To 'remedy' this, the emperor constructed a new city, naming it Aelia Capitolina, to settle retired legionaries, making it a *colonia*.[41] Hadrian erected a temple of Jupiter on the Temple Mount, over the site of the destroyed Second Temple, and banned the Jewish rite of circumcision. In a further affront, according to Eusebius, he installed an idol of a marble pig at the Bethlehem Gate.[42]

This ignited one of the most serious revolts in Roman history.[43] Dio wrote that: 'The Jews deemed it intolerable that foreign races should be settled in their city and foreign rites planted there'.[44] The leader of the uprising was Shim'on Bar-Kokhba whom many Jews regarded as the Messiah. There is considerable speculation that two legions were wiped out – X Fretensis, based in Aelia Capitolina, and VI Ferrata, stationed at Caparcotna on the Sea of Galilee. At the very least both legions were seriously eroded. Hadrian appointed Julius Severus, governor of Britain, the task of quelling the revolt,[45] and systematically the Romans crushed it. Dio estimated Jewish losses to be 580,000, excluding those who died from famine and disease or in villages that were put to the torch.[46] Matters were concluded with another epic siege at Bar-Kokhba's fortress at Bethar near Jerusalem. Eusebius wrote that: 'The siege lasted a long time … before the rebels were driven to final destruction by famine and thirst, and the instigator of their madness paid the penalty he deserved'.[47] Eusebius' anti-Semitic bias is unambiguous here. The revolt culminated in the bloody extermination of the Jewish state and Judaea was incorporated into the province of Syria Palestina.[48]

Not since the War of the Batons in the Augustan period had the spectre of invasion reared its ugly head. However, in 134, the Alans, a Sarmatian nomadic tribal confederacy of Iranian stock, set a dangerous precedent that was to afflict Rome until its eventual collapse. They had established themselves in the Caucasus region between the Black and Caspian Seas by the first century AD, and inflicted a number of defeats inside Parthian territory.[49] Flavius Arrianus, its governor, otherwise known as the Roman historian Arrian, was chosen to repulse them, and matters were concluded with a vintage display of military tactics.[50] Hadrian died in 138 at Baiae on the Gulf of Naples, and was later interred in his mausoleum, visible today as Castel Sant'Angelo in Parco Adriano.[51]

Dio, perhaps, places the judgement of Hadrian's reign in its rightful perspective, and this is echoed in the *Historia Augusta*:[52]

> Hadrian was hated by the people, in spite of his generally excellent reign, on account of the murders committed by him at the beginning and end of his reign, since they had been unjustly and impiously brought about. Yet he was so far from being of a bloodthirsty disposition that even in the case of some who clashed with him he thought it sufficient to write to their native places the bare statement that they did not please him. And if it was absolutely necessary to punish any man who had children, yet in proportion to the number of his children he would lighten the penalty imposed. Nevertheless, the senate persisted for a long time in its refusal to vote him the usual honours and in its strictures upon some of those who had committed excesses during his reign and had been honoured therefor, when they ought to have been punished.

Antoninus Pius (138–161)

The reign of Antoninus Pius, Hadrian's adopted heir, and the 'Fourth Good Emperor', is generally regarded as peaceful.[53] Unlike his predecessors and successors, historical texts that relate to his tenure are scant and we are largely dependent on the *Historia Augusta*, which casts him in a positive light.[54]

Constructions

His economic policy was apparently frugal, considerably benefitting the treasury.[55] In fact, dated building inscriptions in Rome, Italy, and the provinces are the most numerous in the first two centuries of the Principate, and point to buoyant economic conditions in this period. Two of his best-known buildings are in Rome. The first of these monuments was the Temple of the Deified Hadrian, dedicated on the Campus Martius in 145, later incorporated into the Piazza di Pietra (Piazza of Stone), now the Bourse. Part of this is preserved, comprising fluted columns of white marble with Corinthian capitals, and a richly decorated entablature. The *cella* and columns stand on a *stylobate* (platform). The temple was enclosed by a rectangular porticus – some of which survives – possibly the Porticus Argonautarum, built by Agrippa in 25 BC. It derived its name from the paintings on its walls that depicted the adventures of the Argonauts.[56]

The Temple of the Deified Faustina was built by Pius at the entrance to the Roman Forum, and initially dedicated to his wife Faustina, who died in 141, and this is recorded on an inscription on the architrave. Subsequently the temple was rededicated to the emperor and his wife after his death in 161 by Marcus Aurelius. The temple stands on a high platform of large peperino blocks. In the seventh or eighth century it was converted into the Church of Saint Lorenzo in Miranda. Excavations of the temple in 1546 revealed columns of cipollino 17 metres high with Corinthian capitals. The frieze on the sides of the temple was carved in relief with garlands and griffins. The existing remains consist of parts of the peperino wall of the *cella*, built into the church. The second dedicatory inscription on the frieze reads: 'Divo Antonino et Divae Faustinae Ex SC'. ('To the divine Antoninus and to the divine Faustina by decree of the Senate.')[57]

Also, the *Historia Augusta* records that he repaired the Graecostadium after it was burned; the Colosseum was repaired, as was the Mausoleum of Hadrian, the Temple of Agrippa, the Pons Sublicius (Rome's earliest bridge), ports at Caieta and Tarracina, ports and baths at Ostia, the aqueduct at Antium, temples at Lanuvium (south-east of Rome), and the Pharos lighthouse at Alexandria.[58] One building inscription is known in the capital in the reign of Pius.[59]

Several dated building inscriptions are recorded in the Italian regions,[60] and a considerable number in the western provinces.[61]

The Antonine Wall

According to the British archaeologist John Wilkes:[62]

> It is almost certain not only that at no time in his life did he ever see, let alone command, a Roman army, but that, throughout the twenty-three years of his reign, he never went within five hundred miles of a legion.

However, the Caledonian threat in Scotland was deemed sufficient to construct the Antonine Wall between the Firth of Forth and the Firth of Clyde in central Scotland. The *Historia Augusta* hints of a conflict, even if the emperor was not engaged in it personally: 'For Lollius Urbicus, his legate, overcame the Britons and built a second wall, one of turf, after driving back the barbarians'.[63] It should also be considered that the contemporary historian Pausanias wrote of major conflicts in Mauretania and Britain during Pius' reign and the British historians Anne Robertson and Lawrence Keppie have argued that Pausanias' reference was to a revolt in Scotland around 139–142 rather than a supposed revolt of the Brigantes circa 155.[64]

The Antonine Wall was begun around 142 and completed about 154, but abandoned around 162, with Roman forces retrenching south to Hadrian's Wall, a factor that suggests continued hostility in the north. It ran across central Scotland at its narrowest part, from the Firths of Clyde to the Forth, according to Tacitus, in his biography of his father-in-law Agricola: 'Clota and Bodotria, being carried far inland by tides from opposite seas, are separated by but a narrow strip of land'.[65] Archaeological excavations have corroborated the *Historia Augusta*, demonstrating that the wall was made of turf blocks, but underpinned by cut blocks and rough stones. From north to south the wall comprised a bank, V-shaped ditch, a flat area of ground (berm), the wall, and a military road behind that ran along its course (60 kilometres), and the remains of seventeen forts are known.

Legacy

Antoninus Pius apparently died peacefully at his villa in Lorium in Etruria (Tuscany) in March 161. He was succeeded by his two sons Marcus Aurelius, the last of the Five Good Emperors, and Lucius Verus. In *Meditations* Aurelius paid tribute to his late father:[66]

> There was nothing rude in him, nor yet overbearing or violent nor carried, as the phrase goes, 'to the sweating state'; but everything was considered separately, as by a man of ample leisure, calmly, methodically, manfully, consistently. One might apply to him what is told of Socrates . . .

Marcus Aurelius and Lucius Verus (161–180, 161–169)

Their joint reign was baptized by violence, and this was to continue for more than a decade in one of the bloodiest phases in Roman history. With trouble brewing on the Danube, Vologases III of Parthia saw this as an opportune moment to invade Armenia, forcing king Sohaemus into exile. He targeted the legionary base at Elegeia under the command of Aelius Severianus, probably destroying *Legio XXII Deiotariana*, since they are absent on an inscription in Rome listing 28 legions in the later reign of Aurelius.[67] In response, Lucius Verus campaigned with Audius Cassius, governor of Syria on its eastern border (162–164), and then invaded Persia, capturing Ctesiphon, before limping back to Syria, with many losses inflicted by famine and plague.

The Antonine Plague

Commonly known as the Antonine Plague, it proved catastrophic for the population of the Roman empire, spreading its deadly pathogens as the remnants of the returning troops dispersed across the provinces,[68] and this is supported by archaeological and epigraphic data (see below and p. 119). Writing in the fourth century, the historian Eutropius, widely thought to be a credible source, remarked:[69]

> He himself [Aurelius] waged one war against the Marcomanni, but it was greater than any that can be remembered, with the result that it should be compared to the Punic Wars, seeing that it was made all the more serious because entire Roman armies had perished. In fact, under him there was such a terrible outbreak of the plague that, after his victory over the Persians, at Rome and throughout Italy and the provinces a very great proportion of the inhabitants and almost all of the troops died from the enfeebling disease.

An informative study by Dragoș Mitrofan has synthesized the archaeological evidence from mass graves across the Roman empire that furnish evidence for the Antonine Plague in the catacombs of St Peter and Marcellinus in Rome, and a necropoles at Dealul Furcilor and Dealul Podei, in Apulum, Dacia; in the latter instance the graves contained lime, known to be used as a disinfectant. Additional archaeological evidence for the plague has been unearthed at cemeteries at Tomis and Ostrov in Moesia Inferior.[70]

It has been estimated that as many as a third of the urban and rural population perished. This was echoed centuries later as Spanish Flu spread across the world after the return of allied soldiers at the end of the First World War. In the winter of 169, Lucius Verus died in Altinum near Venice, widely thought to have been a victim of the plague. The contemporary accounts of Aelius Galenus, the Greek physician Galen, have led a number of scholars to suggest that the epidemic was smallpox.[71] The plague is sometimes referred to as the Plague of Galen, and Dio mentions a further outbreak early in the reign of Commodus.[72] Historical texts inform that this raged on for the duration of the Danube Wars, and for understandable reasons, the social, economic, and military impact on the Roman empire is considered to have been devastating.[73] The ramifications of the plague on the long-term fortunes of the western Roman empire are fully considered later on, but it is also instructive to examine the epigraphic record in the period in more detail below.

War on the Danube

In 166 Rome was dramatically put on the defensive by a major crisis on the Danube frontier and there followed a protracted series of operations.

This involved the Sueves, Marcomanni, Quadi, and Iazyges, who launched an invasion of Italy, besieged Aquileia and reached the plain of Venice before they were repelled. Aurelius chose the strategic headquarters of *Legio XIV Gemina* as his operational base at Carnuntum in Pannonia Inferior. There, he wrote *Meditations*; the endnote of the first book was entitled: 'Written among the Quadi on the Gran' (referring to the Granua River, a tributary of the Danube).[74]

Aurelius' war effort was sponsored by the proceeds accrued by his predecessor. Antoninus Pius had amassed a great surplus in his reign of 675 million *denarii* (2.7 billion *sesterces*) and this was expended on his Germanic wars.[75] According to the *Historia Augusta*, Aurelius was later forced to sell his wife's furniture, crockery, and clothing at auction in the Roman Forum to honour the expenses of the Roman state.[76]

Eager to bring matters to a conclusion, Aurelius enlisted the support of *Legio XII Fulminata* to deal with a Quadi offensive under Ariogaesus on the Roman side of the Danube. During the course of the pivotal battle that ensued, the extraordinary Miracle of the Rain occurred. No doubt from a Christian-tinted perspective, we are informed of this by Eusebius, Themistius, and Xiphilinus, the latter claiming that it came about after a large contingent of Christian legionaries prayed to God. The event is depicted on the Column of Marcus Aurelius in Rome, along with other scenes from his Danube campaigns. The legion was apparently outnumbered and parched with thirst. Harnuphis, an Egyptian magician and companion of the emperor, is said to have invoked several deities, including Mercury, god of the air, to attract a storm:[77]

> So intent, indeed, were most of them on drinking that they would have suffered severely from the enemy's onset, had not a violent hail-storm and numerous thunderbolts fallen upon the ranks of the foe. Thus in one and the same place one might have beheld water and fire descending from the sky simultaneously; so that while those on the one side were being consumed by fire and dying; and while the fire, on the one hand, did not touch the Romans . . .

It was an incredible twist of fate that the legion involved in this dramatic freak of nature was known colloquially as 'Legion Fulminata' – the 'Thundering Legion'.

Constructions

Building inscriptions in the reign of Marcus Aurelius in Rome, Italy, and the provinces is markedly reduced by comparison with the reign of his predecessor and, curiously, his successor Commodus, an issue that will be revisited below.

The most celebrated monument in Rome in this era is the Column of Aurelius. It is modelled closely on that of Trajan, erected between 172 and

175 to commemorate the emperor's victory over the Marcomanni and Sarmatians. The column is the same height as its predecessor, but tapers to a lesser degree and is more imposing for this reason.[78] Significantly, it is one of the few monuments erected by the emperor. The only significant building from which an inscription is recorded in the capital is the Forum Holitorium, constructed early in his joint reign.[79] Significantly, just one inscription is known in the Italian regions and another in Sicilia,[80] and in the provinces the distribution of building inscriptions is considerably less than for the reign of Antoninus Pius.[81]

The total number of building inscriptions in the western provinces in the joint reigns of Marcus Aurelius is twenty-seven, ten fewer than under Trajan, eight fewer than the reign of Hadrian, and sixteen fewer than their predecessor, Antoninus Pius. This relatively low statistic is telling, especially since Aurelius' reign was quite long at nineteen years. The epigraphic picture does tend to support the historical sources pertaining to the severity of the Antonine Plague, and it should be considered to have had a devastating impact on the urban and rural spheres of the empire, their economy, and population levels.

Legacy

Campaigns were concluded with victory over the Iazyges in the winter of 174–175.[82] Commodus was made co-emperor in 177, Aurelius celebrated a triumph in Rome, and an arch was inaugurated to commemorate the occasion. Its location is not exactly known but elements of its decoration are preserved in the Capitoline Museums and adorn the Arch of Constantine in Rome. He died at Vindobona in 180 and was deified, his ashes interred in the Mausoleum of Hadrian. Dio speculated that the emperor was poisoned by his physicians at the request of Commodus.[83] Ironically, he wrote:[84]

> the corruption of the mind is a pest far worse than any miasma and vitiation of the air which we breathe around us. The latter is a pestilence for living creatures and affects their life, the former for human beings and affects their humanity.

Commodus (180–192)

Marcus Aurelius' death traditionally marks the end of the '*Pax Romana*', yet it is ironic that the tyrannical reign of Commodus that followed was relatively peaceful. It was, however, apparently characterized by megalomania and a ruthless purge of his father's trusted civil and military advisors, especially the senatorial class. Despite this, he was popular with the army and the public, staging a number of lavish spectacles in the Colosseum, of which he sometimes partook as a gladiator. Commodus also had a bloodthirsty penchant for slaughtering exotic beasts, as witnessed by Dio, who was a senator at the time.[85] His hand-outs were excessive, to the extent that the same source indicates that the treasury was virtually depleted after his reign.[86] The historian is one of few sources for understanding his reign, along with the *Historia Augusta*, and the picture they paint is decidedly negative. It should be borne in mind that he was closely allied with Septimius Severus under whom he served as proconsul of Africa, so it would have naturally suited him to be scathing about his former patron.[87]

Constructions

Commodus, although consigned to history as an especially terrible emperor, this point of view should be tempered with the available data set of building inscriptions that point to a reasonable level of imperial patronage in the sphere of monuments, especially in the provinces; however, a good number of these are military in character rather than civic.[88]

Just a few more building inscriptions are recorded in the reign of Commodus, seven more than his predecessor, although this figure weighs in favour of a concentration at Intercisa. The site was a *castrum* (fort), about 70 kilometres south of Carnuntum on the bank of the Danube and is known to have been destroyed around 178 during the Marcomannic-Sarmatian wars with Marcus Aurelius, and the large number of inscriptions here – fourteen in all – record its reconstruction under Commodus. In fact, if this figure is subtracted from the total number in his reign then the figure drops to twenty, and this now modest figure perhaps attests to a lack of building activity in the wake of the Antonine Plague, which continued to afflict this period. This is supported by the fact that only six building inscriptions are recorded in the eastern provinces. These statistics do not add much to the sullied reputation of the emperor.[89]

Legacy

The stability of foreign relations under Commodus was due to his policy with the Germanic tribes on the Danube, signing peace treaties in preference to the continual warfare that he had witnessed under his father, but this was expensive according to Herodian and Dio,[90] but perhaps a necessity given that, as mentioned above, the plague continued to rage on during his reign. Perhaps the most significant military activity was in Scotland, since it is documented that the Antonine Wall was reoccupied under the governor, Ulpius Marcellus, in 184.[91]

Building under *decurions* and other officials

Seventeen building inscriptions are attested in the second century, a manifestation of sponsorship by *decurions* and other officials. Those that are associated with known civic buildings include fora at Herdonia, Apulia et Calabria (Regio II); Aquae Iasae, Pannonia Superior; Singilia Barba,

Baetica; an amphitheatre at Municipium Claudium Virunum, Noricum; a forum at Scarbantia, Pannonia Superior; and a theatre at Leptis Magna, Africa Proconsularis.[92]

The Year of the Five Emperors (192–193)

Commodus' behaviour was deemed intolerable and poison was administered to his wine by his mistress, Marcia, in 192.[93] The last decade of the second century was extremely turbulent, culminating in the Year of the Five Emperors, with Pertinax,[94] Didius Julianus,[95] Pescennius Niger, and Clodius Albinus falling in rapid succession, and Septimius Severus emerging as sole ruler at Lugdunum.[96]

Subsequently, Severus invaded Parthia, with successful campaigns in 197 and 198, and Dio records that: 'Later, upon capturing Ctesiphon, he permitted the soldiers to plunder the entire city'.[97] It is also recorded that '. . . Severus gave the soldiers an enormous donative, none other, in truth, than liberty to plunder the Parthian capital, a privilege for which they had been clamouring'.[98] The booty from these victories enabled Severus, in part, to bankroll his building programme at Leptis Magna, the city of his birth, early in the century that followed.

The burden of the Roman military apparatus

The revolts of the first and second centuries attest to the unwillingness of indigenous provincials to accept the Roman yoke, in spite of the more positive benefits of imperial civilization, such as public bathing and entertainment. Romanization was clearly a 'top-down' phenomenon imposed across the length and breadth of the empire, and often, but never universally, accepted.[99] As future centuries were to prove, the multitude of barbarian peoples were eager to buy into the Roman brand, albeit with devastating consequences for the western Roman empire.

The second century, akin to the first, was a period of almost incessant bloodshed. This had commenced with the Dacian Wars, Kitos revolt, and gathered a violent momentum in the Second Jewish War. There followed the Alani invasion, problems in Britain, and the Parthian and Danube Wars. The downside of this was the loss of *Legion IX Hispana*, and the possible extermination of *X Fretensis* and *VI Ferrata* under Hadrian, as well as the destruction of *XXII Deiotariana* in the reign of Marcus Aurelius. Moreover, the Year of the Five Emperors constituted massive fatalities. The *auxilia* would have also sustained severe losses throughout the period but it is not possible to quantify these.

The broader picture

Collectively, in fact, the whole era was so marred with conflict that the '*Pax Romana*' is in no way an appropriate term to apply to the so-called golden age of the Principate, not even in a relative sense compared with the civil wars of the late Republic or the so-called crisis of the third century that followed. Several books in recent years have chronicled the battles waged in the empire, and the latest of these by Donathan Taylor takes in a broad chronological sweep from 31 BC to AD 565.[100] To put this in context, no fewer than 54 and 10 conflicts are catalogued for the first and second centuries respectively. As for the remainder of the empire, 41 occur in the third century, 56 in the fourth century, and 28 in the fifth. This reality should be set against a recent publication, *Pax Romana*, by the British historian Adrian Goldsworthy, in which he states that:[101]

> ... the Roman Empire was remarkably successful for a very long time, the *Pax Romana* holding sway over much of Western Europe, the Middle East and North Africa for centuries. This area was stable and apparently prosperous, with little or no trace of desolation. Roman peace does appear to have been a reality, for rebellions and large-scale violence were extremely rare. Even critics of empires must concede this about Rome.

This is surely not correct.

These episodes – once again – demonstrated how potentially vulnerable the Roman state was: each conflict demanded a great concentration of military resource, and the tactical movement of legions across the empire like a strategic chessboard – on the frontiers in Britain, the Rhine, the Danube, the east, or in the provinces of Judaea, North Africa, and elsewhere – to deal with major revolts. Despite its size, the army was persistently overstretched. The key to survival was the imperative of maintaining the army with a sufficient capacity to crush further invasions, insurrections, internecine warfare, and also to have the finance in place to recruit a larger force for future territorial expansion when needed. Civic funding, however, was a largely separate matter (see p. 32, 33, 39, 82, 117, 118, 175, 179). However, the empire had already contracted under Hadrian, and the halcyon days of copious booty flowing into imperial coffers had come to an end.

As contended in the previous chapter, the economic fortunes of Rome largely depended on the extraction of minerals to mint coinage, and tax-yields in economic product – cereals, olive oil, wine, and livestock – generated by an unprecedented level of agricultural exploitation across the empire in villas and farms.[102] Something of the scale of agricultural production in the first two centuries AD can be gleaned from the large mound close to the Aventine Hill near the Tiber in Rome, known as Monte Testaccio (Sherd Mountain). This is still visible today and is more than 40 metres in height with a perimeter of over 1 kilometre. It consists entirely of densely packed, broken olive oil amphorae (the 'jerry cans' of antiquity). They were deposited here over a period of some 250 years, beginning in the Augustan period through to the middle of the third century. Recent research has indicated that the mound was formed of an estimated 24.75 million amphorae that once contained

1.7 billion kilogrammes of oil. The remainder was made up of North African oil amphorae (15 to 17 per cent), containers for southern Spanish *garum*, and wine from Gaul and Italy (circa 3.5 per cent). Analysis has shown that more than 80 per cent of the sherds came from the region of Baetica in south-western Spain. Their import peaked in the second century when they constituted between 90 and 95 per cent of the total.[103] From the Severan period onwards the Baetican olive oil trade was dislocated in favour of mass production in North Africa from where it was exported to Rome.[104]

In the military budget a hierarchical scale of pay should be considered, from legionaries with no rank, upwards to general; *auxilia* regiments, discharge imbursements (*praemia*), bonuses (*donativa*), the cost of equipment, and the movement of grain and its consumption. It should also be borne in mind that political circumstances were such that the size of the Roman army increased substantially in the reign of Caracalla and again under Diocletian, with profound implications for the imperial budget.[105] These considerations are developed in the chapters that follow.

Naturally, as long as these demands could be met then the empire was relatively stable. Once again, a healthy economy was central to this, and commodities poured in from the provinces. For instance, grain from Egypt and North Africa; olive oil from Baetica, North Africa, and Syria; and gold and silver from Britain, Gaul, Iberia, Dacia, and elsewhere. Crucially, the ready availability of economic resources across the imperial domain is a prime reason why the empire did not fall, but at times it is clear that it was a close-run thing, with superior military organization and discipline ensuring continued success. In fact, the reputation of the Julio-Claudian, Flavian, and Nerva-Antonine dynasties are not normally equated with the concept of a failed empire, but the truth of the matter is that it could have collapsed in the first or second century.

The proceeds of the late Republican civil wars and the initial expansion under the Principate provided a massive injection of capital into the Roman economy, and epigraphic and written texts record that a considerable number of state-sponsored building projects were *ex manubiis*, built from the spoils of war, especially the Colosseum, imperial fora, and bath-houses. This injection of capital also funded building in Italy and the provinces under Trajan, Hadrian, and Antoninus Pius, and to a lesser extent under Marcus Aurelius and Commodus, whose reigns were afflicted by plague. In many cases where it is not recorded that monuments were built from war capital, this can be inferred; but in some instances buildings were erected under prudent leadership, as in the case of Antoninus Pius, although such occurrences were rare and constructions were on a relatively smaller scale. By the reign of Marcus Aurelius, expansion was impeded, Rome was largely on the defensive, booty was scant, and the prodigious public building projects of his predecessors were not perpetuated. However, a distinction should be drawn at this stage between imperial-funded programmes in the greater cities – such as Antioch, Alexandria, and Rome – on the one hand, and civic-sponsored projects by the *decurions* and other officials in many other cities, which were often paid for by taxes levied from tenant farmers and landowners, a large proportion of which did not go into the state treasury (*fiscus*). In short, however, the flaws of the state infrastructure were plainly exposed in a relatively early phase of imperial history. Fundamentally, the army was persistently overstretched and the impact on the treasury was commensurate. These are pivotal factors when considering the continuity and collapse of the empire.

Notes

1   Marcus Aurelius, *Meditations* (VII.29–31). 1916. Translated by C.R. Haines. LCL 58. For a biography, xi–xxvii.
2   D*RH*, LXVIII.
3   Sim, 2011, 48–50.
4   Pliny the Younger, *Letters and Panegyricus* (X.14). Books VIII–X. 1969. Translated by Betty Radice. LCL 59. *Letters*. Books 1–7. 1969. Translated by Betty Radice. LCL 55. For a biography, ix–xxvi.
5   Platner and Ashby, 1926, 237–245; Gros, 2011, 218–219.
6   Gellius, *The Attic Nights of Aulus Gellius* (25.1). Books I–V, 6–13. 1927. Translated by J.C. Rolfe. LCL 195, 200. For a biography, xi–xxv.
7   D*RH*, LXVIII.16.
8   Curry, 2015, 116–129.
9   AM*H*, XVI.10, 15.
10 Ioannes Lydus, *On Powers or the Magistracies of the Roman State* (II.28). 1983. Translated by A.C. Bandy. Philadelphia: American Philosophical Society. For a biography, ix–lxxv.
11 Platner and Ashby, 1926, 534–536.
12 HD025637 (115).
13 HD025604 (98–117), HD025610 (98–117), HD025616 (103), HD025640 (116–117), HD027374 (98–117), HD065462 (98–117), HD065463 (112), HD065777 (112–117).
14 HD002019 (108–109), HD008880 (106–107), HD020091 (102–103), HD023722 (98–117), HD032467 (104–105), HD032527 (98–117), HD032533 (101–102).
15 HD001314 (100), HD004621 (100), HD020759 (113), HD030757 (116), HD031135 (100), HD031150 (105), HD035406 (98), HD036829 (98–100), HD036945 (103–117), HD037457 (102–106), HD045267 (98), HD045370 (104), HD51847 (102–116), HD58293 (102–117), HD059283 (98–117), HD060140 (98–117), HD065313 (106–117), HD066936 (98–117), HD072446 (103–106).
16 D*RH*, LXVIII.17–23, 25, 26, 28, 29, 31.
17 For an account of this conflict, Horbury, 2014, 257–264.
18 D*RH*, LXVIII.32; Eusebius, *Ecclesiastical History* (IV.2.2–5). Books 1–5. 1926. Translated by K. Lake. LCL 153. For a biography, ix–xxvii.
19 *Mishnah*, Sotah (IX.4). *The Mishnah: a new translation*. 1988. Translated by J. Neusner. New Haven, CT: Yale University Press.
20 Lightfoot, 1990, 115.
21 D*RH*, LXVIII.33.
22 *Historia Augusta* (I.5.). 1921, 1924, 1932. Translated by David Magie. LCL 139, 140, 263. For a critique, Rohrbacher, 2013, 146–180.

23 Platner and Ashby, 1926, 382–386; MacDonald, 2002; Gros, 2011, 174–178.
24 Her paper is a valid critique of the important study of Herbert Bloch, who excluded Trajanic brick-stamps from his study. Bloch, 1959; Hetland, 2006.
25 Platner and Ashby, 1926, 552–554; Gros, 2011, 179–180.
26 D*RH*, LXIX.4.
27 HD025655 (117–138). The other three are HD025673 (128–138), HD025676 (128–138), and HD025679 (117–138).
28 Macdonald and Pinto, 1995.
29 D*RH*, LXIX.4.
30 HD001142 (117–138), HD012580 (121–125), HD023002 (123–128), HD032542 (138), HD032464 (136–137), HD032509 (122), HD032512 (117–138), HD032515 (117–138), HD032542 (138), HD032560 (120–121), HD032620 (117–138), HD032623 (126–127), HD032650 (131–132), HD032659 (117–138), HD032662 (126–127).
31 *HA*, I.19.
32 Opper, 2008, 127–129.
33 Caballos and Pilar, 1997; Boatwright, 2000, 162–167.
34 HD002390 (121), HD002954 (119), HD0011506 (118–138), HD024465 (117–138), HD030787 (137), HD031189 (125–126), HD031192 (125–126), HD031207 (131–132), HD032004 (117–138), HD037458 (132), HD037460 (133), HD051720 (136–137), HD059284 (120), HD059285 (120), HD059286 (120), HD059288 (128–138), HD059289 (117–138), HD069929 (117–138), HD070048 (128–138), HD070210 (117–138), HD070230 (122–138), HD070533 (122–126), HD070810 (122–126), HD071010 (122–138), HD073984 (117–138).
35 D*RH*, LXIX.14.
36 Dando-Collins, 2010, 421–428.
37 *HA*, I.11.
38 Breeze, 2006.
39 Mention is made of the campaign of Count Theodosius in response to the incursions of the Picts in 368, AM*H*, XXVII, VIII.3–8.
40 Faulkner, 2004; Mattingly, 2006.
41 *EEH*, IV.6.4.
42 *Chronicle*, Hadrian, XIX. 1956. Translated by R.J. Helm. *Die Chronik des Hieronymus*, 2nd ed. Berlin: Akademie-Verlag.
43 For an account of this conflict, Horbury, 2014, 278–428.
44 D*RH*, LXIX.12.
45 D*RH*, LXIX.13.
46 D*RH*, LXIX, 14; EC, XVIII–XVIIII; *EEH*, IV.6, 3.
47 *EEH*, IV.6, 3.
48 *EEH*, IV.6.
49 J*JW*, VII.7, 4; D*RH*, LXIX.15.
50 Arrian, *Tactica, Flavius Arrianus, techne taktika* (*Tactical Handbook*) and *ektasis kata alamon* (*The Expedition Against the Alans*). (XI.23, 25, 31). 1993. Translated by J.G. DeVoto. Chicago, Ill: Ares Publishers; D*RH*, LXIX.15.
51 D*RH*, LXIX.22, 23; Aurelius Victor, *De Caesaribus* (XIV). 1994. Translated by H.W. Bird. Liverpool: Liverpool University Press; *HA*, I.25.
52 D*RH*, LXIX, 23; *HA*, I.27.
53 D*RH*, LXX.1.
54 *HA*, III.13.
55 D*RH*, LXXIV.8.
56 Platner and Ashby, 1926, 250, 420.
57 Platner and Ashby, 1926, 13–14.

58 *HA*, III.8.
59 HD025712 (138–161).
60 HD002009 (138–161), HD032428 (138–161), HD032431 (138–161), HD032494 (142–161), HD032542 (138), HD032563 (138–161), HD032569 (139), HD032596 (139), HD032632 (138–161).
61 HD002408 (146), HD002411 (146), HD002454 (150–151), HD002537 (151–152), HD002949 (151–152), HD002952 (158–159), HD002955 (158–159), HD017102 (138–161), HD018203 (143–144), HD021069 (147–161), HD030366 (138–161), HD030817 (157), HD031234 (140–141), HD031243 (143–146), HD031264 (147–148), HD031300 (158–159), HD031306 (158), HD031309 (158), HD033427 (157–158), HD036551 (145–161), HD036557 (138–161), HD036726 (138–161), HD037004 (145–161), HD037051 (146), HD037052 (146), HD058096 (144), HD059297 (138–161), HD059298 (138–161), HD060093 (156), HD067653 (150–156), HD067838 (145–161).
62 Wilkes, 1985, 242.
63 *HA*, III.5.
64 Frere, 1987, 126–153; Fulford, 2000, 559–576; Robertson and Keppie, 2015.
65 T*Ag*, XXIII.
66 *Meditations*, I.16.9.
67 Dessau, 1892, I, no. 2288.
68 *DRH*, LXXI.2; *AMH*, XXIII, VI.24; *HA*, V.8.
69 Eutropius, *The Breviarium ab urbe condita of Eutropius, The Right Honourable Secretary of State for General Petitions: dedicated to Lord Valens, Gothicus Maximus & Perpetual Emperor*. 1993. Translated by H.W. Bird. Liverpool: Liverpool University Press. For the extract about the war of Marcus Aurelius, VIII.12. For a biography, vii–lvii.
70 Mitrofan, 2014, 9–13.
71 Galen, *Methodus medendi* (V.12). 1586. Translated by T. Gale. London: Thomas East; Giardina, 2012, 757. A convincing argument for the identification of smallpox is presented by Littman and Littman, 1973, 243–255.
72 *DRH*, LXXIII.14.
73 Littman and Littman, 1973, 243–255.
74 *Meditations*, I.17.8.
75 *DRH*, LXXIV.8; Shaw, 1999, 142.
76 *HA*, IV.17.
77 For an account of this episode, *DRH*, LXXII.8–10.
78 Beckmann, 2011, 134–140.
79 HD025751 (161–164).
80 HD015189 (161–180), HD032446 (173–174).
81 HD002865 (163–164), HD002961 (170–171), HD007887 (179), HD012533 (175–177), HD017331 (177–180), HD026853 (167), HD030823 (162), HD030832 (163), HD030844 (169), HD031333 (162), HD031426 (172–174), HD031429 (172–174), HD031438 (174), HD031453 (172–173), HD031465 (176–177), HD032589 (172–174), HD035121 (166–169), HD051915 (179), HD054166 (169–170), HD054167 (169–170), HD054168 (169–170), HD055795 (161–169), HD056684 (169–170).
82 *DRH*, LXII.7.
83 *DRH*, LXXII.33–34.
84 *Meditations*, IX.2.
85 *DRH*, LXXIII.18.
86 *DRH*, LXXIV.8.
87 Chapter 1, note 8.
88 HD000231 (182), HD001204 (184–192), HD001269 (184–185), HD005564 (180–191), HD015805 (182–183), HD022455 (184–191), HD025796 (180–191),

HD029874 (182–185), HD030369 (182–185), HD031495 (183–185), HD031498 (183–185), HD031504 (186), HD031513 (188), HD032503 (180–191), HD032671 (185–191), HD036652 (186–192), HD037221 (184–185), HD037222 (184–185), HD037223 (182–185), HD037224 (182–185), HD037225 (182–185), HD037226 (180–183), HD037227 (182–185), HD037228 (182–185), HD037229 (182–185), HD037278 (182–185), HD038547 (185), HD048553 (183–184), HD051713 (182–184), HD053712 (184), HD064639 (189).

89 *DRH*, LXXII.14.
90 Herodian, *Empire* (I.6.9). *History of the Roman Empire: from the death of Marcus Aurelius to the accession of Gordian III*. Books I–IV. 1969. Translated by C.R. Whittaker. LCL 454. For a biography, vii–lxxxvii. D*RH*, LXXIV.5.
91 *DRH*, LXXIII.8.
92 HD001645 (101–200), HD000496 (131–170), HD031121 (131–170), HD048553 (101–200), HD052242 (101–130), HD059298 (138–161).
93 *DRH*, LXIII.22; H*E*, I.17.11; AV*DC*, XVII.
94 *DRH*, LXIV.9–10; H*E*, II.5.8.
95 *DRH*, LXIV.16–17; H*E*, II.13.1.
96 *DRH*, LXVII.14–17; H*E*, III.7.7.
97 *DRH*, LXXVI.9; H*E*, III.9.1–12.
98 *HA*, X.16.
99 Millett, 1990, 40–64.
100 Taylor, 2016, 39–45, 46–187.
101 Goldsworthy, 2016, 2.
102 Bowman, 2013, 219–253; De Vos, 2000, 20, 81–84; De Vos, 2013, 143–218; Esmonde Cleary, 2013, 264–302; Marzano, 2013a, 85–106; Marzano, 2013b, 107–141.
103 Opper, 2008, 36–37.
104 Esmonde Cleary, 2013, 292–293, 399.
105 Duncan-Jones, 1994, 33–37.

3   Crisis! What crisis?

And do not fear the soldiers, either, or regard them in any other light than as guardians of my empire, which is at the same time yours. That they should be supported is necessary, for many reasons, but they will be supported for your benefit, not against you ... This is the reason why the taxes now levied are higher than usual, in order that the seditious element may be made submissive and the victorious element, by receiving sufficient support, may not become seditious.[1]

Roman History
Julius Caesar

If the fall of Rome is to be linked to economic factors, it is instructive to look at what is commonly regarded as the crisis of the third century, an unprecedented period of high inflation, imperial assassinations, protracted civil wars, and foreign invasions.[2] The severity of this crisis has been challenged by some, such as the Dutch scholar Lukas de Blois, who has argued that the phenomenon was confined to areas of conflict.[3] Christian Witschel, the German Romanist, has also viewed this period in a more positive manner than the traditional perspective.[4] While the Romano-British archaeologist Richard Reece has suggested that the third century was more a period of transformation than collapse.[5] It is perhaps no coincidence that these more optimistic interpretations of the third century crisis tend to dovetail with – and prefigure – the 'transformation' of Rome in late antiquity from the perspective of Peter Brown and others.[6]

To reiterate, this is a point of view that the weight of textual and archaeological evidence does not support. Primary texts suggest that there was a fundamental political meltdown in the third century and, while this may have affected different parts of the empire more than others, the point most relevant to the present interpretation of why Rome fell is the extent to which the various factors impacted on the Roman economy. In this context, an examination of the archaeological, epigraphic, and numismatic evidence is key.

In light of the fact that so many emperors came and went in rapid succession, the emphasis in the present chapter is more concerned with the broader economic and political trends rather than a reign-by-reign narrative, although there is some concentration in this context on the more relevant imperators. It is logical that the epigraphic evidence is not included in those cases where these omissions are made, but the epigraphic database is scant in these instances, as one might expect.

Maintaining the Roman army

Dio attributed the onset of the third-century crisis to Commodus, whose inept rule turned the Roman empire 'from a kingdom of gold to one of iron and rust'.[7] The gravity of this statement represented for Gibbon, and others, the beginning of the decline of Rome.[8] However, the increasing burden of the armed forces in this period is a substantial issue here. For instance, under Tiberius, the combined total of the legions, *auxilia*, Praetorian Guard, and navy, was in the region of 300,000 personnel.[9] In the reign of Trajan this figure had reached around 450,000. Under Septimius Severus, this had increased again to around 500,000.[10] Estimates suggest that Severus also increased the military salary by a third. According to Dio:[11]

> There were many things Severus did that were not to our liking, and he was blamed for making the city turbulent through the presence of so many troops and for burdening the State by his excessive expenditures of money, and most of all, for placing his hope of safety in the strength of his army rather than in the good will of his associates in the government.

Herodian affirms this criticism: '. . . he weakened their strict discipline and respect for their superiors by teaching them to covet money and by introducing them to luxurious living'.[12] This is thought to have amounted to a rise from 300 to 400 *sesterces*.[13]

Severus' infamous son, Caracalla, increased pay again substantially after his bloody prosecutions in Egypt, according to Dio: 'He likewise gave prizes to the soldiers for their campaign, to those assigned to the pretorian twenty-five thousand *sesterces*, and to the rest twenty thousand . . .'.[14] Herodian also makes a reference to this pay increase: 'In gratitude for his deliverance and in return for the sole rule, he promised each soldier 2,500 *denarii* and increased their ration allowance by one-half'.[15] This is interpreted as an increase from 400 to 600 *sesterces*.[16] Nigel Pollard is surely correct in his assertion that these sources lead to the perception that the Roman empire was being bled dry to pay the army.[17] Herodian is known to have taken a special interest in fiscal affairs although he is not thought to have had a deep understanding in such matters.

There was a final increase in the military salary under Maximinus Thrax (235–238), with a legionary receiving 7,200 *sesterces* by 235.[18] The strain on the military budget was compounded by the elimination of costs from soldiers' salaries under Septimius Severus, so thereafter, coinage was debased and taxes increased on the civilian population.[19]

According to the calculations of Richard Duncan-Jones, from the Augustan period, and for much of the first century, the annual military salary, including *praemia* (discharge payments), for legionaries and the *auxilia* is estimated at 554 million *sesterces*. This sum had risen to 704 million per annum under Commodus, and 908 and 1,188 respectively under Septimius Severus and Caracalla.[20]

Maintaining the army was in fact the largest expenditure in the imperial budget. Duncan-Jones has estimated that the cost of the army accounted for approximately three-quarters of the empire's budget in the mid-second century (between 72 and 77 per cent). By the mid-Severan period (c.215), the cost of the army equated to around 70 per cent (between 64 and 75 per cent) of state spending.[21] However, Ramsay MacMullen has suggested that military expenditure was much lower, and this issue is discussed in more detail below. It is germane to assess these costs in the fourth and fifth centuries in the relevant chapters that follow. Suffice to say that it was crucial to maintain tax-yields to honour the threshold of military spending, not least since the number of military personnel increased substantially again under Diocletian.[22]

The Severan period: Septimius Severus (193–211)

After his victorious campaigns in the eastern and western provinces, Septimius Severus arrived in Rome in the summer of 202 to celebrate his *decennalia* (tenth anniversary in power). He also took the opportunity to smash the Garamantes, and other desert tribes, who had been a persistent thorn in the side of the province and its neighbours.[23] Severus followed up on this assault by re-fortifying the African frontier, pushing a vast defensive network further into the Sahara. On his return to Rome in 203 the emperor's celebrated arch was erected in honour of himself and his sons Geta and Caracalla.[24] Its reliefs, many of which are not preserved, depicted the capture of Parthian soldiers and booty acquired from campaigns.[25]

Some indication of the wealth accumulated may be gauged by his distribution of largesse to the urban plebs and Praetorian Guard, since Dio says that: 'He prided himself especially on this largess, and, in fact, no emperor had ever before given so much to the whole population at once; the total amount spent for the purpose was two hundred million *sesterces*'.[26]

Constructions

In the following autumn he visited Leptis Magna in Tripolitania (Libya), the place of his birth, where he set out an ambitious building programme, transforming the city as a major urban centre, second only to Carthage.[27] This included a new harbour, an enlarged theatre, ostentatious colonnaded streets, a monumental nymphaeum, and the mighty Severan Forum – modelled on the Forum of Trajan – which was completed by Caracalla and dedicated in 216. The remains are some of the most impressive anywhere within the former bounds of the Roman empire, once ringed by lofty colonnades and paved with Proconnesian marble. At one end, on a transverse axis, the basilica dominated, and at the opposite end stood a large temple, perhaps dedicated to the Severan house, often referred to as the Temple of the Gens Septimia. It is possible that it is the same temple mentioned by Dio, who complained of Severus 'he built a temple of huge size to Bacchus and Hercules'.[28]

In Rome, he built the Septizodium, the Baths of Severus, and the Septimian Baths.[29] Five inscriptions are recorded in Rome and five in the Italian regions.[30] There are more imperial building inscriptions under Septimius Severus than any Roman emperor in the western empire. The lion's share are outside Italy.[31] Epigraphy, taken once more as an index of economic prosperity, appears to suggest that the reign of Septimius Severus represented the waxing of Roman fortunes. However, the record is somewhat skewed by military constructions, such as at Ala, Intercisa, and Carnuntum, but nonetheless the emperor's prodigious building programme certainly spreads to the civic sphere as attested in Rome, Municipium Claudium Virunum, and Leptis Magna.

Legacy

Septimius Severus' military policy echoes that of Trajan in the sense that he overextended the empire, and this was clearly the case in his last operation against the Caledonians in northern Britannia. According to Dio:[32]

> Severus, accordingly, desiring to subjugate the whole of it [Britannia], invaded Caledonia. But as he advanced through the country he experienced countless hardships in cutting down the forests, levelling the heights, filling up the swamps, and bridging the rivers; but he fought no battle and beheld no enemy in battle array. The enemy purposely put sheep and cattle in front of the soldiers for them to seize, in order that they might be lured on still further until they were worn out; for in fact the water caused great suffering to the Romans, and when they became scattered, they would be attacked. Then, unable to walk, they would be slain by their own men, in order to avoid capture, so that a full fifty thousand died ... Having thus been conveyed through practically the whole of the hostile country ... he returned to the friendly portion, after he had forced the Britons to come to terms, on the condition that they should abandon a large part of their territory.

Caracalla (211–217)

Emperors realized how essential it was to curry favour with their troops, especially in this period. In York, February 211, on his deathbed, Severus' advice to his sons and heirs, Caracalla and his brother Geta, was 'Be harmonious, enrich the soldiers and scorn all other men'.[33] And apparently commenting further that: 'Everything have I been, and nothing have I gained'.[34] Caracalla chose to ignore the importance of family relations, murdering Geta before the end of the year in his mother's arms. His tragic last words were: 'Mother that didst bear me, mother that didst bear me, help! I am being murdered'.[35] This act was not surprising, since a short time before Severus' natural death, Caracalla attempted unsuccessfully to murder his father in public.[36]

According to Aurelius Victor:[37]

> On the other hand Antoninus won over the Roman populace with unheard of kinds of gifts since he distributed cloaks which reached the ankles, (for which) he was called Caracalla, although in a similar manner he gave the garments the name Antoninians after his own name.

Constructions

Caracalla appears to follow the trend established by his infamous predecessors in that his building activities were rather modest. No dated inscriptions are attested in Rome, but a few are recorded elsewhere in Italy, and several in the western provinces.[38]

Legacy

Despite his notoriety, Caracalla's greatest legacy was the construction of the second of the great imperial bath-houses (thermae) on the Via Nova, known as the Baths of Caracalla (or the Thermae Antoninianae).[39] These are modelled on the Baths of Trajan and also inspired the design of the Baths of Diocletian, built in the early part of the following century. Brick-stamps dating to 211/212 carry Geta's name and indicate that the baths were commenced before his assassination, in the reign of Septimius Severus. It is thought that the complex was not completed until the time of Severus Alexander, so they also spanned the tenure of Elagabalus. It housed some extraordinary sculptures, such as the Farnese Bull and Hercules, presently displayed in the Naples National Archaeological Museum. In the absence of any mention that the baths were constructed from the spoils of war, there can be little doubt that they were bankrolled from the proceeds of the military campaigns of their senior patrons.

The reign of Caracalla was relatively short, in keeping with many third-century emperors. In April 217, while stopping at a roadside to relieve himself near Carrhae in Upper Mesopotamia, his escort, Martialis, took advantage of his disposition, killing him with a single blow of his sword.[40]

The imperial budget

This is an appropriate chronological place to consider the imperial budget once more, which is naturally very important for the purposes of the overall arguments presented in previous and coming chapters. For these figures I once again cite the astute calculations of Duncan-Jones, although naturally it is unwise to rely on one proposal (see below and p. 134, 135). These incorporate army costs (salary and discharge costs – *praemia*); civilian salaries (citizen procurators, senatorial employees, and non-equestrian procurators); the emperor's household costs; hand-outs to civilians and soldiers (*congiaria* and *donativa*), building, gifts and public spending; and foreign subsidies and gifts.

Military expenditure

The extraordinary statistic of Table 3.1 is the sheer volume of spending on the upkeep of the army at around 75 per cent of the imperial budget, but this should be reconciled with the calculations discussed below. Also, we need to consider that Reinhard Wolters has suggested a lower figure for army pay at 535 million *sesterces* for the second century;[41] nonetheless, this figure is still rather high in the period.

It is logical to draw attention to the increasing size of the militia in the following century and its impact on taxation, and the demand on agricultural productivity to maintain these numbers, as there was a necessity to maintain a monopoly on gold and silver resources to pay the troops. These are crucial considerations that will be assessed in the next chapter.

David Potter arrives at a similar percentage of military expenditure during the Augustan period, around 58 per cent of the total budget, increasing to 71 per cent when retirement bonuses are taken into account. This he compares to actual proportions in the preserved budget from Egypt for 1595/1596, with wages amounting to around 50 per cent of revenue with

Table 3.1 The imperial budget, calculated in millions of *sesterces*

Category	Circa AD 150		Circa AD 215	
	Low figure	*High figure*	*Low figure*	*High figure*
Army	643	704	1,127	1,188
Civilian employees	75	75	75	75
Hand-outs	44	44	140	140
Building	20	60	20	60
Other items	50	100	100	150

Source: After Duncan-Jones, 1994, 45.

a substantial surplus amounting to roughly 20 per cent of revenue delivered in tribute to Istanbul and other cities. Potter also draws on data from Elizabethan England and fifteenth-century Florence. In the first instance military expenditures ranged from 73 to 80 per cent of the budget; in the second, they averaged a little under 50 per cent, but this is skewed since this percentage was much higher in wartime. Also, during the Principate he considers that the cost to the treasury would have been proportionally higher than it was in 14 in light of the 33 per cent salary increase granted by Domitian in 84 and because the cost of food and equipment given to legionaries was deducted from their salaries in the first century but came to be included within their pay packages in the course of the second century.[42]

Potter's observations are important when the military budget is considered. The proportion of men under arms was lower in the Antonine period before the plague compared with the Augustan period (roughly 2 per cent compared with 2.5 per cent) and this would have lowered the military budget: 'Such comparative data acts as a check on speculation – if a model for Roman expenditure fell outside the parameters established by measurable budgets of other pre-modern states then the model would, in my opinion, have to go'.[43]

Potter's figures, while concentrating on the Augustan period, appear to suggest that the figure of around 70 per cent is acceptable when other quantifiable pre-modern budgets are considered. My biggest contention with the suggested estimates of population in the Augustan and Severan periods is that demographic calculations in the Roman empire remain notoriously difficult to calculate despite innumerable attempts and 'best estimates'. This forces a reliance on pre-modern calculations, which appear to accord with the calculations of Duncan-Jones. That stated, we should consider that Ramsay MacMullen considers the level of military expenditure to have been considerably less and some of his points are important.[44]

His conclusions draw on the important work of Tenney Frank and represent a nuanced study of this work, using it as a base point.[45] MacMullen suggests that in the Augustan period the army amounted to half of the expenditure of the Roman state, while in the second century this had reduced to around a third of the total budget. However, this statement is at odds with Potter's suggested expenditure increase in the second century. Moreover, he contends that that: 'even so, the empire could not easily afford great military efforts, and that its size and fortunes were still very closely constrained by considerations of expense . . .'.[46]

This somewhat contradictory suggestion appears to be reconciled by archaeological and literary evidence that points to the fragmentation of military units in smaller forts in the era of the so-called Dominate onwards. His rationale for this is as follows:[47]

> In the earlier period we can easily see what was happening to military costs within the overall-budget: they were held stable, and therefore in

relative terms, as government income rose, they sharply diminished from some 50 per cent of the imperial budget to 33 per cent or less. After the mid-third century, conclusions are more difficult to draw. Nonetheless, in the scattering-about of soldiers in smaller clusters, to say nothing of their emplacement inside some city, there lay a substantial saving in cost; for their distribution thereby conformed better with existing natural patterns of production and distribution. It seems reasonable to find in these savings both purpose and explanation for later Roman troop dispositions.

In all this he is contending that great savings were made deploying men in small, stationary groups at natural market centres (riverine forts, crossroads, and towns), since the movement of grain for troops on the march was expensive. In conclusion, MacMullen states that:[48]

> Imperial forces settled in clusters larger than a single legion, from time to time rearranged into vast armies of campaign, such as had been seen in the first and second centuries, were beyond Rome's means in the fourth and fifth.

At first sight this seems quite plausible, but there are some problems with his suggestions. The first is that he appears to rely on Frank's calculations for the overall cost of the Roman militia rather than arriving at any new calculations. Second, while his assertion that later Roman troop deployments made economic sense, this masks the fact that in the later empire massive armies – larger in fact than in the days of the Principate – were being raised on campaign across vast swathes of the Roman empire, with a preponderance of smaller units and forts on the frontiers (Hadrian's Wall, Rhine–Danube, and Syro-Palestine, etc.), and this factor will be demonstrated in the present chapter and those that follow. Even by his own admission, the military budget is likely to have been higher in times of conflict rather than peace, and the sobering reality is that the empire was rarely at peace in five centuries.

Where does this leave us with the level of expenditure needed to maintain the Roman army? Taking the Augustan period as a starting point, MacMullen's 50 per cent spend level is considerably lower than that of Duncan-Jones and Potter at around 70 per cent. Given that MacMullen's figures are based on those of Frank at the end of the 1930s, it is more likely to envisage that the later studies of Duncan-Jones and Potter hold more weight in light of the fact that this subject has received more attention since the publication of Frank's paper, with greater scrutiny of an increasing number of literary sources. However, as suggested above, we should remain cautious of calculating the number of men under arms as a percentage of the population when the latter cannot be gauged with any certainty.[49]

MacMullen's suggestion that the threshold drop of around 50 to 33 per cent or less on military spend is logical from the point of view that as the wealth of the state increased then the militia would become relatively less expensive to maintain. However, this appears to be a generalized calculation that does not take economic fluctuations into account. It is, though, the case that relative expenditure was lower in times of economic growth. One of the best examples of this phenomenon is examined in the next chapter, in the reign of Constantine, when vast quantities of gold were looted from pagan temples and converted into gold *solidi*. As mentioned in the preceding chapters, this was also evident in the reigns of Augustus, Vespasian, and Trajan, during which time the *fiscus* benefitted from massive injections of gold booty – and of course slave labour.

Really the key in this debate are the levels of pre-modern expenditures as presented by Potter, his calculations for the level of military expenditure in the Augustan period, and those of Duncan-Jones for the first to third centuries. My feeling is that MacMullen's estimates of the threshold of state spending on the Roman army are too conservative and a figure of around 70 per cent is more plausible, perhaps dropping to 60 per cent or less at times of extreme prosperity or peacetime – both variables being relatively short-lived phenomena – but nonetheless these parameters are I think plausible calculations.

However, these figures should be treated as propositions since the debate should be tempered with other observations in this context, especially those of Walter Scheidel.[50] Citing the calculations of Duncan-Jones and Wolters, he has suggested that these totals need to be adjusted for two countervailing factors:

> On the one hand, troops may well have been significantly understrength at least in peacetime (which would have reduced actual costs); on the other, non-salary costs on items such as animals and materials, which are not included in existing estimates (and would have raised costs), also need to be taken into account. We cannot be sure to what extent these two variables would have canceled each other out. Given that the military itself engaged in production and construction, routine non-salary costs need not have amounted to more than a small fraction of salary costs.

Military salaries and their changing character in late antiquity

Peter Herz has addressed the important issue of salary distribution across the Roman empire, and this is of course an important factor and will be examined in Chapter 5.[51] In the course of the present book it is consistently argued that agricultural productivity is one of the crucial pillars of imperial welfare, especially in its necessity to support the army. It certainly appears to be the case that the so-called crisis of the third century led directly to a dramatic shift in the way soldiers were paid, and this of course is a fundamental consideration moving forward.

Military hand-outs

Another factor to be considered in the imperial budget is the long-established custom of imperial hand-outs to civilians and higher-ranking soldiers, *congiaria*, inaugurated by Augustus, and mentioned in the *Res Gestae* and *donativa*. These were normally restricted to special occasions, such as accessions, betrothals, and the naming of heirs. The average amount given by the emperor remained consistent or increased. Duncan-Jones has conducted an incisive and extremely informative account of public and military hand-outs. These payments were restricted to privileged members of society while the citizens (*plebs frumentaria*) received a monthly allowance of corn dole. *Congiaria* and *donativa* tended to be granted at the same time, initially every five to ten years, then every three years per reign. Unfortunately, this information is lacking for much of the third and all of the fourth and fifth centuries. However, the cost of *congiaria* and *donativa* calculated by Duncan-Jones from the reigns of Augustus through to Severus Alexander are especially interesting, and provide an inferential frame of reference for the centuries that follow; these are presented in Table 3.2.

Debasement and weight reduction of coinage

From a fiscal point of view this perhaps qualifies Dio's negative comment on the reign of Commodus and its economic impact. Subsequent events tend to suggest that the rising number of soldiers in the period was a response to the military threat posed by Germanic tribes on the Rhine and Danube frontiers.

Table 3.2 The cost of *congiaria* and *donatives*: schematic estimates, calculated in millions of *sesterces*

Reign	Congiaria cost per reign-year	Congiaria and donatives combined
Augustus	9	18
Tiberius	7	14
Claudius	7	14
Nero	4	8
Vespasian	5	10
Domitian	9	18
Trajan	12	24
Hadrian	22	44
Antoninus Pius	22	44
Marcus Aurelius	25	50
Commodus	39	78
Septimius Severus	41	82
Caracalla	70	140
Elagabalus	113	226
Severus Alexander	42	84

Source: After Duncan-Jones, 1994, 41.

Naturally, the respective increases in military personnel and their salaries created a massive demand for the *denarius* – the staple currency – and resulted in its devaluation. Evidence from a range of coin hoards across the empire informs that it was reduced in weight and debased. The work of Duncan-Jones is instructive once more in this context. This process was certainly not unprecedented. In the Augustan period there were 84.95 silver *denarii* to the Roman pound (322.8 grams).[52] This ratio crept up in the first century with significant increases under Nero, so that by the end of his reign *denarii* were worth 100.7 to the pound. There was a revaluation in the reign of Titus but thereafter its value deteriorated, with a significant drop in the reign of Marcus Aurelius (119.9 to the pound) and an even greater one under Commodus (152.3 to the pound).

In the Augustan era the fineness of the *denarius* was 98 per cent and its debasement thereafter generally mirrors its decrease in weight. For instance, under Nero its silver content was reduced to 93.5 per cent by the end of his reign. However, the raging inflation that followed was more likely precipitated by substantial weight reductions and debasement during the reigns of the early third-century emperors.[53] For instance, by the end of Septimius Severus' rule there were 169.6 *denarii* to the Roman pound and the fineness of silver had dropped to 55.5 per cent. At the end of Severus Alexander's reign there were 226.8 *denarii* to a pound of silver and fineness had plummeted to 45 per cent.[54]

It follows logically that other denominations conform to this general pattern of devaluation. The mean zinc percentage in *orichalum* (bronze), *sestertii*, and *dupondii* was 22.8 in the reign of Augustus. This fell progressively through the first and second centuries to the proportion of 3.4 per cent under Commodus.[55]

Devaluation of coinage was also applied to gold currency, its weight gradually reduced. In the reign of Marcus Aurelius there were 44 *aurei* to a pound of Roman gold. This had increased to 44.5 at the end of Septimius Severus' tenure, and 50 to the pound by the death of Severus Alexander. This indicates that the higher value of gold was considerably more stable through this era.[56] In short, there was a direct correspondence between more military personnel, larger quantities of coinage in circulation, and its reduction in weight and debasement. This forced up prices and resulted in substantial inflation.

Severus Alexander (222–235)

In 224 Ardashir overthrew Artabanus, the last Parthian monarch, and the centralization and territorial expansion that followed brought the Sasanians on an inevitable collision course with the east Roman empire.[57] They invaded Roman Mesopotamia and Syria and Severus succeeded in repulsing them in 231. However, in the following year, the Rhine and Danube frontiers were breached by respective contingents of Germanic and Sarmatian invaders.

Despite rigorous preparation for a campaign on the Rhine, Severus was assassinated by his troops in the spring of 235.[58] Conflict with Rome's deadly new enemy in the east was a further drain on state expenditure, and the temptation of a fresh *donativum* proved too much.

Constitutionally, the Sasanian empire was highly centralized by comparison with the Parthian empire, and was underpinned by Zoroastrianism, the state religion, which was administered by the Magi – a powerful and influential priestly cast, who oversaw the temples dedicated to their primordial god Ahuramazda, and the worship of fire. Other religions were also tolerated, as in the Parthian era, such as Buddhism, Mithraism, and Manichaeism, but the adoption of a state religion helped to cement the empire together.[59] Archaeological surveys have revealed that the Sasanian state invested heavily in a massive programme of irrigation between the Euphrates and Tigris rivers.[60] This boosted agricultural product and substantially increased state revenue to underwrite construction projects and maintain the army.[61]

Constructions

Prior to the period of chronic instability ushered in by the assassination of Severus Alexander, the epigraphic record points to a period of modest building activity in Italy and the western provinces.[62]

The infernal cycle

Severus' death brought to an end the African and Syrian dynasty and sparked the crisis of the third century. His assailant was Maximinus Thrax, the first of the many short-lived soldier emperors who were to live and die by the sword in rapid succession at the behest of the Roman militia, looking for their next bonuses against the backcloth of soaring inflation. This situation, which was to last for 50 years, was aptly described by Michael Rostovtzeff as the 'Military Anarchy', and by Jean-Jacques Hatt as 'the infernal cycle'.[63] The insatiable greed of the army, on the one hand, and the inability of the state to adequately fund it, on the other, has been plausibly cited as a major cause of the crisis by Lukas de Blois.[64]

The soldier emperors: Philip the Arab (244–249)

Philip the Arab had to deal with a serious revolt in Panonnia and Moesia by the legions under Claudius Pacatianus who proclaimed him emperor in 248. This distraction enabled the Quadi and other Germanic tribes to cross the Danube and invade Panonnia. To compound matters, in 249–250 the Goths, under king Cniva, crossed the Danube and invaded Moesia and Thracia; and Marcus Jotapianus led an uprising in Syria, but perished soon afterwards at the hands of his soldiers. Such was the anarchy of the third-century crisis.

From the perspective of Rome, this could not have happened at a worse time – in the face of the omnipotent Persian threat. The first hint of trouble was their appearance in the southern Ukraine by 230. Subsequently, they migrated along the coast of the Black Sea and occupied a large swathe of territory to the north of the Danube by 240. The Goths differed from their Germanic predecessors in terms of their sheer numbers and political organization. This factor was one of the principal differences between the tribal confederations of the second century and those of the third, fourth, and fifth centuries.[65] In a drastic response to the Gothic invasion, Philip appointed the distinguished senator Trajan Decius to deal with the crisis. However, in the true fashion of the era he challenged Philip, and according to some accounts he was murdered by his troops near Verona in September 249.[66]

Constructions

Constructions according to dated inscriptions under Philip total five.[67]

Valerian (253–260)

In 256 Shapur launched an invasion of Armenia and Syria and captured many cities, including Cilicia, Dura-Europos, and Antioch, the capital of Roman Syria. The Persian assault on Antioch is described in the fourth century by Ammianus Marcellinus:[68]

> For once upon a time at Antioch, amid deep silence, an actor of mimes, who with his wife had been presented in stage-plays, was presenting some scenes from everyday life. And while all the people were amazed at the charm of the performance, the wife suddenly cried: 'Is it a dream, or are the Persians here?' Whereupon all the people turned their heads about and then fled in all directions, to avoid the arrows that were showered upon them from the citadel. Thus the city was set on fire, and many people who were carelessly wandering about, as in times of peace, were butchered; neighbouring places were burned and devastated, and the enemy, laden with plunder, returned home without the loss of a single man . . .

Dura, garrisoned by contingents from *Legio IV Scythica, III Cyrenaica*, and *XVI Flavia Firma*, was subsequently abandoned and never reoccupied. The city was an important trading outpost, located on the Euphrates on the Syrian frontier near the modern town of Salhiya and is famous for its well-preserved synagogue wall paintings. Valerian, the latest emperor, left his son Gallienus in charge of the west, and waged a determined campaign against Shapur, forcing him back into Mesopotamia. The preceding and subsequent events are enshrined on the trilingual inscription of Shapur

Figure 3.1 Persian rock-relief at Naqsh-i-Rustam, third century.
Courtesy of Fabien Dany.

I known as the *Res Gestae Divi Saporis* (The Acts of the Divine Shapur). It is carved on the 'Cube of Zoroaster', an Achaemenid tower at Naqsh-i-Rustam, a necropolis of Persepolis.[69] They were also commemorated in rock-reliefs at Naqsh-i-Rustam and Bishapur (Figure 3.1),[70] and by the foundation cities in Iran and Mesopotamia.[71] The relevant parts of this read as follows:[72]

> When at first we had become established in the empire, Gordian Caesar raised in all of the Roman Empire a force . . . and marched . . . against us. On the border of Babylonia at Misikhe, a great 'frontal' battle occurred. Gordian Caesar was killed and the Roman force was destroyed. And the Romans made Philip Caesar. Then Philip Caesar came to us for terms, and to ransom their lives, gave us 500,000 *denars*, and became tributary to us . . . . And Caesar lied again and did wrong to Armenia. Then we attacked the Roman Empire and annihilated at Barbalissos a Roman force of 60,000 . . . In the third campaign . . . Valerian Caesar marched against us. He had with him a force of 70 . . . And beyond Carrhae and Edessa we had a great battle with Valerian Caesar. We made prisoner ourselves with our own hands Valerian Caesar and the others, chiefs of that army, the praetorian prefect, senators . . .

Naturally, as with the *Res Gestae Divi Augustae*, a degree of latitude has to be taken into account for reasons of propaganda, and these numbers are likely to be exaggerated. However, the historical veracity of these three defeats is also attested by a series of engineering projects within Sasanian Persia constructed by the forced labour of Roman prisoners of war.[73] One of the best preserved of these is the dam-bridge of Shushtar in modern Khuzistan. Roman prisoners were also forced to assist with the construction of Shapur's palace at Bishapur.[74] Several floor mosaics were also laid by captured soldier-artisans.[75]

Constructions

The so-called crisis of the third century would appear to be in full swing according to the epigraphic record in the western empire during the seven-year reign of Valerian. However, a new plague scourged the Roman empire in 250 and this continued for some time, so the modest building activity in this period is perhaps explicable for this reason as well. This is discussed in more detail below. Just two inscriptions are recorded: at Isca Silurum, Britannia; and Octodurus Varagrorum (Forum Claudii Vallensium), Alpes Poeninae.[76]

The Plague of Cyprian

These astounding defeats should also perhaps be seen in the context of the plague. This broke out in 250, and in much the same way as the war effort of Marcus Aurelius was severely hampered by the endemic in his reign, so too could it be considered that Roman military capability was impeded by a shortage of manpower.[77] Widely known as the Plague of Cyprian, it swept across the empire until 271, apparently with devastating effect. It derives its name from Cyprian, Bishop of Carthage whose eyewitness accounts were recorded by his deacon Pontius.[78] The symptoms appear to be similar to the Antonine Plague and indicate that it was probably smallpox.[79]

In the summer of 2014 an interesting but gruesome discovery was made by archaeologists in Egypt from the Italian Archaeological Mission to Luxor in the Funerary Complex of Harwa and Akhimenru on the west bank of the ancient city of Thebes. Several bodies were found covered with a thick layer of lime, used in the Roman period as a disinfectant. Pottery evidence enabled the excavators of the site to assign the death of the victims to the third century.[80]

Legacy

The humiliating defeat by the Sasanians was accentuated by the fact that Valerian was the first Roman emperor to be captured alive.[81] Valerian's fate was not unique, since Numerian may have perished in a similar manner. According to the *Historia Augusta*, Victor, and Eutropius, he was murdered (d. 284).[82] However, the sixth-century chronicler Malalas records that he was defeated by the Sasanians and captured at Carrhae: 'The Persians besieged him, took him prisoner and killed him immediately. Then they flayed his skin and made it into a bag, which they pickled with myrrh and kept for their own glory. . .'.[83] The precise fate of Valerian in captivity is no doubt exaggerated by the fact that it was recorded by Christian writers who typically had their own axes to grind, especially Lactantius, whose *De Mortibus Persecutorum* (*On the Deaths of the Persecutors*), written in the Constantinian period, sought to describe the deaths of pagan emperors with a track record of Christian persecution:[84]

> . . . Valerian . . . raised impious hands against God and though the time was short he shed much righteous blood. But God inflicted upon him a new and singular form of punishment, so that he should serve as a warning to posterity that the opponents of God always receive the reward that fits their crime. He was captured by the Persians and lost not just the imperial office which he had arrogantly misused, but even the freedom of which he had deprived everyone else; he lived most ignominiously in servitude. For whenever the Persian king Sapor, his captor, wanted to mount either his carriage or his horse, he would order the Roman to bend down for him and offer him his back . . . When his shameful life had come to its end in these circumstances of dishonor, his skin was plucked off him, and when it had been stripped from his flesh, it was dyed red so that it could be placed in the temple of the gods of the barbarians as a memorial of their brilliant victory, and so that it could be shown to our ambassadors, to deter the Romans from being too confident of their own strength, when they saw the remains of their captive emperor on the altars of the Persian gods. When God had exacted such penalties from the sacrilegious, is it not astonishing to think of acting against the majesty of the unique God who rules and controls all things?

The Gallic empire (260–274)

It is contended that events in the next decade and a half provide the key to understanding why, against all the odds, Rome did not fall in the third century. They are also instructive of its eventual collapse in the fifth century. The first part of this conundrum can be effectively resolved with the revolt of Postumus in 260. Postumus' grip on power was impressive, since he held sway over the three northern provinces of Gaul, the two Germanies, the provinces of Britannia, the Iberian peninsula, and, briefly, Raetia.

The second element in this puzzle is that, ironically, the revolt of Postumus had a positive effect on the fortunes of the empire elsewhere, since it enabled the new usurper to consolidate his Gallic empire while leaving his arch-rival, Gallienus, to deal with the serious threats that confronted him in his portion of the Roman state. These he dealt with systematically. In 261 he wrested control of the Balkans; the usurper Regalian was killed in Pannonia, most likely by the Sarmatians; Valens perished in Macedonia; his generals, Aureolus and Domitianus, defeated Macrianus. Generally speaking, the two factions kept each other at arm's length in the face of pressures from the increasingly centralized Germanic tribal confederations.[85]

The Palmyrene empire (circa 250–272)

King Odenathus died in Palmyra under mysterious circumstances, between August 267 and August 268, and there is universal agreement that he was assassinated.[86] Their capital city rose to prominence in this period (Figure 3.2), and the events that followed the accession of his beautiful wife in 267 not only threatened Rome but are pivotal to understanding its survival and eventual collapse. Zenobia inherited her husband's mantel and wasted little time in promoting his child son Vaballathus. In the meantime, Valerian, the future emperor, serving under Claudius, was occupied combating the Goths, Sueves, Sarmatians, Marcomanni, and other barbarian tribes in Thracia and Illyricum.[87] Exploiting the Roman position, Zenobia's general Zabdas extended the Palmyrene domain by 271 to include the bulk of Asia Minor, Syria, Palestine, Arabia, and Egypt, and this is expressed in coin issues.[88]

Aurelian (270–275)

The ascendancy of Aurelian was commemorated on a new issue of coins minted in Milan.[89] In 271 he implemented a fundamental administrative

Figure 3.2 The Monumental Arch of Palmyra, built in the early third century by Septimius Severus. The city rose to prominence under Zenobia.

Courtesy of Peter Horree/Alamy Stock Photo.

change that entailed the withdrawal of transdanubian Dacia and the creation of a new province (or possibly two provinces) south of the Danube called Dacia Ripensis with its capital at Serdica. This was, perhaps, strategically motivated, enabling the Romans to hold the river frontier with considerably fewer troops. This also led to the evacuation of a substantial element of the civilian population, including local officials, merchants, landowners, and those in charge of the mines.[90] This latter detail is of course significant from an economic perspective, since the mines in Dacia were important sources of gold and silver, especially the large complex at Roşia Montană in Transylvania. The abandonment of this fertile province would also have reduced agricultural product and dropped the tax-yield significantly.

To return to the evidence in Egyptian papyri for agricultural production, there is no evidence of a hiatus. The fact that Zenobia was now minting her own coinage demonstrates once more the simple product–coinage relationship. In this case the fertility of Egypt (benefitting also from the available gold in the mines of the Eastern Desert), and the wealth of the other eastern provinces, was essentially bankrolling Palmyra's newly acquired empire. The political situation was gently poised: Tetricus ruled the Gallic empire, Valerian the middle portion of the Roman empire, and Zenobia held sway over the eastern provinces. Each ruler was represented on their own coinage and economic product split between three large regions. This output was sufficient to underwrite the armies of each protagonist through taxation.

In 272 Aurelian had worked himself into a sufficiently advantageous position to launch a major offensive against the Palmyrenes in Egypt, Asia Minor, and Syria. The successful conclusion of these events is recounted in the *Historia Augusta*:[91]

> After thus recovering Tyana, Aurelian, by means of a brief engagement near Daphne, gained possession of Antioch, having promised forgiveness to all; and thereupon, obeying, as far as is known, the injunctions of that venerated man, Apollonius, he acted with greater kindness and mercy. After this, the whole issue of the war was decided near Emesa in a mighty battle fought against Zenobia and Zaba, her ally. When Aurelian's horsemen, now exhausted, were on the point of breaking their ranks and turning their backs, suddenly by the power of a supernatural agency, as was afterwards made known, a divine form spread encouragement throughout the foot-soldiers and rallied even the horsemen. Zenobia and Zaba were put to flight, and a victory was won in full. And so, having reduced the east to its former state, Aurelian entered Emesa as a conqueror, and at once made his way to the Temple of Elagabalus, to pay his vows as if by a duty common to all. But there he beheld that same divine form which he had seen supporting his cause in the battle. Wherefore he not only established temples there, dedicating gifts of great value, but he also built a temple to the Sun at Rome, which he consecrated with still greater pomp, as we shall relate in the proper place.

In the summer of 274 he began his quest for the supremacy of the Roman empire, marched into Gaul and defeated Tetricus at the Catalaunian Plains at Châlons-sur-Marne. Tetricus' life was spared but he apparently suffered the indignity of being paraded alongside Zenobia, who was apparently led through the streets in gold chains and weighed down by jewels.[92] This 'event' is portrayed in the beautiful oil on canvas entitled *Queen Zenobia before Emperor Aurelianus* by Giovanni Battista Tiepolo (1696–1770), displayed in Prado Museum.

Constructions

In light of the fragmented empire for most of Aurelian's rule we should expect building to be scant, notwithstanding the Aurelian Walls in Rome, finished in the reign of Probus.[93] This project was a vast undertaking, with a circuit of 19 kilometres, encompassing the seven hills, and totalling an area of 13.7 kilometres. A mere three inscriptions survive in the west and east.[94]

Legacy

In the autumn of 275 Aurelian launched a campaign against the Sasanians. However, true to the political climate of the time, he was assassinated. This occurred at Caenophrurium, between Heraclea and Byzantium.[95] With considerable justification, coins minted before his death carry the legend *Restitutor orbis* (restorer of unity in the world).[96] By any calculation his deeds surely enshrine him as one of the most extraordinary emperors of the Roman world, especially given that his reign was short – just five years.

The fiscal reforms of Aurelian were certainly instrumental in beginning the economic healing process, as was his extraordinary reunification of the empire. His defeat of Tetricus was perhaps inevitable. With the capture of Palmyra he was, in effect, in control of two-thirds of the Roman empire and its economic and military resources.

The return of the soldier emperors and the rise of Diocletian (268–284)

Aurelian's rule did not end the crisis of the third century, since several more emperors were to experience short reigns and violent deaths: Tacitus (d. 276),[97] Florianus (d. 276),[98] and Probus (d. 282)[99] were assassinated, while Carus was apparently struck dead by lightning (d. 283).[100] Finally, Carinus was defeated and killed in battle by Diocletian at Margus (modern Morava) near Belgrade in Serbia (d. 285).[101] Inflation was also a problem, although there is scant data from the reign of Aurelian, but useful papyrus evidence a little before. For instance, in Egypt the price of wine in *drachmas* per *keramion* was around 9.4 *drachmas* in 247/248. By 260/264 it had reached around 16.6 *drachmas*.[102]

Constructions

Once again, the epigraphic record provides a useful index that echoes the turbulent political events highlighted above. Just five inscriptions are recorded in the Roman empire from Tacitus to Carinus.[103]

Building under *decurions* and other local officials

Several building inscriptions are attested in the third century, attesting to civic patronage by *decurions* and other officials. However, none of these may be associated with identifiable public buildings. As may be expected, they tend to cluster, although not exclusively, to either the early part of the third century, prior to the assassination of Severus Alexander in 235, or the later part of the century, when the political situation had become more settled; and a number of these record the patronage of military officials (especially tribunes) on Hadrian's Wall and elsewhere in the western provinces.[104]

Agricultural productivity in the third century

This relative, yet fragile stability provides a convenient juncture to take stock of the economic situation in the second half of the 260s. With the exception of the *Agri Decumates*, currently occupied by the Alamanni, it should be considered that the agricultural productivity of the Roman empire – effectively its economic backbone – would have been free to function, although in the theatres of conflict, especially on the Rhine–Danube frontier, economic output must have been stunted. In this context it is important to examine the textual and archaeological evidence below.

We should consider briefly the interrelationship between town and cities in this economic equation. Perhaps the most simple interpretation of this dynamic was presented by Arnold Hugh Martin Jones for the later Roman empire.[105] In general terms he outlined the Roman empire as an agglomeration of cities (*civitates* in the west and *poleis* in the east, administered by a *curia* and *boulē* respectively), self-governing communities responsible for the administration of their territories.[106] In each of these was a town, which functioned as its administrative capital, and economic and social centre, with some exceptions such as Rome and Constantinople, and some settlements in the east. The great majority of the cities were essentially rural, drawing the larger part of their wealth from agriculture, the average town being the market of its territory, where the agrarian population (*coloni*) sold their surplus produce. However, these territories formed a key role in articulating long-distance trade, which was instrumental in stimulating large-scale production in particular regions, especially North Africa and Egypt.[107]

Despite the dependence of cities on their hinterland in an agricultural sense, it should be borne in mind that there is some truth in the argument presented by Peregrine Horden and Nicholas Purcell that some functional similarities may be observed between cities and their hinterland, such as administrative, legal, and educational; along with the presence of civic spaces and buildings: theatres and fora, and, therefore, to some degree they cannot be distinguished from the urban sphere in their broader cultural, economic, and political context.[108] However, this was far from the norm, with the greater concentration of populations and public and religious buildings dominating cities, as attested by archaeological remains.[109]

In the following chapter it is relevant to consider the emerging rural settlement pattern and how this articulated with agricultural production, an important factor since evidence suggests that this involved an increasing monopolization of commodities by a series of wealthy landowning aristocrats, who also exercised considerable fiscal control of gold currency from the late third century onwards.[110]

Tax was also levied in kind from farmers, often as military requisitions. Also, it should be considered that landowners, who were often *decurions*, paid their own taxes to the state in cash and in kind.[111] There was an increasing pressure on them in this sense during the late Roman period to pay for civic building projects (euergetism) and central government demanded increasingly more taxation, forcing an ever-increasing number of officials into the imperial service in order to escape their financial obligations.[112] To add to the two streams of tax from source that flowed to the imperial treasury via the urban sphere, other forms of tax existed, such as poll tax, customs duties, and revenue in kind in the form of public service. Taxation is examined in more detail in Chapter 5.

Logically, cities did not escape the turmoil of the third century, their physical character began to change with the inclusion of defensive walls, and there was a general lack of investment compared with more prosperous phases of the first and second centuries; however, the essential dynamic highlighted above – the symbiotic economic relationship between town and country – was essentially the same.[113]

Material sources

Papyri

The massive demand on imperial expenditure imposed by the state's huge military commitment was largely the driving force of tax revenue. The best evidence for understanding these complexities comes from Egypt by virtue of the wealth of papyrus documents that have survived. Duncan-Jones has conducted an informative study on the material of Middle Egypt.[114] During the Principate and the late empire tax-yield on grain was measured in *artabas* per *arouras*. One *artaba* equated to a 38.78-litre dry capacity measure, equivalent to 30.2 kilogrammes of milled wheat. An *aroura* (literally meaning 'earth' or 'agricultural land' in Greek) was equal to a square with sides of 100 cubits (each measuring 52.5cm) thus 2,756 square metres (0.68 acre, 0.275 hectare).[115]

There was also a dike tax levied in copper *drachmas*. Tax on vines and olives was also raised in this manner. Poll tax varied between 8 *drachmas* (in Coptos) and 40–44 *drachmas* (in Arsinoite) per person annually. Sales tax was 10 per cent levied on sales of land, houses, and slaves. Tolls on goods imported and exported were especially high at 25 per cent. The annual total tax revenue from Egypt during the Principate was 32.4 million *artabas* of wheat and 259 million *drachmas/sesterces*. Agricultural output appears to be strong throughout the era.

A more recent study of Egyptian papyri has been undertaken by Alan Bowman, and his conclusions are again informative of agricultural output. His assessment takes into account data pertaining to the *metropoleis* and villages in the nomes (administrative districts) of Middle Egypt. He too observes a robust agricultural product of cereals and olives.[116] Cereals, and to a lesser extent, vines, prospered in the Mendesian nome of the Nile Delta through the same period, as attested by papyri in the analysis of Katherine Blouin.[117]

Archaeological data

In terms of archaeological evidence, Mariette de Vos has provided instructive evidence for a buoyant economy in the third century provided by an intensive survey of Thugga and its hinterland in the Medjerda Valley in Tunisia. A large number of farms yielded evidence for the processing of agricultural crops, notably the remains of olive oil- and wine-presses, olive-crushing mills, and grain mills. A significant proportion of these are assigned to the middle Roman period.[118] In north-eastern Algeria, de Vos also recorded a substantial number of presses of a similar character, many of which date to the third century.[119]

An especially useful survey of olive oil- and wine-presses was conducted by Annalisa Marzano in southern Gaul, the Iberian peninsula, and the region of the Black Sea. The third century was especially well represented by extant remains of multi-press facilities (two or more wine-/olive oil-presses), in each particular region, although the first and second centuries have more presses.[120] Marzano also surveyed similar installations in the hinterland of Rome and, despite a diminishing number of villas in the period, a buoyant production of oil and wine may be inferred.[121]

Drawing on the surveys conducted by other archaeologists in North Africa, Alan Bowman and Andrew Wilson have highlighted the intensification of wine and olive oil production in North Africa, where the largest and greatest quantity of multi-presses are encountered,[122] for instance at Kherbet Agoub in Numidia,[123] Henchir Sidi Hamdan[124] and Senam Semana[125] in Tripolitania. Archaeological data indicate that these installations enjoyed a healthy production in the third century.[126]

Peter Attema and Tymon de Haas have undertaken a quantitative analysis to the south of the area assessed by Marzano, on the Tyrrhenian seaboard approximately 50 kilometres south of Rome. This survey encompassed villages, but for the purposes of economic output, the most relevant sites analysed were farms, villas, and coastal villas. Their findings suggest a peak of settlement in the first and second centuries and a relative decline in the third century.[127]

The available quantitative evidence does at least hint that economic output was solid in the third century in those areas studied, although there is a reduction of sites in some regions. It seems logical to suggest that different parts of the Roman empire were affected more than others in the third century, with Egypt and North Africa faring better, perhaps, than Italy, Gaul, and the Iberian peninsula. In those areas that show a relative decline it is worth considering whether or not the Plague of Cyprian may have contributed to this trend.[128]

Numismatic evidence

If agricultural product was proportional to tax levied at source, notwithstanding additional taxes and revenue raised in coinage, then the 'end product' was, in effect, minted currency. This is informative for the purposes of unravelling the conundrum mentioned above, and may be considered as the final piece in the 'jigsaw' pertaining to the survival and fall of Rome.

To return to the divided empire under Gallienus and Postumus, it is logical that they both minted their own coins. Gallienus issued coins with his portrait on the obverse, minted in Milan (259–268). Postumus issued coins with his portrait on the obverse, minted most likely in Cologne (260–269) and Trier (268–269).[129] These representations are in effect visual territorial markers and it logically follows that precious metal (where available), agricultural product, and tax revenue were split between the factions, each having sufficient wealth to marshal their respective armies, coinage being the end product.

Subsequently, a series of coins attest to a series of rapid and short-lived successions: Laelianus (269), Marius (269), Victorinus (269–271), and Tetricus (271–273).[130] In spite of these problems, Claudius and Aurelian crushed the Goths in the summer of 270. Claudius fell victim to a new outbreak of plague and died in Sirmium shortly after accepting the title of Gothicus Maximus.

The broader picture

This period saw the end of a large-scale 'booty economy'; since the great building projects of the third century under Septimius Severus and Caracalla, the last of the great imperial building projects that we may infer were bankrolled by the spoils of war until the reign of Diocletian. Collectively, the archaeological, epigraphic, papyrus, and numismatic sources paint an interesting picture of this extraordinary era, as the empire gradually splits into two parts, and then three.

Economic productivity appears to have diminished to some extent in the face of this political turbulence across much of the Roman world, although the impact was more acute in some regions, the North African and Egyptian provinces appear to have been 'insulated' from trouble for the time being.

Public building was certainly affected in the tenures of problematic emperors, such as Caracalla, or in those reigns that witnessed severe political disruptions and short-lived reigns – Valerian, Philip, Aurelian, and others. Notwithstanding the early part of the third century, it would appear that the 'booty economy' came to an end.

Building under the patronage of *decurions* appears to have been limited according to the epigraphic record, and military constructions by officials appear to be localized, most likely according to strategic needs, such as on Hadrian's Wall in Britannia or at Intercisa in Pannonia Inferior.

The factionalization of the Roman empire into three parts resulted in mutually exclusive agricultural product, tax-yields, coin production, and military capability that was sufficient to resist the considerable pressures inflicted by Germanic invasions.

This sequence of events proves that providing agricultural product can be generated at a sufficient output, precious metals are available for extraction, and taxes can be levied in cash and in kind, the army can be maintained as an effective fighting force even when the empire appears to be irreparably fractured. This, it is contended, provides the key to its survival in the third century and its destruction in the late fourth and fifth centuries, and it is fruitful to pay close attention to the economic output of this fundamentally agrarian and mineral dependent empire in the chapters that follow.

Notes

1 Julius Caesar, according to D*RH*, XLIII.18.
2 Alföldy, 1974, 89–111; Watson, 1999, 1–20.
3 De Blois, 2002b, 204–227.
4 Witschel, 2004, 251–281.
5 Reece, 1981, 27–38.
6 Brown, 1971; 1978.
7 D*RH*, LXII.36.
8 Gibbon, I.4.95–109.
9 T*An*, IV.5.
10 Le Bohec, 1994, 19–35; MacMullen, 1980, 451–460.
11 D*RH*, LXXV.2.
12 *HE*, III.8.5.
13 Harl, 1996, 216.
14 D*RH*, LXXVIII.24.
15 *HE*, IV.4.7.
16 Harl, 1996, 216.
17 Pollard, 2010, 219.
18 *HE*, VI.8.8. These pay increases under Caesar/Augustus, Domitian (84), Septimius Severus (197), Caracalla (212), and Maximinus Thrax (235) are detailed by Speidel, 1992, 88, Table 1.
19 Herz, 2007, 313.

20 Duncan-Jones, 1994, 36.
21 Duncan-Jones, 1994, 45–46.
22 Jones, 1964, II, 679–686.
23 *HA*, X.18.
24 *HA*, X.16; Birley, 1999, 146–169.
25 Platner and Ashby, 1926, 43–44; Brilliant, 1967; Gros, 2011, 73–74.
26 D*RH*, LXXVII.1.
27 Ward-Perkins, Jones, Ling, Kenrick, 1993.
28 D*RH*, LXXVII.16.
29 *HA*, X.19.
30 HD025853 (198–210), HD025856 (198–210), HD025859 (198–210), HD025880 (202–210), HD025927 (198–211), HD001208 (200–209), HD001660 (200–209), HD018052 (207), HD032545 (195–196), HD032548 (194).
31 HD000905 (209–211), HD001198 (198–209), HD008060 (197–209), HD011387 (198–202), HD014624 (199–202), HD018264 (208), HD018267 (208–209), HD018270 (208), HD019508 (207–208), HD019511 (205–208), HD020076 (197–209), HD028566 (202), HD029862 (199–202), HD030874 (209), HD030880 (208–209), HD031834 (195–198), HD033301 (204), HD033322 (198–211), HD033460 (197–198), HD033463 (198–199), HD034612 (197–209), HD035594 (205), HD037301 (197–209), HD038313 (205), HD039382 (195), HD047118 (198–209), HD047761 (208–211), HD051714 (201–209), HD052201 (198–211), HD052246 (198–209), HD055852 (195–196), HD060118 (202–209), HD061373 (202), HD067044 (206), HD067056 (197–209), HD067283 (202), HD068482 (195–198), HD069626 (198–209), HD069738 (194–196), HD070000 (205–208), HD071848 (198–202), HD072559 (193–211), HD072560 (193–211).
32 D*RH*, LXVII.13.
33 D*RH*, LXXVII.15.
34 *HA*, X.18.
35 D*RH*, LXXVIII.2.
36 D*RH*, LXXVII.14.
37 AV*DC*, XXI.
38 HD006036 (217), HD007600 (211–213), HD011259 (213–217), HD011488 (211–217), HD013868 (213), HD018563 (211–217), HD019367 (211–217), HD023618 (213), HD030898 (216–217), HD032497 (213–217), HD032901 (213), HD033487 (211–217), HD038464 (213), HD047942 (213–214), HD058131 (213), HD061564 (211–217), HD065124 (216–217), HD070439 (211–217), HD071208 (212–217).
39 Platner and Ashby, 1926, 520–524; Yegül, 1992, 146–162.
40 H*E*, IV.13.4–13.5; *HA*, XIII.7; AV*DC*, XXI.
41 Wolters 1999: 211–218, 223.
42 Potter, 2015, 32.
43 Potter, 2015, 32.
44 MacMullen, 1984, 571–580.
45 Frank, 1940.
46 MacMullen, 1984, 572.
47 MacMullen, 1984, 575–576.
48 MacMullen, 1984, 577.
49 Bowman and Wilson, 2011, 1–14.
50 Scheidel, 2015, 156.
51 Herz, 2007, 314–315.
52 The Roman pound or *libra* equates to 328.9 grams, converted from the imperial table of Smith, 1851, 1024–1030.

53 For inflation, Jones, 2014, 338–339.
54 Duncan-Jones, 1994, 213–237.
55 Duncan-Jones, 1994, 235–236.
56 Duncan-Jones, 1994, 217–218.
57 Heather, 2005, 58–62.
58 *HE*, VI.9.7; *HA*, XVIII.59; AV*DC*, XXIV; *ETB*, VIII.23.
59 Gignoux, 1993, 31–43.
60 Adams, 1965, 1981; Gibson, 1972; Wenke, 1975–1976.
61 Simpson, 2000, 58; Howard-Johnston, 1995, 198–203.
62 HD005135 (230), HD007911 (229–230), HD010915 (235), HD010918 (235), HD011837 (233–235), HD018619 (222–235), HD032506 (222–235), HD032575 (231–233), HD039162 (222–235), HD051374 (222–235), HD058143 (226–235), HD060818 (223), HD063760 (222–235), HD067840 (223–235), HD069622 (234).
63 Rostovtzeff, 1926, Chapters X and XI; Hatt, 1966, 227.
64 De Blois, 2002a, 90–107.
65 Heather, 2005, 84–94, 97–98.
66 Zosimus, *Historia Nova* (I.21–22). *New History*. 1982. Translated by R.T. Ridley. Canberra: Australian Association for Byzantine Studies. For a biography, xi–xv. AV*DC*, XXVIII.
67 HD007026 (248), HD021232 (244–246), HD033394 (247–249), HD035507 (244–246), HD054536 (244–247).
68 AM*H*, XXIII.5.3.
69 Howard-Johnston, 1995, 161.
70 Vanden Berghe, 1993, 81, Figure 68.
71 Howard-Johnston, 1995, 161.
72 *Res Gestae Divi Saporis* (VI–X). In *The History of Ancient Iran*. 1984. Translated by R.N. Frye. Appendix 4. Munich: Beck.
73 Vogel, 1987, 47–56.
74 Huff, 1993, 45–61.
75 Ghirshman, 1956; Balty, 1993, 67–69, Figures 51–54.
76 HD069627 (255–260), HD001117 (253).
77 *ZNH*, I.20, 21, 24. For diminished military resource, Boak, 1955.
78 Pontius, *The Life and Passion of Cyprian, Bishop and Martyr* (9). Ante-Nicene fathers V. 1886. Translated by R.E. Wallis. Buffalo: Christian Literature Publishing Co.
79 Sherman, 2006, 431; Littman and Littman, 1973, 243–255.
80 Tiradritti, 2015, 15–18.
81 AV*DC*, XXXII; *ZNH*, I.20.
82 *HA*, XXX.12; AV*DC*, XXXVIII; *ETB*, IX.18.
83 *The Chronicle of John Malalas* (XII.35). Books I–XVIII. 1986. Translated by E. Jeffreys, M. Jeffreys, and R. Scott. Melbourne: Australian Association for Byzantine Studies. For a biography, xxi–xxv.
84 Lactantius, *De Mortibus Persecutorum*, V. 1984. Translated by J.L. Creed. Oxford: Oxford University Press. For a biography, xv–xlv; AV*DC*, XXXII; *ZNH*, I.20.
85 For an outline of these events, Watson, 1999, 34–37.
86 Zonaras, *The History of Zonaras from Alexander Severus to Theodosius the Great* (XII.24). 2009. Translated by T.M. Banchich and E.N. Lane. London: Routledge. For a biography of Zonaras, 1–15.
87 *HA*, XXVI.22, 23.
88 *HZ*, XII.27.
89 Drinkwater, 1987, 146–147.

90 Watson, 1999, 55.
91 *HA*, XXVI.25.
92 *ETB*, IX.13.
93 An exhaustive study of the Aurelian Wall is presented by Dey, 2011.
94 HD032455 (276–283), HD043457 (272–275), HD055847 (274).
95 *HA*, XXVI.35; *ZNH*, I.31.
96 Bardill, 2012, 63, Figure 53.
97 *HA*, XXVII.13; AV*DC*, XXXVI; *ZNH*, I.31.
98 *HA*, XXVII.14; AV*DC*, XXXVII; *ETB*, IX.16; *ZNH*, I.32.
99 *HA*, XXVIII.20; AV*DC*, XXXVII; *ETB*, IX.17.
100 *HA*, XXX.8; AV*DC*, XXXVIII; *ETB*, IX.18.
101 *HA*, XXX.18; AV*DC*, XXXIX; *ETB*, IX.19.
102 Rathbone, 1991, 466; Duncan-Jones, 1994, 26.
103 HD002297 (283–284), HD026837 (282), HD033577 (284), HD033580 (284), HD034544 (276–284).
104 HD000887 (219), HD006770 (201–300), HD014839 (201–270), HD024700 (209), HD026845 (228), HD038224 (201–230), HD058832 (222–235), HD059316 (202–209), HD068766 (201–230), HD070224 (200–300), HD070464 (238–241), HD071037 (259–268), HD071039 (259–268), HD071200 (251–253).
105 Jones, 1964, II, 712–714.
106 Ward-Perkins, 1997, 371.
107 Bowman and Wilson, 2013, 19.
108 Horden and Purcell, 2000, 89–122.
109 Esmonde Cleary, 2013, 99–100.
110 Banaji, 2007.
111 Bowman, 2017, 1–31.
112 Ward-Perkins, 1997, 371–410.
113 Esmonde Cleary, 2013, 97–149.
114 Duncan-Jones, 1994, 47–59.
115 Bowman, 2011, 339.
116 Bowman, 2011, 317–358.
117 Blouin, 2013, 255–272.
118 De Vos, 2013, 143–218.
119 De Vos, 2000, 20, 81–84.
120 Marzano, 2013b, 107–141.
121 Marzano, 2013a, 85–106.
122 Bowman and Wilson, 2013, 19.
123 Brun, 2004, 233–238.
124 Oates, 1953, 97–99.
125 Cowper, 1897, 279–282.
126 Bowman and Wilson, 2013, 19.
127 Attema and de Haas, 2011, 97–140.
128 Bowman, 2013, 221.
129 The lack of mint marks in this era makes it difficult to establish the location of mints for certain but a plausible argument for Cologne and Trier has been ascertained by Drinkwater, 1987, 132–147.
130 Drinkwater, 1987, 145–147.

4 The rise and fall of the new golden era

Some people accuse our generals, others their men, asserting that the generals have not properly trained the men under their command, or that the men
are naturally cowards. I however cannot bring myself to say this, in view of
the many battles they have fought and the way they have died in their ranks,
and have stained with their blood Thrace, much of Macedonia and the
greater part of Illyria. Rain and time have erased those stains, but the piles of
bones remain, and among them, so it is said, you can see those of generals
and colonels and those of lesser rank.[1]

Oration to Theodosius
Libanius

Previous chapters have focused on the persistent conflicts across the length
and breadth of the Roman empire, the burden on the military capability of
the state, the concomitant strain on its budget, and the imperative of agricultural output to maintain the army. In the face of growing Germanic tribal
centralization and the threat posed by the Sasanian Persian empire, the spectre
of warfare continued through the fourth century AD, as did the political
turmoil, although it is fair to say that the empire had settled down in relative
terms by comparison with the events of the third century. Archaeological
evidence indicates that the economy was strong, but there is an indication
that agricultural productivity tailed off, and this perhaps relates to barbarian
incursions and settlements. Diocletian was instrumental in this, and clearly
recognized that without a series of drastic measures the empire was doomed.

The present chapter commences with an examination of Diocletian's
administrative, financial, and military reforms; continuing reconfigurations
of the army and its size and increasing barbarization; the settlement of
barbarians in the western empire; and the key episodes of the fourth century: the ascendancy and reign of Constantine the Great; the extraordinary
brief reign of Julian; the split of western and eastern responsibilities under
Valentinian and Valens; and events leading up to the Battle of Adrianople,
and its aftermath, referenced above by Libanius. Imperial patronage is
examined once more by examining dated building inscriptions as an index

of levels of imperial patronage and economic conditions. Inscriptions in the sphere of patronage under *decurions* is again addressed and also under bishops, and these are informative of the historically attested decline of the former and the rise of the latter.

It is also insightful to look at the complexion and movements of Rome's key belligerents in this period, notably the Franks, Sarmatians, and Goths; and also the Huns who forced the first wave of migrations into the Roman empire. The archaeological and numismatic record is also addressed in an attempt to track the movement of barbarian tribes and unravel their identity where possible. Romano–Persian relations are also a crucial factor pertaining to the security of the empire and the nature of these in the fourth century is assessed.

Set against the backcloth of these manifold problems facing the Roman empire, I return once more to the central issue of agricultural productivity and the extent to which it was affected by these problems. I depend heavily on archaeological evidence for the economic output of cereals, olive oil, and wine, but also look at the availability of precious mineral resources in the period. The decline of the so-called 'booty economy' is a key consideration, as is the abandonment of the countryside (*agri deserti*) the nature of rural settlements, *castella*, *fundi*, and *vici*, along with the villa the locus of elite production and aristocratic status in the countryside. Cities and their changing urban character are also addressed.

In order to proceed with my arguments in this context it is necessary to attempt to provide a quantitative model in order to demonstrate that levels of agricultural product fell sufficiently to precipitate the collapse of the Roman empire. This is a process that I believe can be charted through the course of the fourth and fifth centuries. There are several caveats that oppose this suggestion and these relate to the distribution of the archaeological evidence and its interpretation. These will be addressed in their appropriate context. Since the dynamics involved are essentially all about supply and demand, the nature of the Roman economy is implicit and demands further consideration, and it is also important to look at some of the economic theories, both traditional, and more recently modified approaches.

The Tetrarchic period: Diocletian (284–305)

On his accession to the throne in 284 Diocletian was just what the state needed to repair its damaged core. His notorious persecution of the Christians has sullied his reputation as a great emperor; however, the successful implementation of a series of overarching administrative, financial, military, and political reforms characterize him as an enlightened ruler, and shored up the Roman empire in the west and east, for a large part of the fourth century.

From 293 to 305 Diocletian established what is referred to as the Tetrarchy (the rule of four). The Roman empire was governed by two emperors with the title of Augustus. The senior ruler was based in the east, his counterpart

Figure 4.1 Red porphyry portrait of the Four Tetrarchs, early fourth century. San Marco, Venice.

Courtesy of John Pollini.

in the west (Figure 4.1). A Caesar served under each Augustus and was groomed for succession. In 305, Diocletian and Maximian abdicated and were succeeded by their Caesars, Galerius in the east, and Constantius in the west.[2]

Diocletian's reforms were a direct response to the crisis of the third century. In spite of Valerian's military successes, the centralized configuration of Germanic tribal confederacies posed a grave threat along the Rhine–Danube frontier; the might of Sasanian Persia in the east was at least as serious, as the catastrophic defeats of his predecessors had demonstrated. Given the security threat posed by Rome's belligerents on the frontiers, it is logical to examine the military reforms of Diocletian in the first instance, before the important administrative and economic changes are considered.

The reforms of Diocletian

Diocletian had considerable teething troubles early in his reign with conflicts to deal with in the west and east. The main events in the late third century may be summarized as follows: successful campaigns prosecuted by Maximian in Gaul against the *Bacaudae*;[3] a revolt by Carausius in Britain and parts of north-western Gaul was resolved by the seaborne invasion of Maximian,[4] with successes in Gaul against the Burgundiaces/Alamanni and the Chaibones/Heruli, and the Franks on the Rhine.[5] Constantius fought the Carpi and Alammani on the Danube with a successful outcome.[6] Also, Maximian campaigned effectively against the Saraceni in Syria.[7]

Meanwhile, in Persia, the position of Vahram III was threatened by Narses, a rival to the throne. Diocletian took advantage of the situation by restoring the Roman client king Tiridates III to the throne in Armenia with the consent of the monarch.[8] In 293, Diocletian inflicted a major defeat on the Sarmatians on the Hungarian Plain, and subsequently the emperor closed the net on the Carpi along the Danube in 295–296.[9]

The respective operations of the Tetrarchs on four theatres of war logically explains their preferred places of residence in different cities: Diocletian in Sirmium, Galerius in Antioch, Maximian in Milan, and Constantius in Trier. Alan Bowman draws the distinction between regarding these as the location of 'imperial palaces' rather than imperial capitals in this period.[10]

Martial proceedings were largely ended with the decisive Roman–Persian war against Narses in 296–298.[11] These successes enabled Diocletian, while in Antioch, to negotiate a treaty favourable to the Romans.[12] After securing peace with Persia, the empire appeared to be relatively stable, but there were further campaigns enacted by Galerius against the Sarmatians and the Carpi (302 and possibly 303), Constantius in Germany (303–304), and in Britain, against the Picts in Scotland (305).[13]

Military reforms

In fact, the collective military successes of Diocletian and his colleagues should be seen in the context of possessing a formidably large army. Here, Ramsay MacMullen has plausibly estimated the figure to be around 350,000 at the start of his reign to 390,000 around 300, which includes naval marines.[14] This figure is based on a statement by Lactantius, who suggested the army was expanded under the Tetrarchy, although John Lydus provides exact figures of 389,704 for the Diocletianic army and 45,562 for the fleets, but it is not clear at what point in the reign of Diocletian he is referring to.[15]

The army therefore significantly rose under Diocletian, but he increased the number of legions, giving his army greater flexibility, concentrating on the frontiers and aiding the rapid deployment of troops in those areas where they were needed in an emergency.[16] The intense deployment of troops on the frontiers complemented the strengthening of frontier defences. On the Rhine frontier he improved the defences of pre-existing forts. On the further bank of the Danube, the emperor added a new line of forts and rebuilt older constructions.[17] Along the eastern frontier Diocletian constructed the *Strata Diocletiana* (Road of Diocletian), a fortified road that ran the course of the desert border (*limes Arabicus*), protected by a series of forts running from the southern bank of the Euphrates in north-eastern Syria to north-eastern Arabia, and also in Egypt. These were garrisoned mostly by infantry cohorts and some cavalry *vexillationes*. Policy here was very much defence in depth: *Legio I Illyricorum* was based on the frontier at Palmyra, *III Gallica* just behind at Danaba; further north, frontier posts at Oresa and Sura were occupied by *IV Scythica* and *XVI Flavia Firma* respectively; while in Osrhoene the critical part of the frontier at Circesium was garrisoned *IV Parthica*.[18] This important stronghold was constructed in the reign of Diocletian.[19] Also in this period, some of the best-known installations in England are the Saxon shore forts along the south and east coast, such as Porchester.[20]

His military constructions and deployments are recorded by the sixth-century writer John Malalas:[21]

> Diocletian also built fortresses on the *limites* from Egypt up to the Persian borders and stationed *limitanei* in them, and he appointed *duces* for each province to be stationed further back from the fortresses with a large force to ensure their security.

The most flattering account of Diocletian's military reforms was penned by Count Zosimus, who was resident in Constantinople during the reign of Anastasius (491–518), although for the period 270 to 407 he drew on the work of his contemporary Eunapius, and from 407 that of Olympiodorus:[22]

> Constantine did something else which gave the barbarians unhindered access to the Roman empire. By the forethought of Diocletian, the frontiers of the empire everywhere, were covered, as I have stated, with cities, garrisons and fortifications which housed the whole army. Consequently, it was impossible for the barbarians to cross the frontier because they were confronted at every point by forces capable of resisting their attacks. Constantine destroyed this security by removing most of the troops from the frontiers and stationing them in cities which did not need assistance, thus both stripping of protection those being molested by the barbarians and subjecting the cities left alone by them to the

outrages of the soldiers, so that henceforth most have become deserted. Moreover, he enervated the troops by allowing them to devote themselves to shows and luxuries. In plain terms, Constantine was the origin and beginning of the present destruction of the empire.

As Douglas Lee has suggested, this polemical tone betrays the author's antagonism towards Constantine, since Zosimus was a committed pagan:[23]

who was therefore predisposed to admire Diocletian, persecutor of the Church, and revile Constantine, the first emperor to lend his support to Christianity. The passage's sharply drawn contrast between a Diocletian who strengthened frontier defences and a Constantine who neglected them is belied by archaeological evidence which shows Constantine to have been energetic on this front.

Administrative reforms

Diocletian's main administrative reforms involved the major reconfiguration of the provinces around the time of the creation of the Tetrarchy in 293. This involved the grouping of provinces into a number of larger units comprising twelve dioceses, which were attuned with new arrangements for the minting of coinage and fiscal administration.[24] Within each diocese the provinces were split into smaller units, *Britannia*, for example, comprised the provinces of Britannia Prima, Britannia Secunda, Maxima Caesariensis, and Valentia.

Economic reforms

In 297, Diocletian promulgated a fundamental tax reform now calculated on the basis of units of land and individuals (*iuga* and *capita*). Coinage was reformed, the first, circa 294 involved the raising of the weight of gold coins from 70–72 to the Roman pound to 60. This act of remonetization was deemed necessary as a response to the inflation caused by the monetary reforms of Aurelian in the 270s; it was also a crucial piece of legislation to rationalize the imposition and collection of taxes in light of increasing military needs.[25]

In 301 Diocletian introduced a more radical reform of the currency, revising the absolute and relative values of the gold *aureus*, the silver *argenteus* (100 *denarii*), and the smaller bronze denominations (25 and 4 *denarii*), which can be linked to the value of bullion. The silver-washed *antoninianus* was abolished and replaced by the silver *denarius* of 96 to the Roman pound, and the copper *follis* was introduced.[26] This reform has been plausibly regarded by Bowman as an effective measure of remonetization, reasonably effective until the *solidus* under Constantine. The Edict on Maximum Prices was implemented in the same year but was only promulgated in the east and was essentially a failure.[27]

Constructions

In terms of public works, his greatest tangible legacy is his monumental bath-house built near the Viminal Hill in Rome – a city that he never visited – in the latter part of his reign.[28] These were the largest of the great imperial thermae, occupying a rectangular area about 356 by 316 metres, about the same as the Baths of Caracalla, on which they were modelled; they also served as the inspiration for the Baths of Constantine, built in the capital a short time afterwards. The central hall is well preserved, due to its conversion to the church of Santa Maria degli Angeli by Michelangelo, and this comprises a massive vault divided into three bays, equipped with the facilities that are typically associated with the imperial thermae. The dedicatory inscription suggests that the baths were finished in 305 or 306; it reads as follows:[29]

> Our Lords Diocletian and Maximian, the elder and invincible Augusti, fathers of the Emperors and Caesars, our lords Constantius and Maximian and Severus and Maximin, noblest Caesars, dedicated to their beloved Romans these auspicious Baths of Diocletian, which the divine Maximin on his return from Africa ordered to be built and consecrated in the name of his brother Diocletian, having purchased the premises required for so huge and remarkable work and furnishing them with the most sumptuous refinement.

The inscription does not mention that the baths were built from the spoils of war but it may be inferred that Maximian's successful campaigns against the Berber tribes, concluded in 298, may have helped finance the project.[30] This was probably only a fraction of the booty accrued from a series of successful military campaigns in the period. According to Eutropis, Galerius seized a substantial amount of booty from the Persians in his campaign against Bahram in Armenia: 'He routed Narses, plundered his camp, captured his wives, sisters and children, in addition to a vast number of the Persian nobility and a huge amount of Persian treasure . . .'.[31]

Lactantius, a Christian author, was explicit about the prodigious building activities of Diocletian across the empire, albeit from a negative point of view:[32]

> Diocletian had a limitless passion for building, which led to an equally limitless scouring of the provinces to raise workers, craftsmen, waggons, and whatever is necessary for building operations. Here he built basilicas, there a circus, a mint, an arms-factory.

In addition to booty, we should consider that his systemization of tax reckoning and its collection enabled him to build on such a great scale, as it did paying for his substantial increase in military personnel. It should be considered that Lactantius was biased towards Diocletian, since he was a staunch Christian who guided the religious policies of Constantine.

In the west, there are nine dated building inscriptions from the reign of Diocletian: one at Rome, the remaining examples in the provinces.[33]

Legacy

The final years of the reign of the First Tetrarchy were tarnished by religious persecutions. First, against the Manichees, followers of the Persian prophet Mani, in 302, in the eastern provinces; then against the Christians, the Great Persecution occurring in the following year, although the severity of these should be tempered by the fact that they are related by Christian writers, notably Lactantius, writing in the reign of Constantine.[34] The persecutions appear to have been promulgated in the eastern empire rather than the west.[35] In 305, Diocletian and Maximian abdicated – the former to apparently grow cabbages in the gardens of his palace at Spalato – the first and last emperors to voluntarily step down.[36] However, the fierce rivalry that subsequently evolved from the constitutional and political arrangement of the Tetrarchy led to its collapse within twenty years of its establishment and an unwelcome phase of civil wars.[37]

Agri deserti

Since agricultural productivity is central to the arguments proposed through the course of this book, due consideration should be given to *agri deserti* – the abandonment of cultivated land – a phenomenon that is attested in late antiquity. There are a few explanations for this, one being climate change, drought becoming increasingly common in the period.[38]

Barbarian raids had of course become a major factor in the west since the third century, as outlined in the previous chapter, and this is clear from the point of view that many cities were fortified in this period. However, the administrative reforms of Diocletian impacted negatively on the rural population in many areas. Lactantius naturally had his own bias with Diocletian after his persecutions, although his thoughts were later echoed by Aurelius Victor, who was more sympathetic. Nonetheless, his comments on the size of the army and its upkeep in the era of the Tetrarchs are relevant here, as it is to the overarching arguments of the present work:[39]

> [Diocletian multiplied] the armies since each of the four [Tetrarchs] strove to have a far larger number of troops than previous emperors had had when they were governing the state alone. The number of recipients began to exceed the number of contributors by so much that, with farmers' resources exhausted by the enormous size of the requisitions, fields became deserted and cultivated land was turned into forest.

Richard Whittaker has suggested that *agri deserti* were in fact areas of land that had traditionally remained uncultivated and that contemporary concerns about the issue are distorted in contemporary texts. However, those accounts relayed above would seem to militate against this point of view, and the picture painted by archaeological data presented below points towards shrinking agricultural productivity in many areas.[40] The situation was however alleviated to some degree by Constantine with remedial action and legislation.

An interesting instance of this was implemented in favour of the city of Autun in Burgundy to assist a reduced number of producers.[41] Constantine also addressed the problem of *agri deserti* by granting this land to retired army veterans with additional grants of money, grain, and also tax relief. In 326 he passed a law that: 'veterans shall receive vacant lands, and they shall hold them tax exempt in perpetuity'. This law was repeated and extended on several occasions.[42]

The Constantinian period: Constantine the Great (306–337)

In the wake of the abdication of Diocletian and Maximian, specifically after the Conference of Carnuntum in 308, there were four members of the imperial college: Galerius (Caesar 293, Augustus 305), Licinius (Augustus 308), Maximinus (Caesar 305), and Constantine.[43] There followed a brutal civil war, culminating in the victories of Constantine over Maxentius at the battle of the Milvian Bridge on the Tiber in Rome in the autumn of 312, and then over Licinius at Cibalae, Dalmatia, in 316 and Chrysopolis, Thracia, in 324. The emperor's military success over Maxentius was commemorated with the construction of the Arch of Constantine erected near the Colosseum.[44] Prior to the first battle, Lactantius, whose ecclesiastical rhetoric was established in the previous chapter, recounted that Constantine was told in a dream to paint the *chi-rho* (the Greek letters corresponding to the first two letters of Christ's name) on the shields of his soldiers.[45] According to Eusebius' account:[46]

> ... Thereupon, as he slept, the Christ of God appeared to him with the sign which had appeared in the sky, and urged him to make himself a copy of the sign which had appeared in the sky, and to use this as protection against the attacks of the enemy ... When day came he arose and recounted the mysterious communication to his friends. Then he summoned goldsmiths and jewellers, sat among them, and explained the shape of the sign, and gave them instructions about copying it in gold and precious stones ... It was constructed in to the following design. A tall pole plated with gold had a transverse bar forming the shape of a cross ... On it two letters, intimating by its first characters the name 'Christ', formed the monogram of the Saviour's title, *rho* being intersected in the middle by *chi*.

Constantine's Christian zeal is further underscored by a programme of ecclesiastical building construction in the capital, including numerous martyr-shrines, the Lateran Basilica, and St Peter's.[47] Inscriptions, some in mosaic, record the names of Constantine and other members of the imperial family, linking them with the construction of the building and its cult.[48]

Following the Council of Nicaea, convened and attended by Constantine in 325, a number of important churches were built under the patronage of his mother, Helena, including the 'Golden' octagonal church or Domus Aurea at Antioch, the Church of the Nativity in Bethlehem, and the Church of the Holy Sepulchure in Jerusalem.[49] The Council aimed, with limited success, to resolve a number ecumenical controversies pertaining to Arianism and the nature of Christ (the Son) and his formal unity with the Father (God). This was prefigured by the Donatist schism in North Africa.[50]

After Constantine's victory at Chrysopolis, he became the sole ruler of the Roman empire. He is credited with two of the most significant changes in history. First, Christianity became officially tolerated in the Edict of Milan agreed by Constantine and Licinius in February 313, and his conversion led to the adoption of Christianity as the Roman state religion. Second, his foundation of Constantinople at Byzantium in 324 constituted the inauguration of the city as the new capital of the empire, gradually eclipsing Rome to a significant degree.[51]

The momentous foundation of Constantinople is put into the words of Constantine in a fifteenth-century text:[52]

> Therefore we have resolved that it is fitting that my rule and the power of my Kingdom be transferred and transmuted to the regions of the east and that in the province of Byzantia, on an excellent site, a city be built in my name and my rule be established there; since it is not right that the earthly emperor should have power where the princedom of priests and the head of the Christian religion has been established by the heavenly emperor.

During Constantine's lifetime, the urban prefect and poet Optatianus Porfyrius called Constantinople *altera Roma* (a second Rome).[53] Subsequently, in 357, Themistius the orator, and imperial 'spin-doctor', was predictably upbeat referring to the city as *nea Rōmē* (new Rome).[54] The new Rome was modelled on its namesake, with an urban prefect, a corn dole (*annona civica*), supplied from Egypt, and a Senate.[55] The archaeological remains of the Byzantine city are problematic, since they are mostly obscured by Ottoman buildings. For instance, the Church of the Holy Apostles, which served as the burial place of the imperial dynasty, is buried under the mosque of Mehmet the Conqueror, and the location of the Church of Saint Mokios, mentioned by Procopius, is unknown.[56]

Constructions

For this reason we are largely dependent on the *Notitia Urbis Constantino-politanae*. This is a text of a technical and administrative nature, transmitted by fifteenth- and sixteenth-century copyists from a lost Carolingian manuscript once in the Cathedral Library of Speyer. This divides the city into fourteen regions, akin to Rome. The original part of the city on the eastern sector of the promontory is thought to have been established in the Severan period. Here, the area of the Great Palace adjoined the Hippodrome, and ran up to the Baths of Zeuxippus and the large forum known as the Augusteum, probably a reconfiguration of the Severan-colonnaded forum called the Tetrastoon. Farther west in the undeveloped areas of the city, Constantine's new metropolis emerged. This began at the Severan city gate, and the new Forum of Constantine lay a little beyond this. The most important thoroughfare was the impressive colonnaded avenue known as the Mesē, which ran from the Augusteum through to the new forum. At some distance from this point it divided into a northern branch, past the Mausoleum of Constantine (later the Church of the Apostles); its southern branch led to the Golden Gate.[57]

As the city grew, it was adorned with a substantial number of churches and fora, and an impressive hydraulic system was added comprising several aqueducts, notably the Aqueduct of Valens; also, to the north of the city, there were many cisterns, some of the best known being the Basilica Cistern and the Cistern of Philoxenos (Figure 4.2).[58]

In Rome, at an earlier date, Constantine had also begun the construction of the Lateran Basilica around 313, the Cathedral of Rome, still in use today; and Old St Peter's Basilica around 320 on the site of the Circus of Nero; and Santa Croce in Gerusalemme was consecrated in 325. These were massive constructions, consisting of a central nave with four aisles, and were modelled

Figure 4.2 Basilica Cistern in Istanbul, fourth century.
Courtesy of Denghiū.com.

on the civic basilica, such as the Basilica Ulpia in the Forum of Trajan[59] and Constantine's Aula Palatina at Trier.[60] Another secular building was the Baths of Constantine (Thermae Constantinianae), the last of the imperial thermae, probably built before 315 on the Quirinal. The complex was influenced by the Baths of Diocletian, but they were built on a relatively limited footprint and their design was therefore irregular. Several high-quality works have been found on the site of the baths, including two over life-size statues of Constantine and his son Constans (in the Capitoline Museum); fine bronzes, the Bronze Boxer and the Hellenistic Ruler (in the Museo Nazionale delle Terme); the two large marble river gods, Nile and Tiber (set up in the Palazzo Senatorio on the Capitoline); and two colossal marble statues, most likely of the Dioscuri (displayed in the Piazza Quirinale).[61]

Mention should also be made of the Basilica of Constantine (Basilica Constantini) begun by Maxentius and completed by its namesake in the Roman Forum. This was the last of the great basilicas built in the city, but was modelled more on the halls of the imperial thermae, and a substantial part of its impressive ruins are visible today. It was built on a large rectangular concrete platform 100 metres long and 65 wide, and consisted of a central nave 80 metres long, 25 wide, and 35 in height, with large side aisles, the whole edifice being constructed of brick-faced concrete. In 1487, fragments of a colossal statue of Constantine were discovered in the large semicircular apse at the west end of the nave (now in the Palazzo dei Conservatori). The enormous vaulted roof of the edifice made it one of the most architecturally accomplished buildings in Rome.[62]

In the reign of Constantine there are ten recorded building inscriptions in the west: one at Ostia, another in the Italian regions, the remainder in the provinces.[63]

The last phase of the 'booty economy'

How was this extraordinary programme of public building works across the empire paid for? Constantine would have certainly accrued a considerable amount of booty from his successful campaigns in order to bankroll his extensive building spree. For instance, his victory and its aftermath over the Sarmatians at Bononia in Panonnia Superior (or possibly Bononia in Dacia), is described by the contemporary Christian poet Porfyrius, who mentioned the distribution of the spoils of war after the battle in the summer of 322.[64] However, this is only a part of the overall picture, since it was his victory over Licinius that benefitted the treasury most of all.

His conquest of the east granted Constantine access to the vast reserves of gold accrued in pagan temple treasures and he wasted little time converting this into coin, having introduced the gold *solidus* in 309. This sudden injection of wealth enabled him to use the *solidus* as an effective currency across the empire. Georges Depeyrot has made some interesting calculations in relation to the development of gold currency in this period, which was considerable, as was the dramatic increase in stock of *solidi* in eastern mints. This denomination proved to be an effective means to pay the troops and patronize the Church. His total endowments to churches from 314 to 336 were 963 kilogrammes of gold and 5,300 kilogrammes of silver.[65]

The gold *solidus* largely replaced the pure *argentius* introduced under Diocletian. This is widely regarded as the most important economic reform of the fourth century, involving a simple reduction of Diocletian's gold *aureus* from 6 to 4.5 grams; its purity and weight remained unaltered until the tenth century. Its stabilizing impact on the economy across the Roman empire characterizes it as a rare example of successful monetary reform in antiquity. The essential characteristics of the new system was essentially a duality that entailed the mass production and weight reduction of bronze denominations in subsequent reforms, and an increased production of stable gold *aurei*. This resulted in a drop in the value of bronze currency, and effectively meant that gold coinage became the preserve of soldiers' pay and the middle and upper classes, and the bulk of the population suffered as a consequence and the wealth gap widened at their expense.[66] This aroused criticism in some quarters, not least in the anonymous text *On Military Matters* (*De rebus bellicis*), most likely written in 368:[67]

> It was in the reign of Constantine that extravagant grants assigned gold instead of bronze (which earlier was considered of great value) to petty commercial transactions; but the greed I speak of is thought to have arisen from the following causes. When the gold and silver and the huge quantity of precious stones which had been stored away in the temples long ago reached the public, they enkindled all men's possessive and spendthrift instincts. And while the expenditure of bronze itself . . . had seemed already vast and burdensome enough, yet from some kind of blind folly there ensued an even more extravagant passion for spending gold, which is considered more precious. This store of gold meant that the houses of the powerful were crammed full and their splendour enhanced to the destruction of the poor, the poorer classes of course being held down by force.

In the western empire during fourth century, coins were struck in gold and silver under the authority of the *comes sacrarum largitionum* at various mints depending on the emperor or emperor's whereabouts, primarily to pay the army.[68]

Military reforms

In light of the military instabilities of the period, Constantine deemed it necessary to overhaul the configuration of his armed forces. He increased the size and importance of the field army (*comitatenses*) – distinguishing it from the frontier troops (*riparienses* or *limitanei*) – which consisted of smaller infantry legions, new infantry *auxilia*, and cavalry *vexillationes*. The Praetorian Guard, so often directly responsible for the assassination of numerous emperors, was abolished and replaced by the *scholae palatinae*.[69] Occasionally, contingents could be withdrawn from the frontiers for short periods to support the field army, and were termed *pseudocomitatenses*, although frontier deployments remained broadly similar to those established by the reforms of Diocletian.[70]

Legacy

After the death of Constantine in 337, his sons Constantine II, Constantius II, and Constans, declared themselves Augusti. In the autumn of that year they met in Pannonia to divide the empire between them: Constantine took control of Britain, Gaul, and Spain; Constantius, the eastern provinces and Thrace; Constans, the remainder of the Balkan peninsula, Italy, and North Africa. A predictable civil war followed, with much bloodshed, and these events should not detain us, merely that their culmination left one victor, Constantius, who appointed Julian, nephew of Constantine I, to rule in the east in 354.[71] Only one dated inscription is known from this era of political turbulence, and this relates to Constans, in the Theatre at Leptis Magna, Africa Proconsularis.[72]

Julian (361–363)

Julian established an administrative and military track record that, in my opinion, singles him out as one of the most successful Roman leaders, despite his short-lived achievements; he may perhaps be regarded as the Aurelian of the fourth century. In 351, Julian travelled to Athens where he studied Neoplatonism, becoming a pagan convert. His rejection of Christianity is logically regarded as a protest against the imperial circle of Constantius, who had murdered his half-brother, Gallus, whom he replaced, and father, Julius Constantius, a former consul. For this reason he was called Julian the Apostate by ecclesiastics, a person who has abandoned his religion and its principles.

His track record on the battlefield was impressive before his accession to the purple in the western empire: in 357 he defeated the Alamanni at the Battle of Strasbourg; the Franks on the Rhine in 358; and invaded Persia in 362, with much success. Ultimately, however, a contemporary Christian writer Gregory of Nazianzus, chronicled that: 'from this point on, like sand slipping from beneath his feet, or a great storm bursting upon a ship, things began to go black for him'.[73] After initial success, Julian died from a spear wound in the Battle of Samarra in June 363.[74]

Legacy

Jovian, the new emperor, whose reign was short-lived, effectively was forced to sue for peace and the retreated into Roman territory.[75] Perhaps the most extraordinary legacy of his reign is the fascinating chronicle of Marcellinus, a military officer, who penned an eyewitness account of events in this era more generally. This is especially significant for the purposes of the present book, since he also sheds light on the nature of agricultural settlements in this crucial period before the serious political crisis of the fifth century.

Rural settlement: *castella, fundi,* and *vici* and the villa

Marcellinus indicates that agricultural landscapes were diverse across the empire, such as rich, cultivated farms around Amida, Mesopotamia,[76] villa wine estates on the Euphrates,[77] well-ordered cultivated fields in Palestine,[78] wealthy villages in Thrace,[79] fertile estates in the hinterland of Heraclea,[80] and rich suburban countryside near Leptis Magna.[81] In Mauretania, there are several references to *castella*, the most common type of agricultural settlement in North Africa during the early Roman period.[82] In the fourth century there were an increasing number of large private villa estates known as *fundi*. This trend appears to be echoed across the Iberian peninsula[83] and Panonnia.[84] In Britain, the fourth century is widely attested as a time of great economic prosperity, with some of the more grandiose villas expanded or built *de novo* in this period, presiding over large estates.[85] In the western provinces, villas are the symbol of Romanization par excellence, owned by elites who were essentially Romano-British, Romano-Gallic, and the same principle applied elsewhere.

Simon Esmonde Cleary makes the point that:[86]

> By the fourth century, the rural residence or villa as a *locus* for the display of power and wealth had become a major investment among the aristocracies of certain regions of the west. These were above all south-western Gaul; north-eastern, north-central and south-eastern Iberia; and southern Britain . . .

However, the various settlement types and the agricultural territories they exploited is rather complex, with a mixture of agricultural exploitation by *castella, fundi,* and *vici*,[87] and a hierarchy of establishments from grandiose villas down to simple farms, and this issue will be discussed in its appropriate context in the next chapter.

The general picture at the time Marcellinus was writing appears to be a monopoly of agricultural production by elites on a vast scale, involving the exploitation of considerable tracts of land for their financial aggrandizement. Also, as outlined above, gold coinage was now the dominant means of conducting financial transactions across the Roman empire, and the textual and archaeological data suggest that the fourth century was a time of general prosperity. The importance of gold in this period is underscored by Jairus Banaji:[88]

> It has been a major argument of this book that the emergence of gold as a stable high-value coinage revolutionized the economic conditions of

the late empire. In gold the aristocracy rediscovered a powerful medium of accumulation, and the state a medium of taxation that would progressively displace taxes in kind as the dominant form of public revenue.

On the face of it this all boded well for the fortunes of the Roman empire in the fourth century. However, the aristocratic dominance of land was essentially a centralization of agricultural productivity in a series of 'blocks' that were dependent on gold for stability. This socio-economic structure was also vulnerable from the point of view that, on the one hand, gold still needed to be extracted, despite the fact that it remained in circulation; on the other, the political dislocation of elites had serious ramifications for the generation of product across large tracts of land.

Valentinian I (364–375)

Julian's death marked the end of the Constantinian dynasty and the demise of Jovian ushered in the new world order of the Valentinian dynasty in what was essentially a relatively successful 'rebirth' of the Tetrarchy. Conventionally, the split of the Roman empire is often attributed to the succession of Theodosius I in 395, Arcadius ruling the east and Honorius the west.[89] Robert Errington emphasizes the point that the empire was divided on the accession of Valentinian I, who ruled in the west, and Valens, who governed the east. This was essentially a practical solution to the governmental challenge of administering such a large empire.[90]

In this period the empire faced some serious problems: incursions of Salian Franks and Saxons on the lower Rhine; the Alamanni on the middle and upper Rhine and upper Danube; the Quadi and Marcomanni on the middle Danube; and the Goths on the lower Danube. These threats were suppressed in the short term by a combination of military campaigning, peace treaties, and enlisting barbarians in the army as *foederati*.[91] Marcellinus commented that 'During this time, when the barriers of our frontier were unlocked and the realm of savagery was spreading far and wide columns of armed men like glowing ashes from Aetna [Etna]. . .'.[92]

Constructions

Relatively stable economic conditions in the reign of Valentinian I are attested by eleven building inscriptions, more than any other emperor in the fourth century: two in Rome, one at Ostia, the remainder in the provinces; building inscriptions are thereafter scant.[93]

The Roman army in the late fourth century

It is important to consider the complexion and strength of the Roman army in this period. In this context, scholars have rightly concentrated on the

Notitia Dignitatum ('list of offices'), thought to date to the late fourth or early fifth century. This permits the identification of legions and other units added under particular emperors. For instance, legions named as *II, III,* and *VI Herculia* and *I, IV,* and *V Jovia,* adjectival epithets Jovius and Herculius, aligning themselves ideologically with Jupiter and Hercules,[94] added by the two Tetrachs.[95] Likewise, *Legio I* and *II Flavia Constantiniana, Constantini seniores, Constantini iuniores,* and *Constantini Dafnenses,* incorporated by Constantine.[96] A similar pattern is discernible under Valentinian I and Valens, and his sons Gratian and Valentinian II, with the addition of *vexillationes Equites constantes Valentinianenses seniores* and *iuniores; I* and *II Felix Valentis Thebaeorum;* and *Auxilia palatina Valentinianenses seniores* and *iuniores* (some examples of many more additions to the Roman forces).[97]

This demands the question of the numerical strength of the Roman army before the Battle of Adrianople. Above it was contended that the size of the army probably rose under Diocletian to over 400,000. Lee has plausibly argued that it increased again through the course of the fourth century, possibly to around 500,000 personnel, although he is rightly cautious to identify a distinction between 'paper' numbers and physical deployment. He also draws attention to the tax burden that such a large force would have had on the financial resources of the Roman state.[98] This brings us back to the issue of economic product. On the face of it, the formidable size of the Roman army in the third quarter of the fourth century suggests that the economy was thriving in this sense, and the armed forces of the empire were numerically capable of defeating the Goths at the Battle of Adrianople.

A geo-political excursus

This mass exodus of barbarians infiltrating the Rhine–Danube frontier was only the beginning of a greater problem, and it is appropriate to turn briefly to the geo-political map of the known world in the broader period, since this gives a clearer picture of why this situation occurred (Map 1). With some exceptions, there were a series of powerful civilizations spanning from the Pacific to the Atlantic Oceans. The eastern Han Chinese occupied the first block of territory, the Satavahana empire, which included much of India (for much of the period), and the Kushans to the north-west inhabited a swathe of modern Pakistan and parts of Afghanistan. Their empire interfaced with that of the Sasanians, which, of course, bordered the eastern Roman empire.

Over the vast territories of Asia, this situation 'squeezed' a series of nomadic peoples into the Eurasian Steppe, the grassland corridor that lay between the various empires and the Arctic Circle.[99] Naturally, the political turbulence that could all too frequently result from this cultural contact had an impact on tribal movements, and these tended to gravitate west, in search of pastures new. Perhaps the best-known example of this is the Xiongnu, a powerful nomadic confederacy who dominated the Asian Steppe from the third century BC to the first century AD. They were in conflict with the Han Chinese for much of this period and were subsequently forced west, and are now, not withstanding 'resolved' controversies, identified with the subsequent appearance of the Huns on the northern Black Sea coast and Europe in the third century AD.[100]

A similar situation arose in those territories to the north of the western Roman empire, where the various Germanic tribes were, in a sense, geographically and politically poised between each other and the might of Rome, and were, in a sense, 'boxed-in' between the Arctic wastes and the fertile lands of their southern neighbours. Through the course of the Roman period it is possible to discern a growing centralization of these various confederacies for defensive reasons, and also because of the trade advantages that derived from cultural contact with the Romans. The catalyst of the tumultuous barbarian incursions of the late fourth and early fifth centuries was undoubtedly the Huns, whose ferocity forced large-scale migrations that pressed them against the Rhine–Danube frontier.

The Gothic and Hunnic issue

One of the most significant events of the fourth century was the settlement of a substantial number of Goths on the Roman side of the Danube in Thrace in 376. This was narrated in considerable detail by Edward Gibbon,[101] based largely on the account of Marcellinus.[102] Their arrival on the far side of the river was a direct consequence of a migration west by the Greuthungi and Tervingi. The movements of the confederacy in response to Hunnic pressure north of the Black Sea resulted in the collapse of the Tervingi under king Athanaric from 372.[103]

Marcellinus, in keeping with Roman perception of barbarian tribes, describes the Huns as exceeding 'every degree of savagery',[104] his judgement colouring the writing of Gibbon:[105]

> The numbers, the strength, the rapid motions, and the implacable cruelty of the Huns were felt, and dreaded, and magnified by the astonished Goths, who beheld their fields and villages consumed with flames and deluged with indiscriminate slaughter. To these real terrors they added the surprise and abhorrence which were excited by the shrill voice, the uncouth gestures, and the strange deformity of the Huns. These savages of Scythia were compared . . . to the animals who walk very awkwardly on two legs, and to the misshapen figures, the *Termini*, which were often placed on the bridges of antiquity.

Their formidable reputation is underscored by the development of a lethal asymmetrical recurve cavalry bow, a composite of sinew, animal bone plates, and wood, and superior in power to its predecessor, the Scythican bow.[106] It is perhaps true to say that the Huns, above any other barbarian tribal confederacy, struck terror into those who were unfortunate enough to confront them. According to Marcellinus:[107]

> When they fight they are fanatical. They ride into battle in a wedge formation each warrior yelling out blood-curdling war-cries. They are lightly armed and so fast and unpredictable that they will scatter suddenly and gallop here and there chaotically, inflicting untold slaughter. They are so fast that they can burst through a rampart or raid an enemy camp before anyone has spotted them. You would rightly say that they are the fiercest of all fighters – they can fire missiles from far off, arrows tipped not with the usual arrowheads but with sharp splintered bones, which they attach onto shafts with extraordinary skill . . .

The origin of the Huns has been debated since an important five-volume publication by the French scholar Joseph Deguignes between the mid-eighteenth century and first quarter of the nineteenth century.[108] He suggested that the Huns were the political and physical descendants of the imperial Chinese Xiongnu, a theory that has been fiercely debated and rejected by prominent historians of the Huns and central Asia. One of the principal problems with this suggestion is that Chinese sources place the Xiongnu in the region some 300 years before they are recorded on the Black Sea. This is emphasized by Peter Heather:[109]

> The ancestors of our Huns could even have been a part of the Xiongnu confederation, without being the 'real' Xiongnu. Even if we do make some sort of connection between the 4th century Huns and the 1st century Xiongnu, an awful lot of water has passed under an awful lot of bridges in the three hundred years' worth of lost history.

Without wishing to become engaged too deeply in this debate, an interesting recent publication by Hyun Jin Kim has presented an incisive argument for a cultural, physical, and 'genetic' link between the Xiongnu and the Huns. The first strand of this is a letter written by a Chinese merchant about the fall of the Chinese capital of Luoyang to the Southern Xiongnu in 311. This explicitly calls the Xiongnu the Huns. Further textual evidence from India (dated 280) and Tibet (308) identify the Huna (Huns) with the Xiongnu. Finally, Kim notes the archaeological concordance between Hunnic cauldrons and those of the Xiongnu in the Ordos region of Inner Mongolia.[110]

Identifying the origin of the Goths is less problematic. They are first mentioned in the territory of modern Poland in the first century AD. The definitive historical text on the Goths is the *Origins and Acts of the Goths*, otherwise known as *Getica*, written in Latin by Jordanes (of Gothic descent), in Constantinople in the later reign of Justinian around 550.[111]

This is not the place to discuss the anthropological ethnic connotations of labelling individual groups on particular criteria, such as race, language, and culture.[112] Archaeological evidence in particular has demonstrated that material culture can mask ethnic identities. Burials in the first Gothic kingdom, centred in Toulouse in the early fifth century are a case in point, since they exhibit more recognizably Roman material than identifiably Gothic artefacts. This reflects their cultural contact with Rome and only in the later fifth century did their culture crystallize into manifestly recognizable Gothic material, for instance, distinctive belt buckles inlaid with garnets and other semi-precious stones.[113]

Archaeological evidence generally associates the Goths with the Wielbark and Cernjachov cultures in the region of the Baltic Sea in Poland in the Roman Iron Age of the fifth to first centuries BC, spreading south-east towards the Black Sea in the first to third centuries AD. Heather has demonstrated that the texts of Jordanes and Marcellinus are misleading in terms of establishing the terms 'Visigoth' and 'Ostrogoth' as distinctive tribal confederacies before the fifth century AD. Before this period they were an amalgam of Tervingi and Greuthungi.[114]

Barbarian settlements in the Roman empire

As outlined above, the settlement of Germanic peoples in Roman territories was an established practice in return for military assistance. The policy of settling peoples can be traced at least as far back as 180 BC when a substantial number of Ligurians from north-western Italy were installed in Samnium in southern Italy, albeit against their wishes. This practice continued in the late Republic and imperial periods, mainly in those provinces that bordered the Rhine–Danube frontier, but also in Britain. In the reign of Marcus Aurelius, Dio records that the Sarmatian Iazyges provided 8,000 horsemen; 5,000 of these were sent to Britannia to serve in the Roman army rather than constituting *foederati*.[115] Gallienus is said by Victor to have given land to the Marcomannic king Attalus in Pannonia for settlement, presumably as *foederati* under their leadership.[116] According to Zonaras, Severus Alexander settled around 400 Persians in Phrygia to farm there.[117] Imperial policy was essentially three-fold: settling foreign peoples into Roman units, embracing them as *foederati*, or accommodating them as farmers.[118] In the latter case, they would have contributed to the all-important production of agricultural yield for taxation. This policy, which seems to have gathered momentum in late antiquity, perhaps implies that the 'indigenous' population of the Roman empire was in decline, an issue that is addressed below.

The gathering storm of Adrianople

Valentinian I died of a stroke in the summer of 375 after losing his temper during peace negotiations with the Quadi on the Danube.[119] Valentinian II was elevated to the purple, but aged a mere four years old, his elder brother Gratian was elected to rule in his place.

This is a convenient juncture to look at the events surrounding the settlement of the Goths in 376.[120] The Tervingi, under Alavivus and Fritigern, were the first to arrive on the further bank of the Danube, followed shortly afterwards by the Greuthungi led by Alatheus and Saphrax, regents of king Vitheric, sons of the late king Vithimer. Embassies of the Tervingi sent a request to cross the Danube via local Roman commanders who in turn passed this request on to Valens. The emperor at this time was in Antioch overseeing the preparations for an expedition against the Sasanians. Tensions were inflated by Roman interference in Armenia and Shapur II was threatening to invade the eastern empire. Valens was therefore obliged to make a peace treaty with the monarch before he could risk turning his attention to the Gothic problem. It appears that Valens agreed to the settlement of the Goths because they promised to provide military assistance and gold. No formal treaty was apparently signed, although the fragmentary history of Eunapius, who was a contemporary, indicates that one of the terms insisted on by Valens was that they should be allowed on Roman soil without weapons and settled as *coloni*.[121]

The Tervingi constituted a large group of people and naturally this made Valens unwilling to grant permission to admit the Greuthungi as well.[122] However, it is evident that the Tervingi were unfavourably treated, deprived of food, and were becoming unruly as a consequence. For this reason, Lupicinus, the senior Roman commander, moved them from the frontier to the city of Marcianople to the south. The vacuum left by their departure led to the crossing of the Greuthungi without imperial agreement, and the disagreements that followed culminated in the Battle of Adrianople.[123]

The course and outcome of the Battle of Adrianople on 9 August 378 has often been outlined and discussed that it is appropriate to omit its finer details, suffice to say that it resulted in one of the heaviest defeats in the history of Roman military conflict.[124] It is generally considered that as many as two-thirds of the Roman field army was destroyed. However, it is widely accepted that the animosity felt by Valens towards Gratian, and his unwillingness to wait for his military support, was a decisive factor in the eventual outcome. The ill sentiment of the emperor and its consequences are perhaps best expressed by Marcellinus:[125]

> In those same days Valens was troubled for two reasons: first, by the news that the Lentienses had been defeated; secondly, because Sebastianus wrote from time to time exaggerating his exploits. He therefore marched forth from Melanthias, being eager to do some glorious deed to equal his young nephew, whose valiant exploits consumed him with envy.

Adrianople and its aftermath

If the scale of the Roman losses is considered, perhaps in the region of 10,000 soldiers,[126] I do not think that the battle *per se* was as catastrophic for Rome as many have considered, bearing in mind the total imperial army was around 400,000 or more in this period. With the policy of absorbing foreign peoples as *foederati*, these numbers would have been replenished relatively swiftly. The problem for the Romans was more a matter of deployment at Adrianople, with so many troops stationed on the frontiers of the Rhine–Danube, and the east; we should also consider that a substantial number of personnel were garrisoned in North Africa, Egypt, and Britannia. These regions exacted a considerable strain on Roman military resources in this era.[127]

The barbarization of the Roman army

It is often claimed that the crushing defeat at Adrianople was a consequence of enlisting too many barbarians into the Roman army and so impairing its performance on the battlefield. This so-called barbarization theory in fact is also seen as a key factor in the eventual collapse of the western empire.[128] This issue is readdressed in the next chapter but it is also relevant to comment on it here.

The root of this derives from Gibbon. It is certainly true that the influx of barbarian troops into the Roman army reached an unprecedented level in the fourth century. The loyalty of these vast contingents of men under arms has been traditionally questioned, logically because they originated in tribes that were enemies of the Roman state and colluded with invading confederacies, or were previously hostile, and their barbarian habits and relatively poor military skills weakened the Roman army.[129]

These assumptions have been rejected by Lee, who asserted that the Roman army remained largely effective in the western empire after Adrianople and well into the fifth century.[130] Based on the *Notitia Dignitatum*, and other sources, Hugh Elton has presented an informative study of the deployment and recruitment of barbarians across the empire. His conclusions are that numbers remained consistent through the fourth and fifth centuries but the analysis of names suggests that barbarians numbered around one man in four, whom primary texts imply were loyal.[131] The substantial Germanic constitution of the army did not go unnoticed by some commentators. It was recorded by a panegyrist that:[132]

> O event worthy of memory! There marched under Roman leaders and banners the onetime enemies of Rome, and they followed standards which they had once opposed, and filled with soldiers the cities of Pannonia which they had not long ago emptied by hostile plundering.

The late Roman army was clearly barbarized, but a sensible distinction should be made between, on the one hand, the ethnic component of loyal troops of barbarian birth, or former invaders who seized the economic opportunity to join the Roman army and remained faithful to the cause of the Roman state; and on the other, the hordes of invaders who wreaked havoc in the western empire from the late fourth century onwards and remained bitter enemies.

Forced Gothic settlements in the west

In January 379, Gratian appointed Theodosius as emperor in the east, and the Gothic War raged on until 382. Roman operations were relatively successful. The Goths had failed to take Constantinople after Adrianople, with its extraordinary fortifications deeming it impregnable.[133] From 378 until the end of the war, the main problem, it is contended, was the Gothic impact on the Roman economy, with tens of thousands of warriors and their families rampaging through Thrace denuding its crops. Perhaps for this reason they felt it prudent to divide themselves. In 380, the Greuthungi under Alatheus and Saphrax split, moving into Pannonia and were defeated by Gratian, and a peace treaty concluded matters, with Gratian granting them land in Pannonia and Upper Moesia. The Tervingi under Fritigern moved into Greece.

In the following year, the forces of the western emperor drove the Goths back into Thrace and a second peace treaty was agreed with Theodosius in 382, accommodating them with land and as *foederati* on the lower Danube and elsewhere in the Balkans. Later, in 386, the emperor settled more Goths in Phrygia, but in 399 they revolted under Tribigild and proceeded to ravage the territories of Asia Minor. This event most likely prompted the passionate outburst of the speech delivered by Synesius to Arcadius, emperor of the east at Constantinople in 399, in which he condemned both the widespread use of non-Roman troops and their settlement on Roman soil.[134] As Gibbon so aptly put it: 'the court of Arcadius indulged the zeal, applauded the eloquence, and neglected the advice of Synesius'.[135]

As had occurred in the third century, the empire was once more split into three: Magnus Maximus held sway over Britain and Gaul; Valentinian in Italy, Pannonia, Spain, and North Africa; Theodosius ruled in the east.[136]

As indicated above, it is logical that Germanic settlements contributed to Roman agricultural productivity when conventional farming practice was observed. However, the impact of the Goths on the generation of cereal product in particular in the provinces of Thrace and Asia Minor must have substantially diminished crop yields and lowered tax revenue to a considerable extent in this period.

The late Roman economy and economic theory

The primitivist/modernist debate

Any considerations of demographic fluctuations are naturally linked to the Roman economy more generally. In doing so it is not fruitful to be drawn into various conceptual and theoretical debates that are inherent in this sphere; however, it is sensible to embrace their current understanding. The first of these is the primitivist/modernist debate, espoused by Moses Finley in his well-known Sather lectures on the ancient economy. The essence of his thoughts was that 'ancient society did not have an economic system which was an enormous conglomeration of interdependent markets'.[137] Subsequent research, informed by archaeology, has fundamentally challenged this assumption. In fact a recent book by Peter Temin argues a persuasive case for the existence of a fully-fledged Roman market economy.[138] The constitution of the Roman economic system was I think correctly characterized by Chris Wickham, who described it as follows: 'The Roman Empire was a coherent political and economic system, operating on a scale that has seldom been matched in Europe and the Mediterranean'.[139]

Some of the most important work marshalled together on the Roman economy is the recent series under the general title of *Oxford Studies on the Roman Economy*, edited by Alan Bowman and Andrew Wilson. These draw on quantitative archaeological data collated from excavations and surveys in the cities and countryside of the Roman empire. Collectively, this information, albeit proxy, provides a useful insight into demographics, economic conditions (relative growth and decline), urban construction, agricultural productivity, industrial production, and trade.[140] With regard to the important concept of Roman economic policy, they make a particularly important statement: 'We do not need a single explicit "policy" or a consistent policy to demonstrate integration, merely an array of integrated economic institutions or patterns of behaviour'.[141] It is also important to stress at this stage that any discussion of demographic decline needs to take into account that many attempts have been made to estimate the size of populations in the urban and rural sphere across the length and breadth of the Roman empire, and this is hampered by an incomplete archaeological record and the latitudes inherent in sampling methods, resulting in a number of interesting theoretical studies in addition to quantitative estimates based on raw data sets (principally pottery and settlements). However, it is still far from clear how large the population was in the Roman period.[142]

The Malthusian economy

The second economic concept that should be mentioned is that of a Malthusian economy, espoused by Thomas Malthus in the late eighteenth and early nineteenth centuries.[143] This has been especially influential and has dominated economic theory to the extent that it permeates literature in this sphere today. In short, Malthus argued that the size of the population was limited by the resources available to feed it, the 'Malthusian equilibrium'. If the resource constraint improved through regional specialization in trade, or technical change as argued by Wilson,[144] as occurred in the first two centuries AD, then for any given population size product and per capita income rise.[145]

Developing the taxes and trade model of Keith Hopkins (discussed below), Richard Saller also viewed the correlation of technological improvements and economic growth, plotting gross domestic product (GDP) per capita from AD 100 to 300, which reached a peak in the first century, returning to its original value by the end of this period.[146] This is compatible with the Malthusian model in which incomes and population continue to rise until what Temin describes as 'the pull of the Malthusian equilibrium is felt' – the so-called 'Malthusian Trap'. The latter would have occurred if there was a one-time increase in productivity whose effects gradually died out during the early Roman empire, or there was continuing productivity growth in this time but it was interrupted by the plague and political events in the third and succeeding centuries. Temin makes the important point that data are two sparse to differentiate between the two theories.[147]

The taxes and trade model

An especially well-known and informative paper on the Roman economy was published by Hopkins in 1980 that examined taxes and trade between 200 BC and AD 400.[148] The central tenet of this was that: 'the Romans' imposition of taxes paid in money greatly increased the volume of trade in the Roman empire'.[149] With the work of Jones, mentioned in the previous chapter, each scholar provides a basic insight into what is a difficult subject area.

Returning to Jones, he outlined a basic symbiotic relationship between the town and the country in which agricultural product – principally cereals, olives, and wine – were produced on villa estates and farms and sold in city markets. Of course, it is necessary to include *castella*, *vici* (villages), and *fundi* as additional components in the configuration of agricultural units across the empire, as discussed above,[150] although for the purposes of the arguments presented, it is appropriate to concentrate on the western empire.

Hopkins makes some interesting points:[151]

> ... the economy of the Roman empire, in spite of its sophistication in some respects, was predominantly a subsistence economy. The monetary economy constituted a thin veneer of sophistication, spread over and tied to the subsistence economy by the liens of taxes, trade and rent.

If this was the case, and there is every reason to accept this as being so, how was the all-important taxation raised in coin to pay the troops and other principal expenditures? This is a basic but important question that is often glossed over. The explanation, at least in part, is provided by Hopkins: 'In economically unsophisticated regions, peasant tax-payers increasingly sold some of their primary produce in local markets in order to raise money with which to pay taxes'. What followed was 'a significant increase in agricultural production, an increase in the division of labour, growth in the number of artisans, in the size of towns where many of them lived, development of local markets and of long-distance commerce'.[152]

It is important to remember that taxes were also levied in cash and kind and there was manifold direct and indirect taxation. The recent work of Alan Bowman in particular has revealed some important deficiencies in Hopkins' taxation model.[153] Of course, also co-existing with this system was the *annona civica* grain levied directly from North Africa by the state to feed Rome, and later Constantinople, principally from Egypt,[154] and to a lesser extent North Africa, but also olive oil from Baetica (southern Spain).[155] A substantial proportion of grain requisitioning from these regions was the *annona militaris*, used to feed the army; this last factor should be considered in a little more detail since it is directly relevant to the arguments presented through the course of this book.

Taxation in the late Roman period

Any discussion of a correlation between agricultural productivity, tax, and its maintenance of the army should naturally address the rate of taxation and its character, and in light of more recent scholarship, it is necessary to refine certain suggestions by Hopkins, but in doing so this by no means rejects his basic model. In a forthcoming paper by Bowman he rejects the Roman imperial economy as a 'low-tax economy', as for instance suggested by Elio Lo Cascio,[156] with levels around 10 per cent of GDP.[157] This study is important for the purposes of my central arguments.

Several further points are made. With reference to Hopkins' paper, he has drawn attention to the difference between raising revenue by direct taxation and by management and rental. Tax collection became centralized in the Principate, local collection being managed by communities through appointed officials (*liturgists*) or local contractors. A large proportion of the direct taxes raised (in cash and in kind) was spent in the provinces where they were raised, obscuring the relationship between what was raised and what was 'sent to Rome'. It is difficult to gauge tax revenues from individual provinces (except Egypt) or to know if the state attempted to calculate budgetary needs on an empire-wide basis. The reforms of Diocletian (mentioned in the previous chapter) are simplified as comprising: a regularization of exactions for the army; and an overhaul of the methods of assessing the taxability of land and people, using a system of taxable units (*iuga* and *capita*).

Customs duties were especially lucrative, although there is a lack of evidence in this sphere in late antiquity; however, the few textual sources that exist for earlier periods are informative in this context. For instance, Frank estimated that provincial dues in 63 BC totalled about 40 million *denarii* (160 million HS), of which about 10 million (40 million HS) would come from 'customs dues at harbours, and other less important sources like the monopolies on public forests, and the fishing, river and salt taxes'.[158] Bowman has studied a number of customs-house registers from the Arsinoite nome in

Egypt.[159] One register from the village of Bacchias, dating to 114, shows a high accumulation of tax income from internal transportation of routine goods at one station in one month, worth about 2 talents (12,000 *drachmas*) annually if replicated across the whole year. Moreover, as for the duties on external trade, the 'Muziris' papyrus indicates a high value for Indian trade in the mid-second century AD. The calculations of Dominic Rathbone show a payment of the 25 per cent export tax for a single cargo totalling about 2,308,950 *drachmas* (the equivalent in *sesterces*).[160]

The main elements of the imperial tax-system, already touched upon in the work of Duncan-Jones, is summarized as follows:[161]

- Direct taxes (*tributum soli*) paid in both cash and kind on privately owned land;
- Direct capitation taxes and taxes on persons (*tributum capitis*), mainly poll tax;
- Rents on various categories of public land, which are effectively direct revenue;
- Indirect taxes, mainly customs duties, taxes on inheritances, sales, manumissions;
- Military requisitions in cash and in kind (either raised as irregular tax impositions or paid for at below-market rates);
- Revenue in kind in the form of public service (*munera* and *liturgies*).

The *collatio lustralis*, levied on trade and industry, should also be considered.[162]

Bowman emphasizes the three important infrastructural features to be borne in mind that relate to the balance and fiscal effects of taxation:[163]

- The greater proportion of tax raised was on land and some of that but not all was paid in kind (with much regional variation); there was also significant money taxes on land, best attested in Egypt but not unique.
- Even at the climax of the so-called crisis of the third century, there was not a great reversion to payment of tax-in-kind. Currency, though massively debased, continued to circulate and capitation taxes are recorded as cash payments.
- Most taxes were paid to the imperial government but there was a significant (under-emphasized) sector of municipal taxation.

There are two crucial points: first, that per capita tax levels were around 20 per cent; second, Hopkins failed to take into account two categories of taxation: military impositions and requisitions for military purposes, which contributed to imperial revenue, and compulsory public service delivered both in money (*munera patrimonialia*) and in service (*munera personalia*), some of which contributed to imperial revenue, some to civic or municipal. These constituted an extra layer of taxation, and would have had a cumulative impact.

This last point underpins the military burden of the state in terms of its obligation to maintain a massive armed force. It is also clear that the system of taxation was wholly dependent on its manifold extraction of taxes that, with the exception of custom duties and tolls, sales tax, and tax raised from trade and industry, derived from the rural sphere. It therefore logically follows that the security of the countryside was crucial to the integrity of the empire, each *civitas* functioning as a collective economic 'dynamo'. Under these circumstances, Bowman's suggestion of a higher rather than a lower rate of tax is surely correct, since the imperial authorities would have had a vested interest in extracting a higher revenue given its military priorities:[164]

> a very low figure, of significantly under 10 per cent in the high empire, presents us with a conundrum: namely to explain how the state could have functioned and survived after AD 300 with what appear to be much lower rates of central revenue.

Theodosius I (379–395)

Religious policy

It is appropriate at this stage to briefly touch on the religious policy of Theodosius I, which had fundamental ramifications for the administration of the empire and its territories, and any discussion of perceived economic patterns should inevitably be tied in with socio-religious factors.

In February 380, Theodosius promulgated the Edict of Thessalonica, ordering all subjects of the Roman empire to profess Nicene Christianity, thus making it the official state religion. However, this did not solve the doctrinal tension pertaining to the precise relationship of the Holy Trinity to each other. The split between the east and west under Valens and Valentinian embraced the almost universal acceptance in the west of the Nicene formula and the almost universal acceptance of the so-called *homoian* formula in the east.[165]

The demise of civic sponsorship under decurions *and other local officials and the rise of patronage under bishops*

The significance of Theodosius' Edict is, however, important from an administrative point of view, since it paved the way for the permanence of ecclesiastical officials. Mark Whittow has in fact demonstrated that the ruling elite officials of the towns and cities across the Roman empire in the pagan period – the *decurions* – belonged to the same aristocratic families as the ecclesiastical officials of the Christian period, the bishop, clergy, and landowners.[166] Early incidences of official Christian patronage are expressed in the basilica of St Peter's in Rome, on mosaics, marble, and liturgical objects;[167] and, also, a church floor mosaic in Aquileia in Venetia et Histria (Regio X), dating to the Constantinian period. This Latin inscription gives the name of its founder, Theodosius, Bishop of Aquileia between 314 and 320, and begins with the *chi-rho* monogram:[168]

> XP Theodosius, happy one with the help of God the Almighty and of the flock entrusted to thee from on high, thou hast made all felicitously and hast gloriously dedicated it.

It appears that the majority of the colleagues of Martin, the third bishop of Tours (circa 371–397), were members of aristocratic families that had exercised local authority in Roman Gaul.[169] Interesting evidence from rural villas in the western empire in the fourth century points to ecclesiastical ownership, with the inclusion of churches, such as at Torre del Palma in Lusitania.[170] In the canton of Geneva, the villa at Vandoeuvres included a small chapel.[171] The fourth-century floor mosaic at Hinton Saint Mary in Britannia expresses a well-known example of Christian symbolism.[172] Also in the British context, the villa at Lullingstone preserves the decoration of liturgical furnishings, indicating that a church once formed part of the complex.[173]

As alluded to above, churches came to increasingly dominate the late Roman civic landscape in the fourth century, and were as much a product of Romanization as villas.[174] However, it is generally accepted that the munificence, or euergetism – that is their obligatory sponsorship of civic building construction and upkeep – became an ever-increasing financial burden in the late Roman period at the hands of the central imperial administration, who also demanded increasing taxation.[175] This appears to be supported by the silence of the epigraphic record for building inscriptions. In short, there are none recorded in the fourth century in the western or eastern empire, and this pattern is repeated in the fifth century. The decline of dated building inscriptions may point to the militarization of elites in the western empire,[176] and also the unsustainable burden imposed by the central state.

The decline of *decurions*, as attested in building inscriptions and also historically, merits further comment. Simon Loseby has shown that inscriptions recording the patronage of *decurions* tail off as early as the later second century in some areas, a relatively short time after classical urbanism had been fully realized.[177] The trend becomes increasingly widespread in the fourth and fifth centuries, as demonstrated by the epigraphic evidence above and in the next chapter. This appears to be linked to a general decline in what Ramsay MacMullen has termed the 'epigraphic habit'.[178] Prior to the late Roman period, the undertaking of curial office had become a source of resentment rather than civic pride. Increasing administrative centralization made civic office-holding increasingly expensive and diminished its dwindling prestige.[179] The *Theodosian Code* in fact contains 192 laws dating between 315 and 436 under the rubric 'concerning the *decurions*'. Many of these were designed either to narrow the many avenues of escape from *curial* office, by promotion to senatorial rank, the fulfilment of civil or military service to the state, or membership of the clergy. In the fifth century *decurions* were described by emperor Majorian as the 'sinews of the state and the vital organs of the cities',[180] but the reality, as borne out by the epigraphic record, is one of a severe decline in this civic office.[181]

It is clear that the prestige and responsibilities of bishops grew as a consequence of the power vacuum of civic *decurions* in the western and eastern empire that occurred in the third century and that they were well established in the fourth. Essentially, they were the highest moral authority within Christian communities. Their duties were manifold, insuring the physical wellbeing of their congregations. Since they were expected to be inspired by the Holy Spirit, the bishop was obliged to set a high example of moral and virtuous conduct. Most importantly, he was the administrator and guardian of the community chest, who managed those funds in order to support his own clergy and distribute offerings for charity.[182]

The economy of the fourth century

Archaeological data

To return to the issue of demographic growth and decline there are sufficient archaeological data to make some suggestions by proxy. In the previous chapter it was suggested that these indicated a peak in the first and second centuries AD and a relative decline in the third century. It is logically important to view the observable pattern in the fourth century before some concluding remarks are made.

The contraction of the GDP per capita curve suggested by Saller around AD 300 seems to be borne out by empirical archaeological evidence, and it is possible to suggest further stagnation or economic shrinkage in certain regions. However, the random nature of this material across the empire should be regarded as suggestive rather than conclusive. The work of Marzano in the hinterland of Rome, outlined in the previous chapter, shows the number of oil- and wine-producing villas to peak in the first century to nearly 300, that number decreasing to under 200 in the second century, falling to just over 100 in the third century and to around 70 in the fourth century.[183] The 'pattern' above is generally echoed in Marzano's analysis of olive oil- and wine-pressing farms and villas in Gaul, the Iberian peninsula, and the Black Sea region, although there are some expected gaps and fluctuations in these data.[184] The surveys of Attema and de Haas pertaining to rural settlements (farms and villas), and their populations, hit a peak in the first century BC, fall slightly in the late first century AD, and drop markedly from the second half of the third century to the end of the fourth, with estimated populations following this trend.[185]

In North Africa, the work of de Vos in the rural landscape of Thugga (Tunisia), pertaining to villa and farm olive oil- and wine-presses and cereal-producing mills, yielded a relatively prosperous second and third century, and increased output before the Vandal invasion of the fifth century. This information being based on the chronology of surface pottery finds.[186] In Egypt, Bowman's study shows an increasing surplus of wheat production in the fourth century compared with that of the second century. This, he suggests, is in large measure due to a substantial drop in taxation levels.[187]

In terms of quantifying Roman trade more generally Wilson has paid rightful attention to the quantitative data presented by Anthony Parker in a series of informative graphs.[188] His graph of shipwrecks in the Mediterranean by century shows a substantial peak in the last two centuries BC and the first two centuries AD; thereafter, the number of wrecks fall by around a half in the third century, and by about a half again in the fourth century. He makes two important observations about this data set. First, the information points to amphora usage, and conceals the fact that from the second century onwards wooden barrels were employed to store commodities and do not survive on shipwrecks. Second, this is supported by Parker's regional breakdown, which shows a greater number of shipwrecks continuing through the late antique period in the eastern Mediterranean, where amphorae remained in use longer than in the central and western Mediterranean.[189]

Regional declines in quantitative data can be misleading for other reasons. For instance, in the Guadalquivir valley of the Catalonian littoral, in north-eastern Spain, there is substantial archaeological evidence for olive oil production from the first century BC through the first and second centuries AD, as recorded by Michel Ponsich between the 1960s and 1990s.[190] Esmonde Cleary has noted that, thereafter, production continued at a much-diminished rate in the Iberian peninsula. This is explicable from the point of view that the region was used to supply the oil *annona* to Rome. From the Severan period onwards, the Baetican olive oil trade was reoriented, with the creation of the so-called 'tax spine' from North Africa to Italy, as central North Africa became a bulk supplier of olive oil and grain to Rome from the 320s.[191]

Epigraphic data

The process of urbanization should also be considered. Wilson has conducted an especially useful analysis in this sense, recognizing the correspondence between this phenomenon and its direct correspondence with per capita incomes. These data are presented in a useful series of graphs. For instance, the chronological distribution by ten-year periods of building inscriptions datable to within twenty years (data provided from the *Epigraphische Datenbank Heidelberg*). These show a gradual increase over the early and mid-first century BC, a sharp rise in the early Augustan period, it was more or less sustained over the first half of the first century AD, a drop under Nero and Vespasian, an erratic climb to the mid-second century, and a dramatic fall in the 160s (probably due to the Antonine Plague). It is observed that from this point there is a peak in the mid-180s, a decline under the Severans, a sharp drop in the third century, and a decline thereafter. There is a mini peak in the 360s, which could correspond with the earthquake and tsunami of 365.[192]

This picture is not entirely correct since, as observed in the previous chapter, building inscriptions show a peak under Septimius Severus, and while there was a marked decline under Caracalla, Severus Alexander was also quite active in the sphere of building. However, it should always be borne in mind that inscriptions are not a mere index of new constructions but also of repairs and embellishments.[193] The Roman Forum is a case in point, although originally constructed in the first century BC, dedicatory building inscriptions are recorded there in the first, third, and fourth centuries. The other factor that should be reiterated is that building inscriptions are often military in character and tend to follow the same pattern as civil inscriptions, for instance, at Intercisa in Pannonia Inferior, representing embellishments and repairs rather than constructions *de novo*.

The broader picture

There are several propositions that may be drawn from these data and also the general political events of the fourth century, although it should be reiterated that these are propositions rather than definitive conclusions.

Archaeological data support the idea that the economy was slowing down in the fourth century in those areas that were directly affected by the incursions and settlements of barbarians in the fourth century (Italy, Gaul, Iberian peninsula). In those areas not affected by these problems (Egypt and North Africa), data indicate a prosperous economy. The former regions appear to corroborate the Malthusian equilibrium, the suggestions of Temin, and others, who have argued for a correspondence of population increase relative to agricultural resources and technological advances (first century BC and first and second centuries AD), resulting in a growth of GDP per capita. Conversely, in this region, the apparent economic slowdown (third and fourth centuries) logically suggests that GDP per capita fell.

It is clearly the case that the size of the Roman army increased considerably from Diocletian through the fourth century under Constantine and his successors. It seems likely that Constantine's monetary reforms solved the spectre of aggressive inflation. However, the economic slowdown suggested above came at precisely the wrong time in the Roman period: when the army was at its zenith and a high economic product was essential to raise the necessary taxation to maintain its cost and also to feed and mobilize it. However, it would seem that the reigns of Diocletian and Constantine benefitted from booty extracted from their successful military campaigns and this is manifest in building constructions.

In the sphere of non-imperial civic patronage under *decurions*, inscriptions disappear in the fourth century, but bishops emerge as powerful elite sponsors in the cities and countryside. This socio-political shift is recorded epigraphically on buildings and artistic media as well as being supported historically.

It is clear that the army – despite its size – was needed mostly on the frontiers; and raising a sufficient field army to deal with any threats within these areas demanded sizeable contingents from the east and west, as proven by the failure at Adrianople, on the one hand, and the later successes in the Gothic War on the other. This raises an important question: 'did the Roman empire decline before it fell?' The unchecked movements of the Goths within Roman territory in the later part of the fourth century certainly did not help, although these were relatively short term, and their overall impact was probably quite minimal; however, they certainly set a dangerous precedent. It is contended that the overall picture from the archaeological data and epigraphic evidence in proxy, and the economic theories presented above, suggest that parts of the empire were in a decline relative to the last century of the Republic and the first two centuries of the Principate. It remains now to examine the extent to which the political turmoil of the fifth century affected the generation of economic product, and the extraction of mineral wealth, and precipitated the collapse of the western Roman empire.

Notes

1 Libanius, *Selected Orations* (XXIV). Vol. I. 1969. Translated by A.F. Norman. LCL 451. For a biography, ix–xlv.
2 *ETB*, IX.22; *LDMP*, XVIII; Sarris, 2002, 19–20.
3 *Panegyrici Latini* (X.II.4). *In Praise of Later Roman Emperors. The Panegyrici Latini*. 1994. Translated by C.E.V. Nixon and B.S. Rodgers. Berkeley, CA. University of California Press. For an exegesis of this work, 1–37.
4 *ETB*, IX.22; *PL*, X.2.12.
5 *PL*, X.2.5.
6 *PL*, VIII.5.1–5.2.
7 *PL*, XI.5.4.
8 *PL*, VIII.3.2–3.3.
9 *PL*, V.III.5.1.
10 Bowman, 2005, 76.
11 *ETB*, IX.25.
12 Bowman, 2005, 82.
13 For a summary of these events, Bowman, 2005, 85.
14 MacMullen, 1980, 451–460.
15 John Lydus, *De Mensibus* (I.27). A.C. Bandy, *Ioannes Lydus. On the Months (De mensibus). The Three Works of Ioannes Lydus, 1*. Lewiston: Edwin Mellen Press, 2013. *LDMP*, VII.
16 Nischer, 1923, 1–11.
17 Luttwak, 1979, 176.
18 Campbell, 2005, 125.
19 Bowman, 2005, 73.
20 Scullard, 1991, 66–68; Campbell, 2005, 125.
21 *Malalas Chronicle*, XII.40. In all, for the purposes of Diocletian's military programme of defence, there is no reason to doubt its veracity, although he does rely on earlier sources for this period.
22 *ZNH*, II.34.

23 Lee, 2007, 413. For the archaeological evidence of Constantine's defensive programme, Johnson, 1983; Whittaker, 1994, 207–208.
24 Bowman, 2005, 76.
25 Bowman, 2005, 76–77.
26 Sutherland, 1955, 116–118.
27 Bowman, 2005, 83–84.
28 Platner and Ashby, 1926, 527–530.
29 For a later description of the baths, Yegül, 1992, 163–169.
30 Odahl, 2004, 58.
31 *ETB*, IX.25.
32 *LDMP*, VII.
33 HD027125 (293–305), HD025803 (297), HD028157 (293–305), HD033577 (284), HD033580 (284), HD057687 (311), HD058327 (293–305), HD066887 (290), HD067598 (305–306).
34 *LDMP*, X–XVI.
35 Bowman, 2005, 85–86.
36 *AVDC*, XXXIX; *LDMP*, XVIII, XIX; *ZNH*, II.40.
37 Sarris, 2002, 19–20.
38 Leclercq, 1907, 371.
39 *LDMP*, VII; *AVDC*, XXXIX.
40 Whittaker, 1976, 137–165.
41 *PL*, V.4, 5.
42 *The Theodosian Code, and Novels, and the Sirmondian Constitutions* (VII.20.3, 4, 8, 11). 1952. Translated by C. Pharr and M.B. Pharr. Princeton: Princeton University Press.
43 *ETB*, X.1; *LDMP*, XX, XXIV.
44 Platner and Ashby, 1926, 36–38.
45 *LDMP*, XLIV.
46 Eusebius, *Life of Constantine* (I.29–31). 1999. Translated by A. Cameron and S. Hall. Oxford: Clarendon Press. For their critique on Eusebius as a source, 46–48.
47 Cameron, 2005, 96.
48 *Inscriptiones christianae Urbis Romae*, ii, 4092–4095; Trout, 2009, 183.
49 Krautheimer and Ćurčić, 1986, 39–92.
50 These issues are complex and beyond the scope of this book. For an outline of the First Council of Nicaea, Papadakis, 1991, 1464–1465; the Donatist schism, Cameron, 2005, 95.
51 Grig and Kelly, 2012, 3–30.
52 *Donation of Constantine, 18*. This passage was in fact exposed as a forgery in the fifteenth century, see G. Bowersock. 2007. *Lorenzo Valla: On the Donation of Constantine*. Cambridge, MA: Harvard University Press. Grig and Kelly, 2012, 3 and the translation by Bowersock, 2007.
53 Mango, 2002, 1; Ward-Perkins, 2012, 53; Optatianus Porfyrius, *Carmina* (IV.6, XIX.34), Vol. I. 1973. Translated by J. Polara. Turin: G.B. Paravia.
54 Themistius, *Orationes* (III.42a, c). 1965–1974. Translated by H. Schenkl, G. Downey, and A.F. Norman. Deutsche Akademie der Wissenschaften zu Berlin, 3 vols. Leipzig: Teubner.
55 Grig and Kelly, 2012, 6–18.
56 Ward-Perkins, 2012, 55; *On Buildings*, I.4.27.
57 For a study of Constantinople according to the *Notitia Urbis Constantinopolitanae*, Matthews, 2012, 81–115.
58 For a comparison between the facilities of Rome and Constantinople, Ward-Perkins, 2012, 53–78. An important article on the water provision of Constantinople is provided by Mango, 1995, 9–18. The extraordinary aqueduct system feeding

the city from Thracia is revealed by Çeçen, 1996. The water supply of the two cities is compared by Merrony, 2009, 30–34. For a definitive study on the water supply to the city, Crow, Bardill, Bayliss, and Bono, 2008.

59 Gros, 2011, 218–220.
60 Krautheimer and Ćurčić, 1986, 39–67.
61 Platner and Ashby, 1926, 525–526; Yegül, 1992, 169–172.
62 Platner and Ashby, 1926, 76–78.
63 HD008799 (324), HD001875 (313–324), HD000647 (308–324), HD004408 (326–331), HD004474 (317–324), HD008799 (324), HD021549 (324–326), HD026977 (324–326), HD057687 (311), HD064415 (314–316).
64 Porfyrius, *Carmina*, VI, 3.26–3.28; Kovács, 2013, 198.
65 Depeyrot, 2006, 237–240.
66 Banaji, 2007, 39–60.
67 *De Rebus Bellicus* (II.1–2). *A Roman Reformer and Inventor: being a new text of the Treatise De Rebus bellicis*. 1952. Translated by E.A. Thompson. Oxford: Clarendon Press.
68 Esmonde Cleary, 2013, 330.
69 Bingham, 2013, 50.
70 For the military reforms under Constantine, Nischer, 1923, 12–49; Campbell, 2005, 127–128.
71 AM*H*, XIV–XIX. For an outline of these events, Sarris, 2002, 26–27. A comprehensive account of Julian's career is presented by Hunt, 1997, 44–77.
72 HD059368 (340–350).
73 Nazianzus, *Orationes*, V.10. *Translation in the Roman Eastern Frontier and the Persian Wars AD 226–363: a documentary history*. 1991. Edited by M.H. Dodgeon and S.N.C. Lieu, 249. Routledge: London. B.E. Daley, 2006, *Gregory of Nazianzus*. London: Routledge.
74 AM*H*, XXV.3.3–3.23.
75 AM*H*, XXV.5, 6, 7.
76 AM*H*, XIX.2.2.
77 AM*H*, XXX.1.9.
78 AM*H*, XIV.8.11.
79 AM*H*, XXXI.6.5.
80 AM*H*, XXXI.16.3.
81 AM*H*, XXVIII.6.4.
82 AM*H*, XXIX.5.25. See Banaji, 2007, 6–7.
83 Gorges, 1979.
84 Biró, 1974, 23–57.
85 Millett, 1990, 186–211.
86 Esmonde Cleary, 2013, 215 (215–236 for the broader discussion).
87 Banaji, 2007, 6–15.
88 Banaji, 2007, 213.
89 Blockley, 1997, 111.
90 Errington, 2006, 1–2, 79–110.
91 Errington 2006, 47–54.
92 AM*H*, XXXI.4.9.
93 HD004683 (364–375), HD008796 (365), HD027281 (364–375), HD000453 (364–367), HD008057 (371), HD009544 (372), HD021132 (365–367), HD038310 (371), HD062461 (371), HD062462 (371), HD067299 (370).
94 Bowman, 2005, 70.
95 Nischer, 1923, 3.
96 Nischer, 1923, 16.
97 Nischer, 1923, 50–51.
98 Lee, 1997, 219–220.

99   Masson, Puri, Edmund, Habib, 1992.
100 Kim, 2013, 26–31.
101 Gibbon, III.26.19–33.
102 For a more detailed description of the Huns, AM*H*, III.31.2.1–12.
103 Heather, 1996, 130–132; 2005, 145–154.
104 AM*H*, XXXI.1.
105 Gibbon, III.26.30.
106 Heather, 2005, 154–158.
107 AM*H*, XXXI.2.7–2.9.
108 Deguignes, Saillant, Durand, 1756–1824.
109 Heather, 2005, 149.
110 Kim, 2013, 26–31.
111 Heather, 1996, 9, 10; 2005, 351–360. For the primary source, *Jordanes Getica*.
     1915. Translated by C.C. Mierow. Princeton, NJ: Princeton University Press.
112 This 'Gothic problem' is clearly outlined by Heather, 1996, 1–7. Also, a rational
     outline of the problem of assigning ethnicity to Germanic and non-Germanic
     tribes, more generally, has been presented by Pohl (2015, 256–257): 'Odoacer
     is variously identified in our sources as Scirian, Turcilingian, Thuringian, Herul,
     or Goth, but not as a Hun . . . This is what makes understanding late ancient
     ethnicity so difficult: ethnic identities were not clearly circumscribed and could
     change. They might matter to some and not to others, and they were distorted
     by outdated conventional names, ethnographic perceptions, and literary fabrica-
     tions. Last but not least, we have relatively little evidence what people called
     themselves.'
113 Esmonde Cleary, 2013, 359–364.
114 Heather, 1996, 130–132; 2005, 145–154.
115 D*RH*, LXXI.16.2.
116 AV*DC*, XXXIII.
117 H*E*, VI.4.6; *HZ*, XII.15.
118 A study of the settlements through the Roman period is provided by De Ste.
     Croix, 1981, 509–518.
119 AM*H*, XXX.6.3.
120 An outline of the settlement of 376 is provided by Heather, 1996, 130–134;
     2005, 145–154.
121 The writings of the chronicler who lived in the fourth and early fifth centuries
     survive in his own fragmentary works, and were also drawn upon by Zosimus
     in the sixth century. See Eunapius, *Fragment* (XLII). 1982. Translated by
     R.C. Blockley. *The Classicising Historians of the Later Roman Empire: Eunapius,
     Olympiodorus, Priscus, and Malchus*, Vol. 2. Liverpool: Cairns.
122 Events leading to the revolt of the Tervingi in 377 and the Battle of Adrianople
     in 378 are detailed by Heather, 1991.
123 AM*H*, XXXI.5.3.
124 Heather, 2005, 176–181.
125 AM*H*, XXXI.12.1–12.3.
126 Heather, 2005, 181.
127 Errington, 2006, 43–75.
128 Ferrill, 1986, 167–169.
129 Goldsworthy, 2003, 208–209.
130 Lee, 1997, 232–237.
131 Elton, 1996, 128–152. Marcellinus, for instance, does not mention any disloyalty
     among barbarian troops serving in the Roman army (I.16.12).
132 *PL*, II.32.4.
133 Ward-Perkins, 2005, 34–35, Figure 3.2; 2012, 62–64, Figure 3.3.

134 Synesius, *On Kingship* (XIV–XV). *The Essays and Hymns of Synesius of Cyrene*. 1933. Translated by A. FitzGerald. London: Oxford University Press. De Ste. Croix, 1981, 514–515.
135 Gibbon, III.30.204.
136 Blockley, 1997, 111–137.
137 Finley, 1973, 22–23.
138 Temin, 2013.
139 Wickham, 2005, 10.
140 Bowman and Wilson, 2009, 2011, 2013.
141 Bowman and Wilson, 2009, 21.
142 A number of studies are presented in Bowman and Wilson, 2011.
143 Malthus, 1798 (published anonymously); 1826.
144 Wilson, 2002, 1–32.
145 Temin, 2013, 220–239.
146 Saller, 2002, 251–269.
147 Temin, 2013, 232–234.
148 Hopkins, 1980, 101–125.
149 Hopkins, 1980, 101.
150 Banaji, 2007, 6–15.
151 Hopkins, 1980, 104.
152 Hopkins, 1980, 102.
153 Bowman, 2017, 1–31.
154 Carrié, 1999, 301–302.
155 Esmonde Cleary, 2013, 293.
156 Lo Cascio, 2007, 623.
157 I follow here elements of Bowman's incisive paper on this topic, Bowman, 2017, 3–4.
158 Frank, 1933, 324; 1940, 6–7, 49–50.
159 Bowman, 2017, 12–13.
160 Rathbone, 2001, 39–50.
161 Duncan-Jones, 1990, 188–193. This summary of points follow the more concise breakdown by Bowman, 2017, 5.
162 Jones, II, 1964, 769.
163 I paraphrase his points here, Bowman, 2017, 5–6.
164 Bowman, 2017, 15.
165 Errington, 2006, 212–259.
166 Whittow, 1990, 3–29.
167 *Inscriptiones christianae Urbis Romae, ii*, 4096, 4097; Trout, 2009, 183.
168 Van der Meer and Mohrmann, 1958, 65.
169 Sulpicius Severus, *Life of Saint Martin* (X). *Sulpicius Severus: the complete works*. 2015. Translated by J.R. Goodrich. New York: The Newman Press.
170 Maloney and Hale, 1996, 275–294.
171 Terrier, 2005, 72–81.
172 Henig, 2003, 238; Neal and Cosh, 2005, 156–160.
173 Meates, 1987.
174 Esmonde Cleary, 2013, 150–197.
175 This issue is addressed by Ward-Perkins, 1997, 371–410.
176 Whittaker, 1994, 243–278.
177 Loseby, 2009, 143–145.
178 MacMullen, 1982, 233–246. See also, Trout, 2009, 170–186.
179 Garnsey, 1974, 229–252; Brown, 1978.
180 Majorian, *Novella Maioriani, De curialibus et de agnatione vel distractione praediorum et de ceteris negotiis* (VII, AD 458); This translates to *Decurions, Their Children and The Sale of Their Landed Estates*, and was apparently given

in Ravenna, in November 458 to Basilius in the name of Leo I. *The Theodosian code and Novels, and the Sirmondian Constitutions.* 2001. Translated by C. Pharr, 557-560. Union, NJ: Lawbook Exchange. The status of *decurions* in the view of the emperor is perhaps wishful thinking given the epigraphical testimony for their decline.
181 Loseby, 2009, 143–145.
182 Testa, 2009, 527.
183 Marzano, 2013a, 85–106.
184 Marzano, 2013b, 107–141.
185 Attema and de Haas, 2011, 97–140.
186 De Vos, 2013, 143–218.
187 Bowman, 2013, 219–253.
188 Parker, 1992, Figures 12 and 13.
189 Wilson, 2009, 219–229.
190 Ponsich, 1974–1991.
191 Esmonde Cleary, 2013, 292–293, 399.
192 Wilson, 2011, 163, Figure 7.1.
193 Beltrán Lloris, 2015, 91–94.

5 The plight of Rome

> In the hour of savage licence, when every passion was inflamed and every restraint was removed, the precepts of the Gospel seldom influenced the behaviour of the Gothic Christians. The writers best disposed to exaggerate their clemency have freely confessed that a cruel slaughter was made of the Romans, and that the streets of the city were filled with dead bodies, which remained without burial during the general consternation. The despair of the citizens was sometimes converted into fury; and whenever the barbarians were provoked by opposition, they extended the promiscuous massacre to the feeble, the innocent, and the helpless.
>
> *History of the Decline and Fall of the Roman Empire*
> Edward Gibbon, 1781

As outlined in the previous chapter, the prelude to the fourth century witnessed an extraordinary administrative, fiscal, military, and political overhaul of the imperial infrastructure under Diocletian, which successfully re-established Roman supremacy in the face of adversity; and this situation was consolidated in the reign of Constantine, with a substantial public building programme and an inrush of gold currency, converted from looted pagan treasures. Later, under Theodosius' successors, Honorius and Arcadius, the situation began to deteriorate rapidly, with increasingly centralized and potent Germanic and non-Germanic tribes breaching the Danube and Rhine on an escalating scale, the impending menace of the Huns; and a fresh round of internecine warfare, at times surpassing the intensity of the third century, culminated in the sack of Rome.[1] These events, and those that surpassed them in the course of the fifth century, are carefully scrutinized. Special detail is paid to the relationship between agricultural output and military capability in this period, as is the availability of gold, the singular most crucial mineral resource required to pay the army.

The political situation in the early fifth century

Given the political turbulence of the era, Rome was fortunate that the situation on the eastern frontier was relatively stable. From 379 to 399 the Sasanian monarchs were dealing with internal political problems, and the threat of Hunnic aggression; and there was more of the same for much of the fifth century, with the Hephalites, a nomadic tribe from central Asia, also known as the White Huns.[2] The fifth century, notwithstanding some minor periods of hostility between the Romans and Sasanians, was one of détente.[3]

In 395 Theodosius I appointed his sons Honorius (aged 10) and Arcadius (aged 18) emperors of the west and east respectively, based in Milan and Constantinople.[4] Stilicho, of Vandal descent, the senior general of the west, was entrusted as his advisor, and effectively became the power behind the throne, but after remarkable military successes and some intrigue, Honorius had him put to death.[5]

The second great migration

Things reached a critical head in the early part of the fifth century, when Hunnic pressure forced the second great wave of migrations, resulting in the crossing of the Rhine by the Alans, Vandals, and Sueves (and probably the Burgundians) on 31 December 406. They moved through Gaul and systematically ravaged it in 406–409, and in the latter year doing more of the same in the Iberian peninsula (discussed below). The impact of the Gallic invasion, perhaps somewhat exaggerated, was recorded in a contemporary poem by Orientius, plausibly identified as the bishop of Auch:[6]

> Some lay as food for dogs; for many, a burning roof. Both took their soul, and cremated their corpse. Through villages and villas, through countryside and market-place, through all regions, on all roads, in this place and that, there was Death, Misery, Destruction, Burning, and Mourning. The whole of Gaul smoked on a single funeral pyre.

The Gothic sack of Rome in 410

These events paved the way for the unthinkable, and the episode that followed was foretold in the preceding century by the ecclesiastical chronicler Lactantius:[7]

> . . . the slide into ruin will come soon, except that no part of it seems fit to fear as long as Rome is intact. But when the chief city of the world does fall . . . then the end will be there without doubt for deeds of men and for the whole world. Rome is the city which has kept everything going so far, and we must pray to God in heaven with due adoration – if, that is, his statutes and decisions can be deferred – that the awful tyrant does not come sooner than we think, that loathsome tyrant with his great task to achieve and the famous light to put out, at whose death the world itself will collapse.

On 24 August 410, a large force of Goths, led by Alaric, sacked Rome and captured Galla Placidia, the future empress (daughter of Theodosius I); Alaric later married her. The essence of this event is graphically portrayed on a late nineteenth-century oil on canvas by the French painter Joseph Noël-Sylvestre (Figure 5.1). This sent shockwaves around the Roman world: not since the sack of Rome in 387 by the Gallic chieftain Brennus had the

Figure 5.1 The sack of Rome by the Barbarians in 410, Joseph Noël-Sylvestre (1890). Oil on canvas.

Courtesy of Musée Paul-Valéry, Sète, France.

city fallen to a foreign enemy. In 402, Rome had been replaced by Ravenna as the capital of the western empire, but symbolically it was still widely regarded as 'the Eternal City'. The impact on the psyche of writers at the time is expressed by St Jerome, who lived in Bethlehem:[8]

> . . . a dreadful rumour reached us from the West. We heard that Rome was besieged, that the citizens were buying their safety with gold, and that when they had been thus despoiled they were again beleaguered, so as to lose not only their substance but their lives. The speaker's voice failed and sobs interrupted his utterance. The City which had taken the whole world was itself taken.

Augustine was more philosophical, citing a number of calamities that had occurred before the birth of Christ, such as the first sack of Rome – God was not to blame: 'Where were they when the Gauls took, sacked, burned Rome and filled it with slaughter?'[9]

The fragmentation of imperial power

How was this allowed to happen? Ironically, perhaps, the simplest explanation harks back to those words famously attributed to Julius Caesar some 450 years earlier: '*Divide ut Regnes*' – 'Divide and Conquer'.[10] In Chapter 3, the disintegration of the Roman empire into three parts and its subsequent reintegration was outlined. It was argued that each faction was able to sustain itself with sufficient agricultural product and mineral wealth to maintain an army to keep its enemies in check.

This was largely the case in the reign of Arcadius and his successors in the east. However, the situation in the west during the reign of Honorius was of a different magnitude. It is significant that in this critical period there were no fewer than nine usurpers: in Britannia, Marcus (406–407), Gratian (407), and Constantine III (407–409), who also established himself in Gaul, as did his son, Constans II (409–411); in northern Gaul, Jovinus and his co-emperor Sebastianus (412–413), both with Burgundian support (411–413); with Visigothic support in the Iberian peninsula, Maximus (409–411) and Priscus Attalus (409, 414–415); and in North Africa, Heraclianus (412–413).

Coins, once more, are informative, and may be regarded as the visual 'end product' of political and economic control in terms of transmitting the resources of agricultural product – cereal, olive oil, wine, and livestock – into taxation and a surplus. The 'reigns' of Marcus and Gratian were fleeting, and no coins are currently associated with them. However, the other usurpers referred to all issued their own coinage. In 411 there were five pretenders to the purple, Honorius, the one legitimate emperor in the west, and Theodosius II in the east (Arcadius died in 408). A slightly later source recorded: 'This emperor, while he never had any success against external enemies, had great good fortune in destroying usurpers'.[11] This is a bit of a paradox, since this pattern of usurpation, and hence factionalization, was to prove as grave a threat to the existence of the western empire as that posed by the barbarian invaders.

The erosion of the Roman empire in the early fifth century differs considerably with that of the third. In the former instance, it was not formally split into west and east, its temporary 'tripartite' structure represented three massive geo-political blocks, each dealing with their own external threats successfully. In the latter case, the eastern empire was financially independent from the west to a considerable degree, and remained largely unaffected by the troubles of the west. As for the former, its economic, and thus military, resources were in the worst point of crisis split 'six-fold', and to compound matters there were innumerable barbarians rampaging through Gaul, the Balkans, Iberia, and Italy.

The effect on the countryside in those areas afflicted would have severely impeded agricultural production, the levying of taxes, and the concomitant number of soldiers necessary to form an effective fighting force. Italy is a case in point. In 413, according to the *Theodosian Code*, Honorius instructed the praetorian prefect of Italy to reduce the taxes of Tuscany, Campania, Picenum, Samnium, Apulia, Calabria, Bruttium, and Lucania by four-fifths. In response to the impending invasion of Radagaisus, new recruits were offered ten *solidi*, but the payment of seven was deferred. The situation was so desperate that slaves were enlisted with the offer of two *solidi*.[12] In a second law of 418, Campania's taxes were reduced to one-ninth of its previous levels and the other provinces to one-seventh.[13]

The availability and distribution of gold

It is also important to consider that soldiers had been paid in gold *solidi* since its introduction by Constantine. What was the availability of this precious mineral in the period?

One aspect of Roman archaeology and history considerably overlooked is the extent of the Roman occupation and 'Romanization' of Wales, which was considerable. The conquest of the region was no doubt incentivized by the presence of gold. In fact, the gold mines at Dolaucothi are the only known Roman gold mines in Britain. The *Geography* of Strabo, published in the early first century AD, mentions gold as an exported commodity from Britain.[14] Excavation and survey work in the 1960s, and from 1987 to 1999, revealed a series of large opencast pits, trenches, and underground galleries, and several leats (aqueducts) supplying water to a system of tanks, reservoirs, and processing mills.[15] Evidence from the associated fort and settlement indicate occupation from the last quarter of the first century AD to the first quarter of the second. However, pottery recovered from the water tank of the Melin-y-Milwyr cascade attests to its use through the remainder of the Roman period.[16]

Numismatic evidence there extends to the reign of Gratian.[17] This suggests that the mines were a crucial source of gold at a time when the importance of the gold mines in northern Spain had diminished, those in Transylvania were not available, and production in Dalmatia had ceased in the third century, with a brief flurry of activity again in the fourth. In Egypt, the Eastern Desert mines were the preserve of the eastern empire, as were other sources attested in the *Theodosian Code*, in Illyricum, Pontus, Thracia, and Asia.[18] The usurpation of Constantine III would have secured this resource, and the abandonment of Britain in 410 of course meant that another vital gold supply was lost.[19]

Other sources of gold are attested archaeologically, such as at Limousin in southern Gaul in the late fourth and early fifth centuries, and they remained in use during the Merovingian period.[20] The key remaining gold ores were in Upper Moesia.[21] It was, however, unfortunate that this region lay on the path of the Goths en route to Italy, and it can be surmised that production there was seriously disrupted in the period. So large-scale exploitation of gold diminished at precisely the time Rome needed it to mint coins to pay the army. This is borne out by textual evidence.

Pliny the Elder is perhaps our most informative source on the extraction of gold in the western empire, especially since he served as *procurator* in Hispania Tarraconensis, and his description of gold mining techniques was probably based on personal observations in 72–74 at Las Médulas:[22]

> Gold dug up from shafts is called 'channelled' or 'trenched' gold . . . These channels of veins wander to and fro along the sides of the shafts, which gives the gold its name; and the earth is held up by wooden props. The substance dug out is crushed, washed, and fired and ground to a soft powder.

Pliny also gives an account of the sheer quantity of gold mined in the region:[23]

> According to some accounts Asturia and Callaecia and Lusitania produce in this way 20,000 lbs weight of gold a year, Asturia supplying the largest amount. Nor has there been in any other part of the world such a continuous production of gold for so many centuries.

It is not the intention here to dwell on the processes of gold mining, its subsequent distribution being more important for its supply to pay the army. Naturally, gold and silver mines were under state control and bullion was sent directly to the principal treasuries from where it was transferred to the mints for conversion into new coinage and transferred to pay the army in the frontier regions where the bulk of the army was billeted.[24] Mines were worked by private contractors under imperial authority, who used gangs of slaves toiling under harsh conditions. Some gold ingots are preserved but these were in fact currency bars marked with assayers' stamps to ensure they were composed of high-quality coins rather than forgeries. These were produced at Hermopolis, Egypt (late third century), Sirmium, Upper Moesia, and at Krazsna, Dacia (later fourth century). It was more practical to test a smaller number of large bars than vast quantities of coin. Subsequently, they were melted down again and reminted.[25] For pragmatic reasons, treasuries and mints tended to be in close proximity, and in the western empire in the early fifth century, they were still present in Rome, Mediolanum, Arelate, Lugdunum, Treviri, Aquileia, Siscia, and Salona.[26]

Pliny's figure for gold production is interesting, and it is fruitful to reflect on this briefly. His calculation of 20,000 pounds per annum equates to around 6,578 kilogrammes. When it is considered that Constantine felt it was imperative to plunder 963 kilogrammes of gold from pagan sanctuaries between 314 and 336, this could suggest that the extraction of gold had dropped significantly in the period as mineral availability began to dwindle and progressively more mines were no longer available to exploit.

The impact of conflict on the Roman army in the early fifth century

It should be considered that the Roman army would have suffered substantial losses in this period of dire conflict, with extraordinary levels of violence on all fronts. The *Notitia Dignitatum* is informative in this regard, which was updated until the death of Theodosius I in 395, in the east; in the west, this provides a record until 408, and in a partial manner down to the early 420s.[27] On the basis of his analysis of this important source, Peter Heather has calculated that nearly half of the western regiments (47.5 per cent) had been destroyed in the first two decades of the fifth century, losing around 30,000 troops.[28] In this sense we should envisage the terrible bloodshed as a consequence of highly trained *auxilia* and legionaries going head to head in combat. However, this should be tempered with the suggestion that the drastic reduction in the size of the militia could also represent a parlous imperial treasury.

The distribution of military salaries

It follows that the distribution of salaries to the troops would have been problematic in this turbulent period. As mentioned briefly in Chapter 3, Peter Herz has addressed this fundamental issue in different regions of the Roman empire, and this is of course an important factor.[29] He draws attention to the fact that, logically, troops were paid in the area where they were stationed and this would have been a relatively straightforward process in most cases, the wealth of individual regions financing the army with available tax revenue, in Egypt, North Africa, the Iberian peninsula, and the eastern borders (Syria, Cappadocia, Arabia, Judaea-Palaestina). He suggests that the financing of troops based on the Rhine and Danube was more of an issue, since the economic potential of this region was not so developed, and there were eight legions stationed there in the early imperial period.

At face value this would seem to be a valid claim, but if the epigraphic record for dated building inscriptions is considered along the Rhine–Danube frontier this idea does not hold water, since there are numerous buildings attested in the first three centuries, both civil and military, which broadly speaking may be taken as an index of economic conditions. Two provinces serve to illustrate this point. In the Rhine province of Germania Superior (western empire), there are 34 imperial inscriptions from the accession of Augustus in 27 BC to the end of the fourth century AD; while in the Danube province of Dacia (eastern empire) there are 46 from the beginning of the princeps' reign until the withdrawal from the province under Aurelian.

There is substantial archaeological evidence for vast quantities of coinage recovered from military camps along the Rhine.[30] On this frontier Herz logically assumes that soldiers were paid in coin levied from taxes from most if not the entire region of Gaul, entrusted to the *procurator Galliarum*, who controlled the revenue of the *fiscus Gallicus* in Lyon, where coinage could be minted for the army's wages. A similar system of administration was probably in place in the Danube region. The factionalization of the army in the early fifth century would have thrown this system into disarray, with salaries paid on a geographically circumscribed basis. For instance, at the peak of the crisis in the first decade and a half of this era, each usurper was dependent on the agricultural product that could be extracted by taxation or requisition from specific territories, with precious metal extraction diminished and unavailable in some regions.

Military pay in the late Roman period

Peter Kehne has established some relevant facts.[31] Perhaps the most important of these is the creation of the *annona militaris*. The key point suggested here is that soldiers' annual pay in money (*stipendium*), previously given to them by the *aerarium* or the provincial *fiscus*, reverted largely, but not completely, to the Republican system of official tax-in-kind. Included in the *annona* were a soldier's food allotment, fodder allowances, military clothing, and several other items of military equipment. One of the implications of this, of course, is that, on the one hand, the demand for coinage needed to pay the army dropped significantly in the fourth and fifth centuries; on the other, the demand for grain became even more important. If this was indeed the case then it challenges one of the fundamental arguments of this book – that the western empire fell because the high military expenditure of around 60 to 70 per cent of the state budget could not be maintained. This naturally demands further discussion.

It is widely thought that late Roman soldiers were entirely reliant on the *donativa*, cash bonuses that were paid by emperors periodically in gold *solidi.* This amounted to five *solidi* every five years of a reign (one *solidus* per annum). The accession of a new emperor was also commemorated by the payment of five *solidi* and a pound of silver to each soldier. Collectively, soldiers received on average around two *solidi* each year.[32] By comparison with the pay of soldiers in the second century this was considerably less, the latter receiving around eight *solidi* per annum. However, it should be borne in mind that the scale of pay would have been greater as one ascended the pyramid of seniority. Infantry soldiers (*pedes*) were at the base of this pay scale, it then rose progressively with *limitanei* (frontier troops), *comitatenses*, *palatini*, and the elite *scholae*. Unfortunately, the pay differentials are largely unknown, except that the quartermaster (*actuarius*) of a *comitatus* regiment was paid 50 per cent more than his counterpart in a *pseudocomitatenses* regiment.[33]

It is difficult to understand how it may be inferred that soldiers were paid less in the late Roman period when we lack comprehensive knowledge of pay scales across the hierarchical spectrum. Bearing this factor in mind it is surely not appropriate to claim that the military budget would have been less in the late Roman period. To return to the figures suggested by MacMullen and Duncan-Jones, they defined expenditure on the army at around 1 billion *sesterces* per annum by the early third century out of a total of about 1.5 billion total in state revenue.[34] Also taking into account Potter's estimates, as in Chapters 1 and 3, the overall expenditure is still rather high at around 60 to 70 per cent.[35]

This suggestion is supported by Warren Treadgold, Brent Shaw, and others, who maintain that military expenditures for the late Roman and Byzantine states remained at a similarly high level of about three-quarters of the state budget.[36] Their calculations are confirmed by an anonymous author of the manual *Peri strategias* (*On Strategy*) in the sixth century, in which it is stated clearly that the wages of soldiers consumed a large proportion of the annual state revenue.[37]

This tends to gravitate against the dependence of soldiers on grain provided from the *annona militaris* or requisitions more generally in the late Roman period. The old saying that an army marches on its stomach, attributed to Napoleon Bonaparte, implies that an army can only operate effectively if it is well supplied with food.[38] While this was certainly the case, what possible incentive to recruitment would a food allowance over and above a financial reward tempt a citizen to join up? This is an especially relevant question when it is considered that the bulk of the Roman population lived in the countryside where grain was readily available. However, this does not countervail the reality that the army required huge requisitions of grain to feed it. The problem, touched on above, was more a question of supply: with intense civil wars, barbarian incursions, and the 'insulation' of the eastern from the western empire, the base of availability of grain must have been massively reduced. Of course this problem became especially serious when North Africa was annexed by the Vandals.

Agricultural productivity and the beehive metaphor

At this stage it is relevant to return to the administrative structure outlined by Jones in the previous chapter and the economic model presented by Hopkins, notwithstanding of course the refinements that have been adapted to this model.[39] To reiterate, Jones defined the Roman empire, with few exceptions, as an agglomeration of cities and territories, modelled on the principle of the Greek city-state: *civitates* in the west and *poleis* in the east. For the sake of the arguments pertaining to the collapse of the western empire, it is appropriate to concentrate on this part of the imperial domain, although the same processes were broadly similar in the east. Each city or town provided the market for its territory and generated economic product. Taxes were direct, paid in both cash and kind on privately owned land; direct capitation taxes and poll tax; rents on public land (direct revenue); customs duties, taxes on inheritances, sales, manumissions (indirect taxes); military requisitions in cash and in kind; and revenue in kind in the form of public service.[40]

It logically follows that the welfare of the western empire depended on the collective healthy functioning of each *civitas* to contribute to the tax obligation of the state in order to maintain an effective fighting force. As emphasized persistently, the cost of the army accounted for around 60 to 70 per cent of the state's overall budget. Put another way, the failure to maintain this threshold meant that levels of military personnel could not be maintained at requisite levels – theoretically, and surely in practice, the lower the revenue the smaller the army.

Bryan Ward-Perkins has made an especially relevant comment in this regard:[41]

> In my opinion, the key element in Rome's success or failure was the economic wellbeing of its tax-payers. This was because the empire relied for its security on a professional army, which in turn relied upon adequate funding ... The number of troops under arms, and the levels of military training and equipment that could be lavished on them, were all determined by the amount of cash that was available. Military capability relied on immediate access to taxable wealth.

Also, however, a substantial proportion of agricultural produce could be requisitioned for this purpose and precious minerals – gold and silver – could be used, as long as they were available, to pay the troops, irrespective of the tax base.

It is not possible to calculate the contribution of each *civitas* towards the state treasury due to a lack of textual information and an incomplete archaeological record, and it is of course obvious that different geographical regions would have been more productive than others, so there would have been a great variability in yields of cereals, olive oil, and wine, the latter two products thriving in the Mediterranean, below the 'olive and wine lines' in southern Gaul. One way of looking at this issue is to use what I often think of as the beehive metaphor, considering the *civitates* as individual cells of a great honeycomb that contributed in a collective manner to the benefit of the '60–70 per cent tipping point', thus preserving the wellbeing of the queen bee and the hive, in this case the emperor and the western empire.

The territorial loss of *civitates* and the economic ramifications of this are examined in more detail below. With the splintering of imperial authority caused by the usurpations of the early fifth century, it would have been impossible to sustain a collective 60–70 per cent on military spending because of the administrative, economic, political, and territorial fragmentation of the western empire; this all being precipitated by the most severe Germanic and non-Germanic, incursions in Roman history. Also, there was a good deal of social unrest caused by a rebellious group known as the *Bacaudae*. This situation resulted in a fresh bout of imperial settlements, and the gradual extinction of the individual cells that comprised the 'imperial hive'.

Barbarian settlements in Gaul

Further settlements should be considered in the first half of the fifth century, but these should be tempered with the recognition that it is difficult to fit historical Roman sources with the archaeological evidence, since it has been plausibly argued that perceived ethnicity and ethnic reality do not equate to the same thing.[42] Within the great mix of Germanic and non-Germanic peoples migrating into the western provinces of the Roman empire, the Alans and Burgundians merit attention, as do the Franks, since all three tribes were initially accommodated and demanded more land at the expense of the Roman state. While this was not of the magnitude of the Goths in southern Gaul and the Vandals in North Africa, their encroachments nonetheless impacted on the imperial tax-yield at precisely the wrong time for their hosts. It is also instructive to examine briefly the impact of the *Bacaudae* on imperial fortunes.

The Goths

It is possible to glean from Hydatius, Bishop of Aquae Flaviae in Gallaecia (the Iberian peninsula), and the theologian, Prosper of Aquitaine (Gaul), that a treaty was agreed between Constantius and Theoderic I (418–419), establishing them in the Garonne valley between Toulouse and Bordeaux.[43]

On the face of it these agreements would appear to support the notion by the Canadian historian Walter Goffart that the Visigoths were peacefully accommodated.[44] However, Ward-Perkins has made the important point that the territory granted to them was small by comparison to what they subsequently took by force, or the threat of force, from the Roman government and provincials.[45] Primary texts make it clear that Gothic aggression and expansion intensified in southern Gaul in 425 and 430,[46] and between 436 and 439, and an agreement in the latter year restored peace.[47] In the Iberian peninsula an additional treaty was brokered with the Sueves between 446 and 448.[48]

It seems that the Gothic settlement in southern Gaul was granted on the basis of '*hospitalitas*', an imperial euphemism which has largely driven the debate as to whether or not they were peacefully accommodated.[49] Whether this was peaceful or violent, it appears that they may have received as much as two-thirds of the land and a significant proportion of tax revenue would logically have been lost to the Roman state.[50] This situation would have been echoed in the Iberian peninsula, with the Vandals, Alans, and Sueves entrenched there.

Archaeological data

As mentioned in the previous chapter, archaeological evidence for the Goths in southern Gaul is elusive and masked by distinctively Roman material culture.[51] Cemeteries in eastern Europe of the later fifth century indicate that Gothic burial rites were evolving towards inhumation with few or no grave goods. A substantial number of mosaics and sarcophagi have been discovered in fifth-century Aquitaine, along with a vast number of villas, all this indicative of a Christianized Gothic elite occupying the region.[52]

Numismatic evidence

Coins once more are instructive of this settlement. In what may be regarded as 'the kingdom of Toulouse', the earliest issues struck are of the so-called pseudo-imperial type, comprising *solidi* and *tremisses*. Tolosa was probably the central mint, but there were most likely other centres of production, such as Narbo, where a mint existed, albeit for a short time in 414. An illustration exists of a lost *solidus* of Athaulf's protégé Priscus Attalus. The earliest *solidi* struck between the 420s and 440s are imitations of Ravennate coins of Honorius, succeeded in the 450s by a new type, imitating coins of Ravenna, with a standing figure of the emperor with his right foot on the head of a human-headed serpent on the reverse. These were first struck in the name of Valentinian III. *Tremisses* attributed to the Visigoths are of three types: the earliest in the name of Honorius, with a Victory advancing right on the reverse, in the same style and lettering as *solidi*; the second group usually bear the name of Valentinian III, with a cross-in-wreath on the reverse; finally, a large group bear the names of Valentinian III, Severus III, and Zeno, with a standing Victory holding a long, jewelled cross on the reverse. The type was used on imperial *solidi* in Constantinople from 420 onwards.[53]

The Alans

Roman texts mention the settlement of the Alans in 440 by Aetius in the middle Rhône valley in the area of Valentia, and in 442 in the Loire valley in the area of Cenabum. It appears that they were under considerable pressure from the growing powerbase of the Huns in this period, who had driven them west. Imperial policy here was a direct act of appeasement, according to the source of the Alans' settlement, the *Gallic Chronicle* of 452: 'The Alans, to whom lands in northern Gaul had been assigned by the patrician Aetius to be divided with the inhabitants, subdued by force of arms those who resisted, and, ejecting the owners, forcibly took possession of the land'.[54]

Archaeological data

Archaeological finds at Calvados in Armorica provide some evidence for their presence in northern Gaul. At Airan, objects from a female burial have Alannic parallels in the Ukraine; and at a large cemetery at Saint-Martin-de-Fontenay, a small number of female skulls had cranial deformation, a practice associated with the Alans (and Huns), known sporadically across eastern and central Europe from the Pontico-Danubian region westwards.[55]

The Burgundians

The Burgundians were an east Germanic tribe, thought to have migrated from Scandinavia, settling in the Vistula basin in the third century AD. They may have crossed the Rhine in 406 with the Alans, Vandals, and Sueves.[56] They were apparently granted land, and the status of *foederati*. In a familiar scenario, the barbarians began to expand their territory, and after the accession of Gunderic, the *Gallic Chronicle* indicates that Aetius resettled the Burgundian remnant in the Sapaudia as *foederati* after 443, where they established a petty state (west of Lake Geneva).[57]

The Franks

Archaeological and textual evidence indicate that the Franks were a confederation of Germanic tribes that settled between the lower and middle Rhine and the Weser rivers, the dominant groupings being the eastern Ripuarians and the western Salians, who began to amalgamate politically in the first and second centuries AD.[58] They are first mentioned in the *Panegyrici Latini* in the late third century.[59] In the late third and early fourth centuries they were serving as Roman *foederati* according to the *Notitia Dignitatum*. In this period the Ripuarians were more concentrated in the area of Colonia Claudia Agrippinensis on the middle Rhine; the Salians occupied the area of northern Gaul known as Toxandria, demarcated by the Rhine to the north, the North Sea in the west, and the Maas to the east.[60]

Archaeological data

Archaeological finds of prestige goods (belt buckles and vessels) in 'row-grave' cemeteries at Vermand (Picardy), Eprave, Samson, and Haillot in the Namur possibly attest to Frankish territorial gains in south-central Belgium.[61] However, we should be cautious in interpreting material cultural items as specifically Frankish in the region based on historical texts, since it has been demonstrated archaeologically that other cultural groupings, notably the Alamanni, shared similar material. Nonetheless, certain finds and burial practices are instructive in this period. One of the most celebrated Frankish sites is at Gellep on the middle Rhine. There, a number of weapon-graves and women's graves appear around 425, the richest of these (grave 43), dating to around 450.[62] It is generally recognized that material from the reign of Childeric onwards in the later fifth century matured into what may be regarded as Frankish.[63]

Bacaudae *rebels in Gaul and the Iberian peninsula*

The problems that beset the western empire in this period were not confined to barbarian incursions and settlements and imperial internecine warfare. An indigenous provincial faction, known as the *Bacaudae*, have aroused considerable debate.[64] They are first mentioned in the third century, but emerge as a disruptive force in 410, and remained problematic until the 440s.

According to the *Chronicle of Hydatius* in 453, in around 435 an individual named Tibatto led a Bagaudic rebellion in Armorica, north of the Loire, and this was crushed two years later. In Spain, Hydatius recorded that the military commander Asterius killed a large number of *Bacaudae* rebels from Tarraconensis in 441, and are mentioned in Aracelli in 443.[65] In 449 Basilius is said to have gathered a group of *Bacaudae* and sided with the Suevic king Rechiarius, killing a contingent of imperial troops as well as Bishop Leo at Tyriasso.[66] *Bacaudae* are described in the *Chronica Gallica* as 'servile'.[67] Salvianus of Marseilles, writing in the 440s, views them as those oppressed by social circumstances, government, and the law (under Valentinian III);[68] a late Roman comedy describes them as a lawless, egalitarian society north of the Loire. While it is tempting from these sources to regard this group as an early Communist society created by the circumstances of a weakened imperial state, Ian Wood has highlighted the bias of these accounts and places them in the context of a broad spectrum of reactions to the failure of Roman rule. Salvianus is a case in point:[69]

> The concerns of the *De Gubernatione Dei* are entirely different: Salvian's explanation for the disasters of his own time, like that of other Gallic and Italian moralists of the period, involved a radical critique of the social, economic and moral structures of the fifth-century empire, and for Salvian the *bagaudae* afforded one opportunity to expose Gallic corruption.

The barbarian occupation of the Iberian peninsula

Athaulf's invasion of the Iberian peninsula in 415 impacted on the Siling Vandals and Alans and they formed an alliance with the Hasding Vandals.

By 422 they held sway over the southern peninsula.[70] The varying reliability of Roman historical texts in this period forces a reliance on archaeology to attempt to paint a fuller picture. However, in the case of the Vandals, their presence in Spain was quite short-lived, and there is a general agreement that their transience is the plausible explanation for the lack of material evidence associated with them.

Archaeological data

We are on firmer archaeological ground with their Iron Age origin, especially pottery, but also place-names, which indicate that the Hasdings were from Norway, central Sweden, and the Danish region of North Jutland; the Silings are thought to have come from the island of Zealand in Denmark. Subsequent material evidence places their migration to Poland and eastern Germany in the second century BC, where they are associated with the Przeworsk culture.[71]

The archaeological picture is especially confusing with the Goths in this period, since many cemeteries contain burials of a Hispano-Roman tradition, such as Duratón and El Carpio de Tajo. Also, material culture that may be associated with the Visigoths, such as the *Adlerfibeln* (eagle fibula), comes from the Pontico-Danubian region to the east rather than to the north of the Pyrenees as one would logically expect, later transmitted in fact from Italy via the Ostrogoths. The whole of the Iberian peninsula was absorbed into the Visigothic kingdom in the century that followed. The complicated archaeological understanding in the broader region reflects the incursion of several Germanic groupings, with a variety of traditions, in a relatively short period of time, overlying a mixture of indigenous practices. The difficulty of squaring this complex material amalgam with texts written from a Roman perspective is perhaps to be expected.[72]

The Sueves

Archaeological evidence for the Sueves, who were confined to Gallaecia (north-western Iberia) and centred round Bracara, is also difficult to establish. However, their dominance was relatively brief, and more recognizably Visigothic material is present here and elsewhere in the later part of the fifth century, reflecting their increasing political dominance.

Numismatic evidence

Suevic kings were, though, minting their own coinage in the fifth century (Figure 5.2). Rechiar (438–455) was in fact the first Germanic king to mint coinage bearing his own name. Coins consist mainly of rather crude gold pseudo-imperial *tremisses* and *solidi*. *Solidi* imitate those of Honorius of the mint of Milan, typically with a bust of the emperor on the obverse, and the

Figure 5.2 Suevic pseudo-imperial gold *solidus* in the name of Honorius, minted in northern Spain. On the obverse, a bust of the emperor; reverse with the emperor standing, holding a long cross and Victoria on a globe, foot on captive. Mid-fifth century.

Courtesy of London Coin Galleries.

reverse depicts the emperor standing with a cross on a shaft in his right hand and a *globus cruciger* (orb and cross) in his left hand. *Tremisses* were copied from those of Valentinian III, often with a bust of the emperor on the obverse, and a cross within a wreath on the reverse, typically inscribed with the name of the king. The letters BR and C are probably abbreviations of mints in Bracara and Conimbriga. The production of coinage continued for over a century.[73]

The Vandal invasion and settlements in Africa

Victor of Vita, Bishop of Byzacena, is a principal source for the unfolding events in North Africa. In 428, Gaiseric, an Arian Christian, succeeded his half-brother Gunderic as Vandal king. In the following year they crossed the Strait of Gibraltar into Mauretania with an estimated body of 80,000 people and 15,000–20,000 troops.[74] Possidius, Bishop of Calama in Numidia and a friend of Augustine, Bishop of Hippo Regius, is another main source, and narrates that the progress of the Vandals through North Africa was violent and bloody. Bonifatius was defeated by the forces of Gaiseric (in 430 and 435): on the first occasion this led directly to the siege of Hippo Regius.[75] This culminated in a peace treaty between Aspar and Gaiseric in the city. According to the terms of the treaty, the Vandals were ceded parts of Mauretania and Numidia, but the Romans were able to retain most of Numidia and the rich provinces of Proconsularis and Byzacena.[76]

The final stage of the Vandal conquest came in 439 with the occupation of Carthage and in 442 a second treaty was agreed, the details of which are outlined by Procopius.[77] According to its particulars the Vandals took the rich grain-producing lands of Africa Proconsularis and eastern Numidia and were granted jurisdiction over the Roman province of Byzacena – incorporating the rich cereal-yielding territories encompassed by the province – and also the western part of Tripolitania. A legal document confirms that the Romans continued to administer Mauretania Sitifensis and Caesarensis.[78]

On the face of it, this agreement may have been partly beneficial to the Roman cause. Andy Merrills and Richard Miles make the important point that the form of this agreement was new. Previously, the imperial government had granted land to barbarian groups for settlement, but had retained nominal sovereignty in the name of the empire. However, in this case, they were not simply federates of the empire, but it seems that they were given lands of their own, and a proportion of the revenue generated was paid to Rome rather than the reverse, as was usually the case.[79]

However, as mentioned in the previous chapter, from the late second century onwards, under Septimius Severus, the region had been transformed into a formal supplier of cereal and olive oil, levied as taxes to feed Rome and its army, and this process was firmly embedded in the fifth century. Whatever money trickled into the imperial coffers from the newly acquired Vandal territories was massively offset by the loss of the prime tax-yielding provinces of the western empire, and the impact on the economy of Rome would have been substantial, compounding the problem of raising a sufficiently effective army.

The political situation in the era

The 440s were therefore a pivotal time for the western empire given that, in a mere three decades after the sack of Rome, the bulk of the Iberian peninsula and southern Gaul had been ceded to the Visigoths, and what remained of Gaul was being carved up by the Alans, Burgundians, and Franks. Moreover, the Roman army was smaller in size compared with the end of the fourth century, highly factionalized, and dependent on the enlistment of barbarian *foederati*.

The Huns in Europe

Initially in this period, the Huns posed a major threat to the eastern Roman empire. Much of what we know of the culture and activities of Rome's deadly foe in the fifth century is recorded by Priscus who was particularly well informed and met Attila in person while on a diplomatic mission at his camp in the former province of Dacia in 449. Although he was a Christian writer his chronicles are without religious bias and he is generally regarded as a credible source. In a sense his history is a lost work since no manuscript survives that contains all of the eight works that it originally comprised.[80]

The incursion of the Huns under the joint kingship of Attila and his brother Bleda into the Danubian provinces of the Balkans forced Theodosius II to sign the Treaty of Margus in 435. Under the terms of this agreement the Romans were obliged to pay an annual tribute of seven hundred pounds of gold. In 440 this treaty was broken by the Huns who ransacked the Roman fortress of Castra Constantia on the Danube and wreaked havoc in the Balkans, leading to the First Peace of Anatolius in 443. The tribute demand increased to an annual payment of 2,100 pounds of gold. Bleda died after this event, probably murdered by Attila in 444 or 445[81] Subsequently, according to Marcellinus Comes: 'A mighty war, greater than the previous one, was wrought upon us by king Attila. It devastated the whole of Europe and cities and forts were invaded and pillaged'.[82] This culminated in the pivotal Battle of the Catalaunian Plains, with an allied victory, albeit indecisive, in which Theoderic was killed, although this was sufficient to force Attila's withdrawal from Gaul. After the death of their king in 453 the Hunnic kingdom systematically disintegrated under the rule of his sons Ellac, Dengizich, and Ernak.[83]

Archaeological data

As in the case of other barbarian peoples summarized above, it is often difficult to pinpoint the transient presence of the Huns in the western empire. However, a tomb discovered in the Alsace region of France in 2011 yielded a skeleton of a female with an elongated skull along with jewellery and a bronze mirror from the Caucasus region or central Asia. This dates to around the mid-fifth century AD and may possibly be associated with Attila's campaigns in Gaul. Hunnic burials are more common in those areas where they maintained more of a sustained presence, such as in the Volga steppe north of the Black Sea and the Hungary Plain. One such burial was discovered at Budapest in 1961 and contained the remains of a male skeleton, his horse, and a number of artefacts, including garnet-inlaid gold plaques, iron buckles, and an iron horse bit, along with other items.[84] In relative terms, the number of known Hunnic burials is low, but those known from the region are distinguished by their bows, non-standard European forms of dress, cranial deformations, and cauldrons.[85]

Imperial desperation

After the death of Attila, the western empire, and what remained of it, hung by a thread and the eastern empire was hamstrung, at least in the short term. The territories of central and northern Gaul were being swallowed up by the Burgundians, Franks, and Alans, and the agricultural product with it. Also, the havoc wreaked by the *Bacaudae* rebellions exacerbated Rome's problems.

In North Africa, the Vandals had cut off the vital cereal and oil artery that was fundamental to the survival of Rome. The Roman-Gothic alliance perhaps demonstrates, above all, a severely impaired military capability, which must have been a direct consequence of the state's inability to raise tax from the previously embedded market system. It is not possible to gauge this with any degree of precision, but it can easily be imagined. The basic system of producing and distributing agricultural produce from villas and farms in Gaul and the Iberian peninsula must have been severely disrupted.

The end of the gold monopoly

Of course, a weak economy could be circumvented with a ready supply of gold and silver coinage to pay the troops and raise and maintain a substantial army. However, it was emphasized above that the available resources of gold had diminished in the first half of the fifth century – the mines in Britannia and Dacia had been lost; the mines in the north of the Iberian peninsula (and what resources remained) were under control of the Suevic and Visigothic kings; those in Limousin, south-central Gaul, were no longer in use; the same may be said of the principal mines in Dalmatia; and the available gold in Upper Moesia and the Eastern Desert of Egypt was flowing into the treasuries of the eastern empire.

As for silver, the most important sources in the south-western Iberian peninsula were lost at Rio Tinto, Tharsis, San Domingos, and Aljustrel; those in Upper Moesia were operational until the fourth century; Dacia was an important source of silver in the second and third centuries; in Britannia, from the early fifth century the argentiferous lead mines were no longer available.

The decline of operational mints

It is perhaps no coincidence that by the mid-fifth century the number of operational mints had sharply fallen. Even before the loss of Britannia, those of Camulodunum and Londinium had closed in 324. In Gaul, Colonia Claudia Agrippinensis was no longer producing coinage by the later third century, Treveri shut in the 420s, Moguntiacum closed by the end of the third century, Ambianum after 353, Iantium after 294, Lugdunum around 420, while Arelate fell into Gothic hands in the early fifth century. In Italy, the mint at Mediolanum was active until 326 when production of coinage shifted to Constantinople, as did the minting of coinage at Ticinum, while the mint in Aquileia closed around 425, and Ostia had shut in 313, with production shifting to Arelate. The only operational mints in Italy at this time were in Rome and at Ravenna.

In the Balkans, Siscia had closed in the early 390s, while Sirmium was operational in 320–326 and 351–364. This situation was in stark contrast to those mints that continued in production in the eastern empire. While Serdica only struck occasional coinage circa 303–314, and possibly later, Thessalonica continued to strike through the fall of the west and later, Heraclea remained operational until the reign of Leo I (457–474), Constantinople opened in 326 and continued to mint coinage until the city fell in 1453. Other mints include Cyzicus, which apparently closed before the end of Zeno's reign (474–475, 476–491), Nicomedia remained active in 476 and beyond, while in Syria and Egypt Antioch remained operational through Zeno's reign and beyond, and Alexandria functioned through the reign of Leo I.[86]

Of course, we must allow for the fact that coinage often stayed in circulation for periods of time, and this was increasingly the case after the Flavian period at military sites where there was considerable recycling.[87] This is also evident from countermarks and counterstamps, which may be regarded as forms of damage to the 'host' coin, applied to re-value an issue, redefine its area of circulation, extend circulation life, or to propagandize a change in regime, but rarely are gold coins countermarked.[88] So, even coins remained in circulation, for whatever duration; this was economically unsustainable with a lack of newly minted coinage, and the political turmoil of the period must have severely disrupted circulation within the western empire; it is clear that barbarian kings were snapping up minted coins and issuing them as pseudo-imperial currency.

Demography and military recruitment

Aside from a decline in the production of agricultural commodities and a shortage of gold and silver coinage, other factors should be taken into account that would have militated against Rome's fortunes in this period. A fundamental aspect is the issue of a population decrease in the western empire. This, it has been suggested, is a corollary of economic decline. It should be considered that only a relatively small proportion of people served in the Roman army. For this reason, a significant drop in the indigenous population of the western empire should not have affected the ability of the state to maintain the number of troops. The highest estimates of military numbers put the Roman army at around 650,000. Even if this figure was realized, which it probably was not, no more than 1 per cent of the population of the Roman empire were ever drafted into military service.[89] According to Marcellinus, there appears to have been a recruitment problem in Italy, with a general reluctance to join up, by contrast with Gaul:[90]

> All ages are most fit for military service, and the old man marches out on a campaign with a courage equal to that of the man in the prime of life; since his limbs are toughened by cold and constant toil, and he will make light of many formidable dangers. Nor does anyone of them, for dread of the service of Mars, cut off his thumb, as in Italy: there they call such men 'murci', or cowards.

The *Theodosian Code* also refers to the issue of self-mutilation rather than to commit to military service.[91]

All this said, demographic shrinkage would have impacted on the overall farming yield, so one would naturally expect product to drop. Of course, this would have been massively exacerbated by the settlements of Germanic and non-Germanic peoples and the subsequent territory that was wrested from the Roman authorities. The issue here touches on military capability in this period, and the contention is really how effective could an army be, no matter how skilled, with drastically reduced numbers?

Arther Ferrill's military explanation is relevant to the present book.[92] His main line of reasoning is straightforward: 'Many historians have argued ... that the fall of Rome was not primarily a military phenomenon. In fact, it was exactly that. After 410 the emperor in the west could no longer project military power to the frontiers'. He is correct perhaps for the wrong reason, since it has been demonstrated that the lack of military capability was more to do with a loss of booty revenue, gold resource, economic product, and tax revenue than a military failure *per se*.

His arguments continue as follows:

> To be sure, the loss of strategic resources, money, material and man power compounded the mere loss of territory and made military defence of the rest of the Empire even more difficult. It is simply perverse, how- ever, to argue that Rome's strategic problems in the 440s, 50s and 60s were primarily the result of financial and political difficulties or of long term trends such as depopulation.

While the latter may not necessarily affect the military population, if money could be levied to pay the troops, it is difficult to accept that strategic prob- lems were not the result of financial or political difficulties. How else could these have arisen?

Ferrill's overriding argument is that: 'As the western army became barbarised, it lost its tactical superiority, and Rome fell to the onrush of barbarism'. This interpretation is problematic. He bases his explanation partly on *Epitoma rei militaris* (*The Military Institutions of the Romans*) written around 390 by Vegetius. This is a manual of military instructions that defined the apparent weakness of the late Roman army as a pale shadow of its former self, largely due to urban decadence, and set in place a series of recommendations. In the first book, for instance, he says:[93]

> I realize that in the first ages of the Republic, the Romans always raised their armies in the city itself, but this was at a time when there were no pleasures, no luxuries to enervate them. The Tiber was then their only bath, and in it they refreshed themselves after their exercises and fatigues in the field by swimming. In those days the same man was both soldier and farmer, but a farmer who, when occasion arose, laid aside his tools and put on the sword. The truth of this is confirmed by the instance of Quintius Cincinnatus, who was following the plow when they came to offer him the dictatorship. The chief strength of our armies, then, should be recruited from the country. For it is certain that the less a man is acquainted with the sweets of life, the less reason he has to be afraid of death.

This work should also be considered at the time it was written, a mere twelve years after Adrianople; it would have been natural for a contemporary historian to construe the Roman army as weak at this time. However, the reliability of Vegetius as a source is open to question. According to the American historian, George Watson: 'Vegetius . . . was neither a historian nor a soldier: his work is a compilation carelessly constructed from material of all ages, a congeries of inconsistencies'.[94]

Another issue here is that Ferrill cites Jordanes, who wrote a dubious passage about what Attila apparently said about the quality of the Roman army before the Battle of the Catalaunian Plains in 451:[95]

> See, even before our attack they are smitten with terror. They seek the heights, they seize the hills and, repenting too late, clamour for protection against battle in the open fields. You know how slight a matter the Roman attack is. While they are still gathering in order and forming in one line with locked shields, they are checked, I will not say by the first wound, but even by the dust of battle.

In fact, this battle proved to be the undoing of the Hunnic king and his empire, and resulted in a Roman victory, albeit with Visigothic support, so to cite Jordanes is somewhat contradictory.

Some other points should be addressed. First, that at Adrianople it was the eastern army that was defeated, and those failed campaigns of the fifth century were chiefly the eastern army, especially against the Huns and the catastrophe of the Byzantine Armada. As outlined above, the western army was substantially reduced in the early fifth century, and relied often on barbarian support, whether *foederati* or alliances with individual kings. This whole argument in fact is rather circular: if the barbarian soldiery had reduced the tactical capability of the western army, then this suggests that the barbarian tactical capability was limited in its own right, and this does not explain how a Visigothic, Vandalic, or any barbarian contingent had a tactical advantage over a Roman force. In the sixth century, the eastern army was able to reconquer Ostrogothic Italy, parts of Visigothic Spain, and Vandal North Africa, and it was as 'barbarized' as the western army. This continued long after the collapse of the eastern provinces in the seventh century. The ferocious capability and loyalty of Viking mercenaries known as the Varangian Guard are well known in the Middle Byzantine period.[96]

Goldsworthy has made some relevant comments: 'Each civil war cost the empire. Anything gained by the winning side inevitably had to be taken from other Romans and a prolonged campaign was likely to involve widespread destruction within the provinces where fighting occurred'.[97] He has also claimed that: '. . . weakening central authority, social and economic problems and, most of all, the continuing grind of civil wars eroded the political capacity to maintain the army at this level'.[98] These are surely critical points. The factionalization of the western empire as a result of internecine warfare has been emphasized, particularly in the early fifth century, and the impact on agricultural productivity would have been profound. On a gory note, the impact of legion against legion – highly trained forces pitted against each other – should be considered; the slaughter must have been on a truly terrible scale.

The Vandal sack of Rome in 455

That the Roman army was a pale shadow of its former self is attested by the Vandal sack of Rome. According to Hydatius:[99]

> Year 455, Forty-third in line of the Roman emperors, Marcian, now in the fourth year of his reign, ruled alone … Gaiseric entered Rome – according to an evil lie spread by rumour he had been summoned by Valentinian's widow before Avitus became Augustus … and having looted the wealth of the Romans, he returned to Carthage, taking with him Valentinian's widow and two daughters, and the son of Aetius, who was named Gaudentius.

The Vandals apparently encountered little resistance and entered Rome on 2 June 455, razing the aqueduct bridges that fed the city and cutting off its water supply (Figure 5.3). According to Prosper, who is known to have

Figure 5.3 Genseric sacking Rome, 455. Karl Briullov (1833–1886). Oil on canvas.
Courtesy of State Tretyakov Gallery, Moscow.

lived in Rome from around 435 and may have been an eyewitness to the Vandal Sack:[100]

> The holy Pope Leo ran to meet Geiseric outside of the gates and, with God's help, by his supplication so softened him that he abstained from fire, slaughter, and torture, on the condition that all power was given to him . . .

Rome was plundered, although the extent of this has been debated. The gilded roofing tiles of the Temple of Jupiter Optimus Maximus were certainly stripped. Also, the Jewish Temple treasure brought to Rome by Titus, or what was left of it after the Gothic sack of 410, was seized,[101] along with thousands of captives, according to Victor of Vita, including senators and artisans, as well as Eudoxia and her two daughters, Eudocia and Placidia.[102] Subsequently, the Vandals seized Sardinia, Corsica, the Balearic Islands, and dominated Sicily. In 458 the poet Sidonius railed against 'a savage foe . . . roaming at his ease over the unguarded sea'.[103]

End of the empire

Those events left the western empire with one last chance to reverse its fortunes, culminating in a joint expedition sanctioned by emperors Anthemius in the west and Leo in the east in 468; known to posterity as 'the Byzantine Armada', under the command of Basiliscus. The cost of this expensive campaign is known from Candidus, a contemporary generally considered to be a reliable source.[104] This equated to about 169,000 pounds of gold. In the event, the Roman fleet was destroyed off Promontorium Mercurii (Cape Bon) by fire-ships, as recounted by Procopius, although it should be borne in mind that his panegyrical style would have sought to magnify the crisis to further glorify the reconquest of the Vandal kingdom by Justinian.[105]

Candidus relates the following sequence of events. Odovacar, an Arian Roman *foederati* commander of Gothic, Heruli, or other descent, was gradually absorbing what remained of Roman territory in Italy and the northwest Balkans, emerging as the power behind the throne. Finally, Flavius Orestes, who ruled in Roman Dalmatia until 480, appointed his young son Romulus Augustulus ('little Augustus') to the purple on 31 October 475. He was forced to abdicate by Odovacar in Ravenna on 4 September 476 and spent the rest of his life in exile, probably in Campania. The imperial regalia – purple cloak and diadem – were sent to Zeno in Constantinople, who appointed Odovacar *dux* of Italy, so ending the formal sovereignty of the western empire (Map 2).[106]

Sources

A combination of sources – archaeological, epigraphic, numismatic, and textual – point towards an economic and demographic collapse. As suggested in the previous chapter, it is difficult to quantify the decrease in real terms, since a number of calculations and models have made it clear that we cannot truly know the population of the western, and indeed eastern, empires. For this reason it is fruitless to attempt an estimate here. However, it must have been substantial, and surely commensurate with the overall picture of urban and rural decay outlined below. Particularly instructive in this context are the various papers presented in the edited volume by Bowman and Wilson,[107] as are the arguments of Temin.[108]

The Vandals

After sacking Rome the Vandals consolidated their power in North Africa. The kings ruled from the former Roman palace on the Hill of Byrsa in Carthage. Archaeological remains paint a picture of a prosperous city that adapted Roman civilization, equipped with bath-houses fed by a monumental aqueduct from the Atlas mountains, amphitheatre, circus, odeon, theatre, and opulent private houses with mosaics – some are displayed in the British Museum. Several churches were taken over and adapted for Arian worship.[109] There are considerable remains of agricultural installations in the hinterland of Vandal North Africa.

Archaeological data

Returning to the survey work of Mariette de Vos, the chronology of sites surveyed in the rural sites of Thugga in northern Africa Proconsularis, based on surface pottery, indicate a surge in the Vandal period, with 91 sites dating to the late Roman period and 126 to the Vandal era.[110] This obviously indicates that the Vandals fully exploited the extraordinarily productive cereal and oil-rich provinces wrested from imperial control; and this accords with an attested continuity of trade, as borne out by the distribution of African red slip ware around the west and east Mediterranean, principally amphora sherds, from the containers of olive oil, *garum*, and wine.[111]

Numismatic evidence

Coins shed light on the Vandalic powerbase (Figure 5.4). At the Carthage mint, the first issues, minted circa 440–490, were silver pseudo-imperial *siliqua* depicting Honorius on the obverse; the reverse often showing an enthroned Victory holding the *globus cruciger*. In the period that follows, around 490–533, a number of royal silver issues of *denarii* and *nummi* develop, minted in the name of successive kings with stylized busts on the obverse; the reverses tend to depict wreathes enclosing letters denoting the value of the coins. Municipal copper *nummi* depict a standing figure of Carthage on the obverse or an inscription naming the city and a standing soldier; the reverse has letters and numbers denoting the denomination and value or a horse's head and value mark.[112]

Figure 5.4 Vandalic *siliqua* of Gaiseric minted at Carthage, issued in the name of Honorius. On the obverse, a bust of Honorius; the reverse depicts Carthage holding ears of corn. Struck 443–444.

Courtesy of London Coin Galleries.

The Merovingian Franks

In northern Gaul, the Franks were expanding their domain southwards. In 481/482 Clovis succeeded his father, Childeric, as the ruler of the Salian Franks of Tournai. In the short period that followed, their powerbase expanded. Crucially, the king landed a crushing defeat on the Roman commander Syagrius at the Battle of Soissons in 486 or 487 and compelled the other Salian tribes to submit to his authority, as well as the Ripuarian Franks who were based around Colonia Claudia Agrippinensis. In 496, he conquered the Alamanni to the east and defeated the Visigoths at the Battle of Vouillé in 507, seized Aquitaine, and drove them into Spain. The Burgundians were in turn conquered in 532/534 and their kingdom partitioned.[113]

Archaeological data

Aside from Frankish 'row-graves' and their material culture across the region, the most relevant archaeological evidence in this period was the discovery of the tomb of Childeric, and its rich grave goods, at Tournai in 1653.[114] More prosaic archaeological material is manifest in the appearance of 'Germanic' settlements that slowly supplanted Romano-Gallic villas and non-villas. The most notable examples are the fond de cabane (Grubenhaus), or the sunken-floored building (SFB) – square or rectangular structures, widely thought to be associated with the Alamanni, Anglo-Saxons, and the Franks in particular.[115]

In 1991 Tamara Lewit published a coherent synthesis of survey work in Britannia, Gaul, and the Iberian peninsula, and presented these data in a series of charts and graphs. In the north-western part of Gaul (Belgica), rural sites (small, medium, and large) and *vici* reach a peak in the second century AD, and there is an observable decline in the third century (especially the second half). In the fourth century, there is a further drop (notably in the second half), and a sharp decline in the fifth century, totalling 76 sites. In the broader region of northern Gaul, a similar pattern is evident for small, medium, and large rural sites. [116]

Elsewhere in northern Gaul, data in the Ile-de-France region are telling, largely on the basis of the survey work conducted by Paul Van Ossel, Pierre Ouzoulias, and their associates, the research group Diocesis Galliarum. There, villa and non-villa sites show a clear reduction in numbers in the fifth century compared with the fourth century. At Mauldre-Vaucouleurs 15 per cent of sites date to the fourth century compared with 9 per cent in the fifth century. The reduction is less marked at Pays de France (30 to 27 per cent). At Marne-la-Vallée, 4 per cent of sites date to the fourth century and 2 per cent to the fifth century, while at Sénart 15 per cent of sites date to the fourth century and 8 per cent to the fifth. Finally, at La Bassée, the ratios are 10 to 9 per cent.[117] These proportions indicate significant, but not universal, dislocations of the agricultural system.

Agricultural sites in central Gaul also indicate a relative drop of settlements in the fifth century compared with the fourth. There the survey work of Cristina Gandini has been instrumental in establishing a pattern of decline. At Boischaut nord, more than 20 per cent of sites dated to the fourth century and less than half of that number to the fifth century. The ratio was similar at Boischaut sud, Bourbonnais, Brenne, Champagne, and Sologne. Significantly there were no new constructions in the region after the third century.[118]

Numismatic evidence

Merovingian Franks were minting their own pseudo-imperial coinage from around 500 onwards in northern Gaul, and subsequently in Aquitaine, Burgundy, and Provence (after 507 or post-534), until around 580. The first issues were gold *solidi*, depicting emperor Anastasius (491–518) and his legend on the obverse, and Victory holding a long cross on the reverse. Gold *tremisses* are similar, but reverses tend to depict Victory with a wreath and a palm. A third, royal issue of gold and silver *nummi*, depict the monogram of Thierry I 'King of Metz' (511–534). None of these carry a mint-mark and it is assumed that they were minted in their region of distribution.[119] The Merovingian annexation of the Burgundian kingdom coincides with the disappearance of their coinage, the last issue minted by king Gundobald (473–516). After the consolidation of Frankish power in Gaul, mints were established at Lugdunum, Massilia, Chalon-sur-Saône, and elsewhere in the realm.

The Visigoths in southern Gaul and the Iberian peninsula

Visigothic king Euric extended his rule to encompass most of southern Gaul by 476 and the bulk of the Iberian peninsula in the 480s, except the Suevic kingdom in the north-west.

Archaeological data

This period is represented by a considerable number of 'row-grave' cemeteries ('*Reihengräber*') appearing across Spain dating to the last quarter of the fifth century onwards that tend to yield material associated with the Visigoths. A large burial site is known at Duratón, where females were buried with cloaks fastened with pairs of fibula brooches at each shoulder, and a large rectangular buckle around the waist.[120]

In south-eastern Gaul, some interesting statistics emerge, based on the survey work of the European research project ARCHEOMEDES. There, the sites are categorized as type A (at Alpillies, Comtat, Beaucairois, and Uzège) and type B (at Vaunage, Lunelois, Valdaine, and Tricastain). Collectively, type A sites dwindle from around 6 per cent in the fourth century to around 2 per cent in the fifth century; type B sites from around 8 per cent in the fourth century to around 5 per cent in the fifth century.[121]

In the same region (with the inclusion of the Languedoc), Marzano examined the capital investment in agriculture at a more conservative number of sites. Only one olive oil- and two wine-presses are known in the fourth century but, significantly, none are present in the fifth century.[122]

In the Arrat valley in southern France, the survey work of Catherine Petit paints a similar picture. In the first century 22 villas are dated, most of these occupied through the third century. Only eight survive in the fourth century, and three appear to be occupied in the fifth century.[123]

As for southern Gaul more broadly, Eva Carr based her analysis on the data from the Carte Archaeologique de la Gaule. She found a decline of 70 per cent in the number of identifiable sites between the fourth and the fifth centuries, with more upheaval in the early sixth century after the arrival of the Franks.[124]

In the same region, Lewit collated the occupation of medium and large sites. They reach a peak in the first and second centuries, with a relative decline in the third century (especially the second half), and a resurgence in the fourth century. In the fifth century there is a substantial drop.[125]

In the Catalonian littoral, survey has tended to concentrate more on villas than non-villa settlements. Evidence from pottery and palaeo-environmental evidence (mainly pollen) points to a concentration of cereal-producing villas in the fourth century in the hinterland of Ampurias, Barcino, and Tarraco, with a shift to a more pastoral agricultural regime in the fifth century, and a general contraction and abandonment of villas in this period with a general demographic decline.[126]

Also in northern Spain, in the area of Tarraco, the survey work conducted by Josep Ma Carreté i Nadal, Martin Millett, and Simon Keay in the early 1990s, analysing surface pottery, demonstrated a considerable integration into broader commercial networks (imports). In the fifth century, however, the paucity of ceramics led them to conclude that exchange networks were contracting at this time.[127]

From the late 1960s to the early 1990s, Michel Ponsich of the Casa de Velazquez (the French archaeological institute) in Madrid undertook a comprehensive survey in the Guadalquivir valley covering a large area and recorded thousands of sites.[128] He categorized these as agglomerations, villas, farms, and shelters, dated on the basis of Hayes and Lamboglia pottery forms.

Further analysis of pottery evidence by Eva Carr, and a reappraisal of this work, has enhanced our understanding of the settlement pattern in the region. The Guadalquivir comprises the southern Iberian province of Baetica, and the valley of the Guadalquivir river and the uplands on each side of it, and is flanked by the Mediterranean and Atlantic coasts. This region is well known for its imperial estates, and state monopoly on the production of olive oil for the *annona*. In the fourth century, nearly a quarter of sites showed traces of olive oil-presses. At the beginning of the fifth century, around the time of the Vandal invasion, 37 of these sites disappeared, along with a similar proportion of sites without olive oil-presses. Only three of nineteen new fifth-century villas had olive oil-presses. At the beginning of the sixth century, with the arrival of the Visigoths, less than an eighth of the new sixth-century villa sites yield evidence for oil production. This pattern is also echoed by a chronological shift of settlements to the hills: 41 per cent of sites occupy there in the fourth century, compared with 45 in the fifth century, and 60 per cent in the sixth century, suggesting a preference for safer sites in times of unrest. Carr suggests that the overall picture equates to a substantial demographic decline in the region.[129]

The survey of Marzano revealed a different pattern in the southern coastal region of the Iberian peninsula. Thirty olive oil-presses and 37 wine-presses date to the fourth century, with ten olive oil-presses and 26 wine-presses known in the fifth century. This indicates that similar processes were underway.[130]

An overview for the pattern of rural settlement in the Iberian peninsula is presented by Lewit. In northern regions, the number of sites occupied peaked in the second century, declined in the third century (especially the second half), flourished again in the fourth century, and declined sharply in the fifth, with 54 sites. In southern regions, the pattern is similar, but with a less marked decline in the second half of the third century.[131]

Numismatic evidence

The first issues of Visigothic coinage were considerably earlier than Frankish coinage, as related above, a consequence of their formal settlement by imperial authorities in southern Gaul in the early fifth century (Figure 5.5). After their defeat at Vouillé in 507, the Visigoths consolidated their domain in the Iberian peninsula. The coinage of the period from around 509 to 580 consists of gold pseudo-imperial *solidi* and *tremisses*. On their obverse, these denominations are similar in character and represent and bear the names of successive eastern emperors Anastasius (491–518), Justin I (518–527),

Figure 5.5 Visigothic pseudo-imperial gold *solidus* issued in the name of Valentinian III, uncertain king, minted in southern Gaul. On the obverse, a bust of the emperor; reverse shows Valentinian standing, facing right with his foot on a bound captive, holding a military standard and Victoria on a globe. Struck circa 425–430.

Courtesy of London Coin Galleries.

and Justinian (527–565), and a Victory in profile holding a cross-staff. Visigothic domination is attested by finds across the Iberian peninsula, minted in Bracara, extinguishing the rule of the Sueves in that region, with mints spreading to Caesaraugusta, Eminio, Elvora, Emerita, Toledo, and elsewhere.[132]

Odovacar and the Ostrogoths in Italy

In the meantime, Ostrogothic king Theoderic revolted in the eastern empire, ravaging Thrace, and en route through the Balkans took Italy from Odovacar.[133] He is depicted on a wall mosaic in his great church of St Apollinare Nuovo in Ravenna; another depicts the façade of his palace in the city.[134]

Archaeological data

It is perhaps logical to commence in the heartland of the western empire and re-examine agricultural production in the hinterland of Rome. The work of Marzano, discussed previously, surveyed 169 single and multi-presses in this region that belonged to villa estates. Of these, 14 per cent were wine-presses, 36 per cent olive oil-presses, and 50 per cent uncertain. The interesting statistic, for the purposes of the arguments presented, are the chronological phases attested at elite villas in Latium. More than 60 were operational in the fourth century, in the fifth some 25 of these were in active use.[135]

The case study in central Italy of rural settlement and population extrapolation presented by Attema and de Haas is once again instructive. To reiterate, this focused on the rural settlements of Antium from 350 BC to AD 400, incorporating settlement types including small farms, large villas, and *villae maritimae* (seaside villas). This study plotted around 70 certain and possible sites in the period from the second to mid-third century, this number falling to 40 in the period from the mid-third century to the end of the fourth century. Further east, at Nettuno data are presented that indicate rural settlements (certain and possible) numbered around 45 in the period 250–400, this number falling to around 15 in the fifth century.[136] The concordant population in these sites is calculated as 910 people occupying certain and possible sites from the second to mid-third century and 552.5 from the middle of the third century to the end of the fourth.[137]

In Italy, the large number of field-surveys undertaken in the centre and south of the peninsula suggest that there was a gradual decline in rural prosperity through the third, fourth, fifth, and sixth centuries. A study by the British School of Archaeology at Rome in southern Etruria, soon after the Second World War, has been updated and synthesized by Timothy Potter and Stephen Dyson.[138] After the second century the data plot a continuous decline so that by 500 between 50 per cent and 80 per cent of rural sites in various parts of the survey area had come to an end.[139] Ward-Perkins' survey of southern Etruria echoes this pattern, and he suggests a demographic decline on the basis of diminishing imports of pottery.[140]

In the Biferno valley, on the eastern side of the Italian peninsula, a survey under the direction of Graeme Barker plotted a different chronological distribution. Less than half of the sites occupied in the Republican period continued into the early centuries AD. In this case surviving sites remained in occupation until the fifth century. Thereafter the picture is of a decline.[141] In the Liri valley (about 100 kilometres south-east of Rome), Edith Wightman concluded that the area was colonized in the fourth century BC, with a static settlement pattern into the imperial period, an increase in the second and third centuries, and a decline thereafter.[142]

Information compiled by Lewit from small, medium, and large rural sites in several Italian provinces (Basilicata, Campania, Lazio, Liguria, Marche, Molise, Toscana, Umbria) echoes those general trends above: a first- and second-century peak, a relative decline in the first half of the third century, more so in the second half of that century, a resurgence in the fourth century, and a steep decline in the fifth.[143]

In southern Italy, the archaeological trends are similar in Lucania and Apulia: settlement numbers dipping in the third century; most larger agricultural settlements persisting in the fourth; with some diminution of numbers in the fifth century, but the quality and depth of activity on most sites, especially the larger ones, decline from the fifth.[144]

Numismatic evidence

Coinage in Italy reflects the new world order. First, gold *tremisses* were issued under Odovacar (476–493), minted at Milan, Ravenna, and Rome. These depict the busts of either Zeno or Anastasius on the obverse (with whom the reign of Odovacer overlaps), or Roma; and a cross in a wreath on the reverse, or a figure holding a staff and a cornucopia, or the she-wolf

Figure 5.6 Ostrogothic *follis* issued under Theoderic or Athalaric, minted in Rome. Obverse shows a bust of Roma; the reverse depicts the she-wolf suckling the twins Romulus and Remus. Struck 493–553.

Courtesy of London Coin Galleries.

suckling the twins Romulus and Remus (Figure 5.6). With the accession of Theoderic the same mints produced pseudo-imperial gold *solidi* and *tremisses*, depicting Anastasius and Justin I on the obverse; the reverse depicting Victory in profile holding a cross-staff, or a cross and cornucopia. From the reign of Theodahad, coins tend to show the portrait of the king on the obverse with a range of depictions on the reverse, such as the Victory and staff motif or a wreath.[145]

The economic picture in the west

Shipwrecks

An analysis of shipwrecks, based on the work of Anthony Parker, in the Mediterranean by century shows a substantial fall by around half in the third century, and about a half again in the fourth century. As for the fifth century, the reduction of wrecks goes into free fall.[146]

Building inscriptions

Collective trends from the data presented above, although proxy, and in previous chapters point, generally speaking, to a sustained economic and demographic decline, especially in the second half of the third century, culminating in a fifth-century collapse. This is also borne out by evidence from building inscriptions. To reiterate, based on data provided from the *Epigraphische Datenbank Heidelberg*, there is a sharp drop in the third century after the reign of Septimius Severus; a resurgence under Diocletian, Constantine, and Valentinian I; and a decline thereafter.

To put this into a fifth-century perspective, the epigraphic record is scant in the western and eastern empires, with just eleven building inscriptions, the lion's share of these being in Rome. One of the best-known inscriptions was engraved on the triumphal arch of the tomb basilica outside Rome on the road to Ostia. This was begun under Theodosius I and completed by Honorius.

The inscription reads as follows: 'Theodosius began, Honorius completed this church, consecrated by the body of Paul, teacher of the world'. Further embellishment was completed by Galla Placidia under Pope Leo the Great (440–460) as recorded on the mosaic of the triumphal arch: 'The devout soul of Placidia rejoices to see this edifice radiant in splendour through the devotion of Bishop Leo'.[147]

In the west, four building inscriptions date to the reign of Honorius, three in Rome (the first two from the Curia) and one at Portus in Latium et Campania (Regio I); in the east, one more inscription is recorded in his tenure, at Berkovica in Moesia Inferior.[148] In the reign of Valentinian III, three inscriptions are known in Rome, the first two from the Campus Martius and the Septizodium respectively.[149] In the western provinces just one inscription is known, at Salonae in Dalmatia.[150] A second example at Rome dates to the reign of Avitus, recorded on the Column of Phocas.[151] The final inscription is again from Rome, but has a wide chronological bracket to be of any real use.[152]

Rural settlement

In Italy, the situation, as borne out by the archaeological evidence for rural settlement presented above should be reiterated. Christie has pointed to broadly similar trends in central and southern Italy – a decline of larger settlement numbers in the third century AD, persistence in the fourth, some reduction mainly of larger settlements into the fifth century, and a decline thereafter. By the sixth century, numbers and scale are further reduced, timber usage becomes more dominant, and luxury features such as bath-houses and mosaic floors disappear.[153]

Generally speaking, in hierarchical terms, villas represented the main thrust of rural settlement hierarchy in the western empire, in contrast to the eastern empire, where elites tended to live in luxurious urban houses.[154] The definition of what defines a villa has been endlessly debated. Most studies distinguish between villas and other, smaller and less elaborate dwellings, and the most recent comment in this context by Nigel Pollard seems logical, a distinction 'with underlying social significance, since the luxury materials reflect construction by an individual who, on some level, shared the tastes of urban elites or at least sought to assimilate them'.[155]

In the west, a number of grandiose establishments are attested at the top end of the social spectrum; medium-sized and small villas, and farmsteads, were all greatly dispersed in their respective provinces. These are known from literary and archaeological sources. *Vici* (villages), and *castra* (fortified villages) mentioned in Roman literature are little studied archaeologically, but also formed an integral part of the settlement pattern. *Coloni*, who were essentially tenants of villa estates, either occupied smaller farms there, nearby, or resided in villages, so that villas, although acting as the centre of an estate, were not necessarily linked with settlement patterns in the sense of an overarching ownership, although it should be considered that the collective output of produce represented its own 'block', but the villa may be regarded as the focal socio-economic point.

Villas disappeared when the western empire collapsed and were therefore a universally Roman phenomenon. In Britain, the process of abandonment began in the late fourth century, accelerating in the fifth, and they are absent from the archaeological record by around 450. In northern Gaul, their decline began slightly earlier around 350, and they had all but vanished in the mid-fifth century. In Mediterranean Gaul, the pattern of abandonment is considerably later, in the sixth century and only a small number are attested in the early seventh century, a pattern generally shadowed in Aquitaine. In Italy villas disappear in the late fifth and sixth centuries, but in Sicily a few remain in the seventh century. In Spain, abandonment commenced in the fifth century, few remained by the end of the sixth, some survived until around 700.[156] In Africa, this process is not so well understood but appears to occur around 550.[157] Broadly speaking, a distinction can be drawn between villas in the north – their terminal date clusters to around 400; in the Mediterranean this occurs around the sixth century. The later disappearance of villas in Italy, Sicily, and North Africa of course suggests that a remnant of elite Romans still populated the former territories of the Roman empire, and the same was probably true lower down the social scale.

It is widely thought that a militarization of elites occurred in northern Gaul before the Frankish invasions of the mid-fifth century,[158] resulting in more peasant-like constructions rather than exhibiting 'Germanic' characteristics, and the later pattern of villa disappearance is attributed to the factor that aristocrats were not militarized. It is also curious that *castra* tend to show much greater levels of continuity into the early Middle Ages than villas, perhaps due to the security afforded by their fortifications.

These changes, occurring in different regions at different times, were a basic consequence as Roman culture and its economy unravelled, with a diverse settlement pattern replacing the villa – the aristocratic symbol par excellence – of the rural sphere in the western empire, a dispersal of small villages becoming the norm in the early Middle Ages.

The changing city

The insecurity posed by these troubles in the western empire is manifest in the fortification of a great number of urban centres in the later third century, a trend that was set to continue in the fourth and fifth centuries. Italy, the core of the empire, is instructive in this context. It is especially telling that Ravenna was chosen as the imperial seat under Stilicho and Honorius in preference to Milan, founded as an imperial capital under the Tetrarchs. This was a logical choice; with a coastal location on the Adriatic, a natural defensive marsh, the town was rapidly developed in the fifth century with a circuit wall.[159] At Portus, excavations from the early fifth century show a shrinkage in space to a fortified core,[160] while at Ostia the archaeology points to a rapid decline in the fifth century, both perhaps feeling the impact of Alaric's occupation of Portus and the Vandal Sack of 455.[161] Elsewhere in Italy, fortifications appeared earlier, at Verona under Gallienus, Rome under Aurelian, and Milan under the Tetrarchs, where the physical transformation included high walls, restricted gates, and wide ditches.[162] Naples was refortified to counter the Vandal threat in the fifth century and the walls of Rome were heightened under Honorius. The overall transformation of Italian cities has been summarized by Neil Christie:[163]

> Despite the often substantial problems in exploring sites which have seen continuous urban use, results from major excavations in centres like Rome ... Milan, Brescia, Verona, Naples, and Otranto have done much to chart changing townscapes across the late Roman period and into the early Middle Ages, identifying diverse trajectories in terms of public and private spaces, of reuse or robbing of structures, of organization of civic spaces like markets, of technological change ... Most scholars accept the appearance of much-altered urban innards, with the qualities and technologies much reduced ...

Esmonde Cleary has presented an interesting synthesis of the physical changes of late Roman cities in the north-western provinces, but the picture is by no means homogenous in the third and fourth centuries. For instance, a number of cities in Britannia, southern Gaul, and the Iberian peninsula, show a continuity of the 'classical' past in their overall layout, lack of fortifications, and the variable survival of old civic monuments, religious precincts and buildings, suggesting 'a purposive ideology of maintenance and tradition'. Conversely, in the fourth century, walls characterized cities in northern Gaul, south-western Gaul, and the north-western Iberian peninsula in the early fifth century, where the population was 'militarized', but with more general homogeneity in the fifth century, with walls and churches being the norm.[164] This tapestry of interpretation is difficult to follow in the sense that a number of cities that apparently conform to his first 'category' were fortified. Britannia is a case in point, where urban centres appear to have retained their civic amenities but had circuit walls constructed in the third century, such as Deva, Eboracum, and Lindum Colonia, or the fourth century as in the case of Venta Silurum.

The continuity of imperial patronage in the eastern empire

It is logical to expect that imperial patronage continued in the eastern empire after the western empire had collapsed. A range of archaeological, demographic, epigraphic, ceramic, and numismatic data in fact point to an economic boom in the late fifth and first half of the sixth century AD, this is presented in more detail below.[165] Epigraphy alone provides an insightful snapshot of the economic trends in this era. For instance, the Israeli archaeologist Leah Di Segni applied a quantitative approach to the building inscriptions of Arabia, Palestine, and southern Phoenicia in an attempt to gauge the intensity of building activity in the late Roman period, and the general picture was one of a marked increase in the fifth century, especially under Anastasius I (491–518), with a surge under Justin I (518–527) and Justinian I (527–565).[166]

The social transformation of *decurions*

As for building inscriptions under the sponsorship of *decurions* and other local officials, these are absent in the fifth century in both the western and eastern empires. This no doubt underscores the broadly held view that the increasing burden on this social class squeezed them out of their civic obligations and into the imperial civil service. However, this is only a part of the picture, since the emerging elites in the early Christian period – bishops, priests, deacons, *economoi* – were, as indicated in the previous chapter, from the same social background as *decurions*. In the eastern empire, numerous floor mosaics in ecclesiastical buildings, especially in the later fifth and sixth centuries, record these officials as donors.[167] In the western empire, in the fifth century, a considerable number of new churches were built and older edifices refurbished at the personal expense of bishops or under their sponsorship. This is attested at Arelate, Augustonemetum, Arausio, Divio, Fréjus, Lugdunum, Narbo Martius, Massilia, Reii Apollinares, and elsewhere in Gaul.[168]

A curious inscription on a large stone lintel (*limen*) recovered from the fifth-century cathedral of Narbonne records the commemoration of its reconstruction by the fifth-century bishop, Rusticus, and dates this act precisely during the sixth consulship of Valentinian on 29 November 445. A short time later, Perpetuus, bishop of Tours, inscribed his name in the apse of his new Basilica of St Martin.[169]

Also informative in the context of ecclesiastical patronage is an inscription found in the church of the village of Valentine in the Haute Garonne, and it is thought that Nymfius, the individual mentioned was the patron of a Gallo-Roman villa there.[170] Hagith Sivan has presented an interesting interpretation of its content that names the individual as a *munus* who sponsored the local games in the fourth or possibly the early fifth century. He stresses that, originally, the term retained its original meaning of a spectacle offered in the amphitheatre for public benefit at private expense, and by the fourth century it could be expanded to include a variety of acts, such as the construction and restoration of public buildings, and the upkeep of aqueducts and public roads. His conclusion is that the inscription refers primarily to games given in the past at Nymfius' expense to celebrate his provincial priesthood.[171]

In the rural sphere, the practice of building churches in villas is well known elsewhere, and it is appropriate to mention some fifth-century examples: at the Villa Fortunatus, in the hinterland of Tarraco, so named after a floor mosaic inscribed with this name and a *chi-rho* monogram;[172] also in the same region, the well-known villa of Centcelles is thought to contain a mausoleum and crypt;[173] while at Carranque, south-west of Madrid, a villa was equipped with a basilica and mausoleum.[174] In south-west Gaul the fifth-century phase of the villa at Seviac in the Midi Pyrénées has an oratory and baptistery,[175] while in south-east Gaul there is a possible basilica and mausoleum at a villa near Saint-Maximin in the Var.[176] To the west of the Rhône the villa site at Loupian in the Hérault is associated with a church nearby.[177]

Peaceful accommodation versus hostile takeover

It would seem a little odd if comment was not made on the paradigm that held such massive currency in recent decades: Rome did not fall and the barbarians were peacefully accommodated. This issue was touched on briefly in the Introduction. The notion was iterated by Henri Pirenne and impacted on Peter Brown.[178] Publications by Ward-Perkins and Heather, in particular, have rightly challenged this flawed concept.[179] It is fair to say that Pirenne and Brown were selective in their appraisal of particular historical texts and that archaeological and numismatic evidence do not support the theory. One only has to consider several episodes to support this view: Adrianople, the aggressive barbarian support of Roman usurpers, the Vandal invasion of Africa, the Byzantine Armada – catastrophic for the Roman cause, and these hardly smack of a peaceful barbarian accommodation.

The idea that the western empire fell as a consequence of a hostile takeover gains support from archaeological data. This is particularly the case in the late Roman/Anglo-Saxon transition in Britain, which has attracted a great deal of scrutiny. Shakenoak villa in Oxfordshire is instructive in this regard. The building had towers added to the original villa in the second half of the fourth or early fifth century, and so was militarized in this manner. In the Anglo-Saxon period Germanic belt-fittings from military dress were found and a number of skeletons of young men were discovered. Osteological analysis revealed that in some cases the individuals had clearly met a violent death.[180]

James Gerrard has discussed this phenomenon in some detail, particularly with regard to weapon trauma on late Roman and early medieval skeletons from cemeteries in western and eastern Britain. In the latter region, 40 skeletons had evidence of blade injuries out of a sample of 3,020 (1.3 per cent of the total).[181] His conclusion was that an individual was three times more likely to be wounded with an edged weapon in early Anglo-Saxon England than in fourth-century Britain. He suggests that the percentage may be skewed by several factors, since the cemeteries are predominantly urban, and the real proportion of fatalities could be higher. Even if, taken as a whole, 1.3 per cent seems a low statistic, this should be tempered with the fact that less than 1 per cent of the population ever served in the Roman army, and it would seem logical to expect a similar dynamic in the Anglo-Saxon period.

Perhaps the 'acid test' for hostile takeover is at military sites, and these are well studied in Gaul; although osteological evidence appears to be lacking, the material culture and burial practices are instructive of the Roman militia being supplanted by a Germanic presence. Key excavations took place at Krefeld-Gellep (Gelduba) on the lower Rhine, and more particularly the cemeteries excavated between 1960 and 2000 under the direction of Renate Pirling.[182] Graves and artefacts are generally Roman in character until the turn of the fourth and fifth centuries when non-Roman 'Germanic' material appears from the east of the Rhine. A comparable site on the upper Rhine is Kaiseraugst, where burials and artefacts show a similar trend. The cemetery remained in use until the seventh century by which time it had gravestones with Germanic names.[183] The fort at Alzey on the middle Rhine was partially destroyed around 400 and this has been associated with the Germanic invasion of 406 and Germanic material culture appears thereafter. Around the middle of the fifth century the fort was destroyed by fire.[184]

A common feature of the archaeological sequences at these forts, and in their cemeteries, is an increase in the amount of 'Germanic' material from them after the start of the fifth century. This material forms a significant proportion of the total by the end of the first half of the fifth century and pretty much the total by the end of the century.[185]

The consequence of diminishing agricultural product, taxation, and precious metals

The combination of historically documented events, archaeological, epigraphic, and numismatic data pertaining to the fifth century do, albeit by proxy, point to some general trends. It is clear that the western empire was overwhelmed by a mixture of barbarian tribes that are known by various labels as the Alans, Alamanni, Franks, Huns, Sueves, Vandals, and Visigoths, who first settled then expanded to the detriment of the provincial population and imperial government.

Certainly the archaeological picture is confused when it comes to notions of ethnicity; however, this should surely be a logical expectation in light of similar ritual practices and overlapping material culture (Figures 5.7–5.10), and this is where numismatic evidence helps. Looking at this hypothetically from a contemporary perspective, what would the future excavation of twenty-first century cemeteries in London yield? These would likely reveal a mixture of Buddhist, Christian, Jewish, Muslim, Hindu, and Sikh burial practices, inscriptions, etc. However, any associated coinage would of course depict Queen Elizabeth II, Kings Charles, William, and other future British monarchs on their obverses. So while the ethnic picture may confuse in the future, the collective population would be constitutionally British. As interesting as ethnic definitions are for the purposes of the people who succeeded the Romans in the western empire, for all intents and purposes, it is not especially relevant to the fall of Rome. The real marker here is the coinage, which

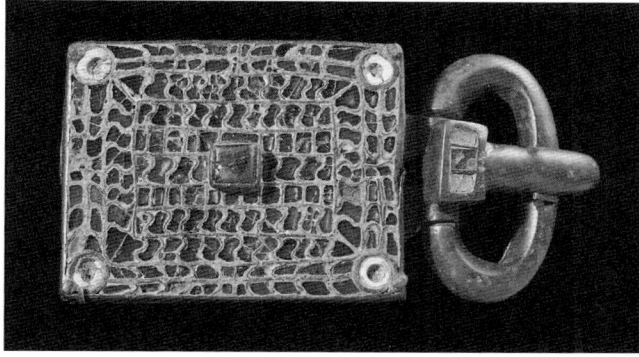

Figure 5.7 Bronze, garnet, and shell belt buckle, Visigothic, sixth century.
Courtesy of a French private collection.

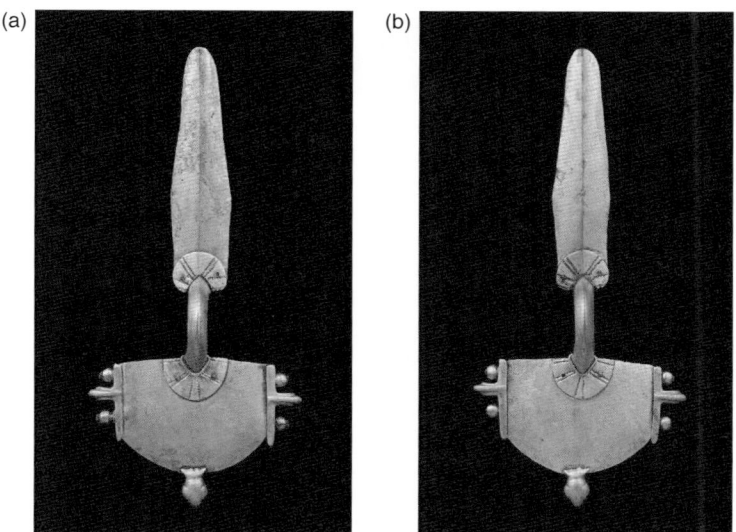

Figure 5.8 (a, b) Gilt silver brooches, Ostrogothic, fifth century.
Courtesy of Ariadne Galleries.

demonstrates that barbarian kings were gaining political supremacy by minting their own coins, first as pseudo-imperial issues, and later in their names.

The central proposition of this book is that the catastrophic events of the fifth century were a consequence of a diminishing 'booty economy', reduced mineral availability, and economic product, leading to a reduction in tax-yields. Also, the greatly reduced availability of precious metals combined to

Figure 5.9 Gilt bronze brooch, Anglo-Saxon, fifth century.
Courtesy of Ariadne Galleries.

impact on the number of soldiers that could be recruited and the military capability of the Roman state. These propositions appear to be plausible as represented by the quantitative data presented. As mentioned previously, a difficulty with this theory is that these data are not complete enough to plot an economic decline with any precision across the temporal and spatial entity that was the western empire.[186] It should remain as a proposal but it is nonetheless suggestive.

How appropriate is the theory of a Malthusian economy to the western empire?

As a base point, it is instructive to return briefly to economic theory, and here the concept of the Malthusian equilibrium is relevant. To recapitulate, Thomas Malthus suggested that the size of the population was limited by the resources available to feed it, with incomes and population continuing in line with productivity growth until it became interrupted by plague and political events when the so-called pull of the Malthusian Trap began to be felt.[187] In the case of the western empire, the picture that emerges from material data makes it clear that large parts of North Africa continued to prosper under Vandal rule; while Italy, Gaul, and the Iberian peninsula were greatly affected

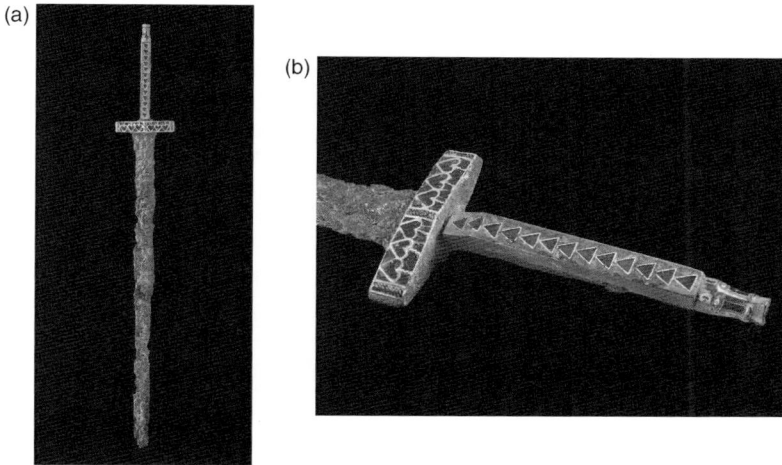

Figure 5.10 (a, b) Iron, gold, and garnet sword, Merovingian, sixth century.
Courtesy of Ariadne Galleries.

by the barbarian incursions and settlements, in conjunction with internecine troubles. These collective problems appear compatible with the mechanisms inherent in a Malthusian economy. The crux of this are the data comparisons between the fourth and fifth centuries that point to a shrinkage in GDP per capita as suggested by demographic and economic decline. In this sense, the trends in those regions affected by foreign and civil wars appear to accord with a Malthusian model, since the interconnected western empire could not sustain itself, whereas the eastern empire could. In the era of growth, during the first two centuries, notwithstanding the plague, technological improvements were most likely also relevant.[188] However, in the period of crisis, the latter would have perhaps been immaterial to the eventual fate of Rome in the face of political turmoil and demographic and economic shrinkage.

A crucial factor is not just demographic and economic decline due to a reduction in agricultural productivity, but also that the most important gold and silver mines either went out of production or were wrested from the Roman authorities, and this is borne out by the number of mints that went out of production in the fourth and fifth centuries. In short, there was a drastic reduction of economic product and precious mineral wealth at more or less the same time that the barbarians were taking control of Gaul, the Iberian peninsula, and Africa. Archaeological, epigraphic, historical, and numismatic sources are helpful in attempting to plot the fall of Rome, but to round this notion out more fully an attempt should be made to address this from a systematic point of view. This brings us back to the basic administrative structure of the Roman empire.

The 'beehive' revisited

It is appropriate to return once more to the basic mechanics of the Roman economy in the western empire: the town–country interrelationship. It has been established that the nub of this was the generation of agricultural product (arable and pastoral) in the countryside of each *civitas*, principally meat, poultry, and cereals, but also wine (where viticulture was possible) and olive oil (in the Mediterranean region). Produce was sold by tenant farmers (*coloni*) in the urban market-place, and from those cash proceeds a proportion of this income would have been paid in taxes. A large proportion of tax was also paid to the state by landowners, and other forms of taxation were based on the land.[189] Collective taxation in *civitates* was also levied to pay the army. Crucially, it has been established, and reiterated, that the cost of the army accounted for around 60–70 per cent of the overall state budget.[190] This being key to maintain the Roman militia at requisite levels, the whole system essentially revolved around the productivity of *civitates* and mineral extraction; booty – precious metals and free labour – was now a thing of the past.

The administrative disintegration of the western Roman empire

The socio-economic and physical changes in the rural and urban sphere, may, it is contended, be related to the administrative collapse of *civitates* as elite militarization occurred and barbarian kingdoms emerged in Gaul during the fifth century. Administratively, a similar process may be observed in North Africa as Vandal hegemony intensified and became consolidated in the fifth century.

Gaul is the best understood region thanks to the the *Notitia Galliarum*, which provides a complete list of the seventeen provinces of Gaul, with their respective metropolitan cities (in most cases) and other *civitates* within each province, along with seven *castra* and a *portus* (river port settlement).[191] The list is further subdivided into two areas corresponding with the Gallic dioceses of Galliae and Quinque Provinciae.[192] Generally speaking, these split Gaul into northern and southern parts with ten and seventeen provinces respectively. This is especially useful since it dates to the crucial period at the end of the fourth century or the beginning of the early fifth. Jill Harries has argued that the document is secular in origin and was adapted for ecclesiastical purposes, most likely in the sixth century. It is therefore accurate for the purposes of the period in question, helping to paint a picture of the structural unravelling of a large region of the western empire. *Castra* are relatively few in number, and originally had military connotations. Their name derives from 'fortified post or settlement' but by the fifth century a *castrum* was no more than a lesser *civitas*, a town lacking independent civic status, and subject to the *civitas* in its territory.[193] We should consider that *castra* would have played a minor role in the economic system of the western empire, and are counted as economic units.

For practical reasons, the ethnic title of each *civitas* is given first, then the ancient name of its principal city, followed by the number of *civitates* and *castra* (and the one *portus*). The provincial sequence runs as follows. Galliae: I. Lugdunensis Prima; II. Lugdunensis Secunda; III. Lugdunensis Tertia; IV. Lugdunensis Senonia; V. Belgica Prima; VI. Belgica Secunda; VII. Germania Prima; VIII. Germania Secunda; IX. Maxima Sequanorum; X. Alpium Graiarum et Poeninarum. Quinque Provinciae: XI. Viennensis; XII. Aquitanica Prima; XIII. Aquitanica Secunda; XIV. Novempopulana; XV. Narbonensis Prima; XVI. Narbonensis Secunda; XVII. Alpium Maritimarum.

From a structural point of view this list is extremely important, since it enables us to conceptualize how the formal administrative territories of Gaul – the 'cells of the imperial beehive' or the economic 'town-hinterland units' – gradually ceased to function to be of benefit to the Roman state. The root of this is the agreement between Constantius and Theoderic I in 418, which settled the Visigoths between Tolosa and Burdigala in the Garonne valley. The total number of *civitates*, *castra*, and *porta* listed in the *Notitia Galliarum* is 113, totalling 61 urban settlements in the northern diocese and 60 in the southern diocese. It is not possible to calculate the exact extent of the Visigothic settlement in the Garonne.[194] However, cross-referencing what is widely regarded as the approximate area of their new territory with the map of *civitates* permits some logical calculations. This encompassed a large area in the Bordeaux region from the Garonne estuary, down the Garonne valley in a south-easterly direction, to the south of Toulouse as far as the Pyrenees. The *civitates* that were probably relinquished in the process are listed in Table 5.1.

As suggested above, it is not possible to calculate the relative productivity of each *civitas*, but the region was certainly a prime cereal- and wine-producing area. The most important factor is the collective loss of eight *civitates*, which is a little over 13 per cent of their total number in the southern diocese. It is impossible to equate this to an exact loss in tax

Table 5.1 *Civitates* ceded to the Visigoths after the settlement of 418

Province	Civitas	City
Aquitanica Secunda	Metropolis civitas Burdigalensium	Burdigala
	Aginnensium	Aginnum
Novempopulana	Ausciorum	Elimberrum
	Vasatica	Cossio
	Lactoratium	Lactora
	Consorannorum	Austria
	Boatium	La Teste de Buch
Narbonensis Prima	Tolosatium	Tolosa

revenue, but it would have been considerable. In the period after the settlement of 418, the Visigoths wrested large swathes of southern Gaul from the imperial government through the course of the remaining century, principally in Aquitainica in the west, Narbonensis in the east, and what remained of the Alpium Maritimarum Provinces in the south-east. The *civitates* lost in this process are listed in Table 5.2.

Through the course of the fifth century, therefore, the Visigoths had wrested an additional 34 *civitates* and a *castrum* from imperial control, which amounted to a little over 58 per cent of the city-states of the southern diocese.

Table 5.2 *Civitates* wrested by the Visigoths after the settlement of 418

Province	Civitas	City
Viennensis	Cabellicorum	Cabellio
	Avennicorum	Avennio
	Arelatensium	Arelate
	Massiliensium	Massilia
Aquitanica Prima	Metropolis civitas Biturigum	Avaricum
	Arvernorum	Augustonemetum
	Rutenorum	Segodunum
	Albigensium	Albiga
	Cadurcorum	Divona
	Lemovicum	Augustoritum
	Gabalum	Anderitum
	Vellavorum	Ruessio
Aquitanica Secunda	Ecolisnensium	Ecolisina
	Santonum	Mediolanum
	Pictavorum	Limonum
	Petrocoriorum	Vesunna
Narbonensis Prima	Metropolis civitas Narbonensium	Narbo
	Beterrensium	Baeterrae
	Nemausensium	Nemausus
	Lutevensium	Luteva
	Castrum Ucetiense	Ucetia
Narbonensis Secunda	Metropolis civitas Aquensium	Aquae Sextiae
	Aptensium	Apta Iulia
	Foroiuliensium	Forum Iulii
	Antipolitana	Antipolis
Novempopulana	Metropolis civitas Elusatium	Elusa
	Aquensium	Aquae
	Convenarum	Lugdunum
	Benarnensium	Beneharnum
	Aturensium	Aturum
	Turba	Turba and Begorra
	Elloronensium	Iloro
Alpium Maritimarum	Saliniensium	Salinae
	Cemenelensium	Cemenelum
	Vintiensium	Vintium

As for the Alans, the two known settlements of circa 440 in and around Valentia and approximately 442 in the area of Cenabum may be equated with the loss of at least those two *civitates* listed in Table 5.3 and these were absorbed soon afterwards by the Burgundians, and later in the fifth century by the Franks. The full extent of additional territories ceded to them by the imperial authorities is not exactly known,[195] but they are thought to have been in Armorica, as evidenced by modern place-names, such as Allainville, Yvelines, Alainville-en-Beauce, Les Allains, and a few other cities, but subsequently these were also to fall under Frankish control.[196]

A similar picture emerges further east with the settlement of the Burgundians after 443, where they established a small state in the Sapaudia. Initially this included an area that stretched from the south-west of modern Geneva to the north-east of Zurich, and in the 460s the Burgundian domain expanded to include the *civitates* and *castra* listed in Table 5.4.

As in the case of the Visigothic settlement of 418, it is not possible to gauge the exact geographical extent of the Burgundian settlement and the area subsequently wrested by force, but some rational calculations can be made from relevant maps. In the southern diocese of Gaul as many as eighteen *civitates* may have been absorbed, and this amounted to a little more than 41 per cent of the total.

In northern Gaul, a not too dissimilar picture emerges with the Frankish settlement and expansion. Initially, in the fifth century, as mentioned above, their powerbase was centred from the 430s around parts of Belgium and the Netherlands (Salians), then in the 450s, Germany (Ripurians). Their settlements incorporated those *civitates* listed in Table 5.5.

Thereafter, as described above, the Frankish domain expanded rapidly under the Merovingian kings to encompass the bulk of the northern diocese of Gaul, excluding those areas under the sway of the Burgundians (Table 5.6).

In the later fifth century the number of *civitates* that were wrested from the imperial authorities by the Merovingian Franks is substantial at 49, which represents a little over 80 per cent of the total number of urban settlements in the northern diocese of Gaul, the remaining few being settled in the 430s or seized by the Burgundian expansion from the 440s. These data for Gaul are the most accurate administrative information for the territorial arrangements at the time of the fall of the western empire.

Also instructive are the lists of ecclesiastical bishoprics in the North African provinces, which Jones lists as cities, and other forms of settlement, such as

Table 5.3 Civitates temporarily ceded to the Alans after the settlements of circa 440 and 442

Province	Civitas	City
Viennensis	Valentinorum	Valentia
Lugdunensis Senonia	Aurelianorum	Cenabum

Table 5.4 Civitates and *castra* wrested by the Burgundians after the settlement of 443

Province	Civitas	City
Lugdunensis Prima	Metropolis civitas Lugdunensium	Lugdunum
	Aeduorum	Augustodunum
	Castrum Cabillonense	Cabillonum
	Castrum Matisconense	Matisco
Maxima Sequanorum	Equestrium	Noviodunum
	Helvetiorum	Aventicum
Viennensis	Metropolis civitas Viennensium	Vienna
	Genavensium	Genava
	Gratianopolitana	Cularo – Gratianopolis
	Albensium	Alba
	Deensium	Dea Augusta
	Valentinorum	Valentia
	Tricastinorum	Augusta
	Vasentium	Vasio
	Arausicorum	Arausio
Narbonensis Secunda	Civitas Regensium	Reii Apollinares
	Vappincensium	Vappincum
	Segesteriorum	Segustero
Alpium Maritimarum	Metropolis civitas Ebrodunensium	Ebrodunum
	Diniensium	Dinia
	Rigomagensium	Rigomagus
	Sanitiensium	Sanitium
	Glanatina	Glannativa
Alpium Graiarum et	Ceutronum	Darantasia
Poeninarum	Vallensium	Octodorus

Table 5.5 Civitates ceded to the Franks after the settlement of the 430s

Province	Civitas	City
Belgica Secunda	Camaracensium	Camaracum
	Turnacensium	Turnacum
Germania Secunda	Metropolis civitas	Colonia Claudia
	Agrippinensium	Agrippinensis
	Tungrorum	Atuatuca

castra, *regiones*, and *saltus*.[197] There are a substantial number of bishoprics, and for practical reasons they are listed by quantity in their respective provinces in Table 5.7. These were seized from the imperial authorities by the Vandals in the fifth century, and to a lesser extent by the Berber princes. These are much more dense and numerous than their Gallic counterparts, attesting to the sheer productivity of the broader region, especially in the first two provincial clusters. It logically follows that some of the larger cities had proportionally greater territories, such as Carthage, Cirta, Cuicul, Thamugadi, Thysdrus, etc.

Table 5.6 Civitates, castra, and portus wrested by the Franks in the later fifth century

Province	Civitas	City
Lugdunensis Prima	Lingonum	Andematunnum
Lugdunensis Secunda	Metropolis civitas Rotomagensium	Rotomagus
	Baiocassium	Augustodorum
	Abrincatum	Ingena
	Ebroicorum	Mediolanum
	Saiorum	Séez
	Lexoviorum	Noviomagus
	Constantia	Constantia
Lugdunensis Tertia	Metropolis civitas Turinorum	Caesarodunum
	Cenomannorum	Suindunum
	Redonum	Condate
	Andecavorum	Iuliomagus
	Namnetum	Condivincum
	Coriosolitum	Fanum Martis
	Venetum	Darioritum
	Osismorum	Vorgium
	Diablintum	Noviodunum
Lugdunensis Senonia	Metropolis civitas Senonum	Agedincum
	Carnotum	Autricum
	Autisiodorum	Autessiodurum
	Tricassium	Augustobona
	Aurelianorum	Cenabum
	Parisiorum	Lutetia
	Melduorum	Iatinum
Belgica Prima	Metropolis civitas Treverorum	Augusta
	Mediomatricum	Divodurum
	Leucorum	Tullum
	Verodunensium	Virodunum
Belgica Secunda	Metropolis civitas Remorum	Durocortorum
	Suessionum	Augusta
	Catalaunorum	Durocatalaunum
	Veromandorum	Augusta
	Atrabatum	Nemetacum
	Silvanectum	Augustomagus
	Bellovacorum	Caesaromagus
	Ambianensium	Samarobriva
	Morinum	Tarvenna
	Bononensium	Bononia
Germania Prima	Metropolis civitas Mogontiacensium	Moguntiacum
	Argentoratensium	Argentorate
	Nemetum	Noviomagus
	Vangionum	Borbetomagus
Maxima Sequanorum	Vesontiensium	Vesontio
	Basiliensium	Basilia
	Castrum Vindonissense	Vindonissa
	Castrum Ebrodunense	Ebrodunum
	Castrum Argentariense	Argentaria
	Castrum Rauracense	Augusta Raurica
	Portus Bucini	Port-sur-Saône

Table 5.7 City territories wrested by the Vandals and Berber princes

Province	Bishoprics by number
Africa, Byzacena, Tripolitania	477
Mauretania Sitifensis, Numidia	725
	(including 1 *castrum*)
Mauretania Caesariensis	218
	(including 5 *castra*)
Mauretania Tingitana	3

Table 5.7 attests to the sheer scale of the economic machine in North Africa, and the archaeological record supports the productivity of cereals, olive oil, and wine on a truly industrial scale. In terms of their tax-yield – arable and pastoral – the loss of over 1,400 cities and their territories (economic units) would have been devastating for the economic fortunes of the western Roman empire. If there was a final nail in Rome's coffin this was surely it.

The beehive metaphor and the fall of Rome

In the present chapter, then, the generally accepted historical picture of events pertaining to the collapse of the western empire have been presented; a broad cross section of archaeological data and epigraphic evidence for barbarian incursions and settlements was outlined; the numismatic record has been examined to give a general impression of how barbarian kings consolidated their power in symbolical terms; and the administrative structure of the empire, and its erosion in Gaul and North Africa was outlined.

This is the appropriate place to contextualize and summarize my central arguments. Perhaps the best place to commence is at ground level, that is, on the land. The focus has been more on the rural sphere than cities *per se* because of the importance of agriculture. In the context of the suggestion that agricultural productivity and the fate of the western empire were linked, it is worth quoting Jones in full:[198]

> The paramount importance of agriculture in the economy of the empire can scarcely be exaggerated. In taxes it provided the vast bulk of the revenue of the state. The most important of the financial ministries, the praetorian prefecture, which supplied all the major needs of the administration, relied entirely on a land tax, which was exclusively assessed on agricultural land, farm stock and the rural population. The much less important department of the *sacrae largitiones* drew much of its revenue from levies, such as the *vestis*, assessed on the same basis, and upon special taxes, such as the *aurum oblaticium* and *coronarium*, paid by the main landowning classes, senators and *decurions*. The third financial

department, the *res privata*, was fed by the rents of imperial lands. The only taxes not levied on agriculture were the customs and tolls (*vectigalia*), the sales tax (*siliquaticum*) . . . the *collatio lustralis* [levied on trade and industry].

However, the administrative role of the city had gained further impetus from the fourth century, placed under increasing pressure of taxation, but the authority of the *decurions* diminished with the increasing centralization of the state, a process that had begun in the third century. A large proportion of civic revenue was directly confiscated for the benefit of the imperial service and land tax increased to fund the ever-increasing size of the army in the third and fourth centuries.[199] Essentially, the ruling elites of late antiquity in the urban realm shifted from *decurions* in the pagan sphere to ecclesiastical officials, notably the bishop, clergy, and wealthy landowners.[200] The patronage of bishops is attested in inscriptions in this era and the epigraphic record does not record any *decurions*.

In its totality, taxation included: direct taxes, paid in cash and kind on privately owned land; direct capitation taxes, mainly poll tax; rents on different types of public land, another form of direct revenue; indirect taxes, mainly customs duties, inheritance tax, those on sales and manumissions; military requisitions in cash and kind; and public service revenues.[201]

Customs duties defy a loss of agricultural product to some degree, but all revenue streams, however, depended on the political health of the state, and with the disintegration of the agricultural infrastructure in the fifth century, and long-distance trade, the collection of customs dues would have broken down across the western empire. It may therefore be envisaged that the bountiful revenues attested would no longer have flowed into the imperial treasuries of the empire (the *aerarium* and *fiscus*), and the same would have applied across the full spectrum of direct and indirect taxation, notably a diminishing poll tax revenue as the population shrank, and a greatly reduced revenue from agricultural produce sold in the market-place, an erosion of tenants' ability to pay their rents, and the inability of landholders to pay theirs to the state, the latter having a knock-on effect in the urban sphere to the detriment of civic tax. This may provide an explanation, at least in part, why *decurions* were unable to sustain their euergetism.[202]

Of course, tax levied by requisition in money and in kind should be considered, but the question is surely, what would have been left to draw on, given the serious territorial losses attested above? Those measures implemented by Diocletian, notably the regularization of exactions for the army, and the refined methods of assessing the taxability of land and people, by the units of *iuga* and *capita*, would have broken down.

This inevitably brings us back to the size and burden of the army and the calculations of Lee, Heather, Duncan-Jones, MacMullen, and Potter in this context.[203] These are key to the arguments presented and it is pertinent to revisit them briefly. Lee suggested that the size of the army increased in the fourth century, possibly to around 500,000, but this was their number on paper rather than physical deployment[204] and, of course, this applied to the western and eastern empires: it is probably safer to say that the actual number deployed was somewhere between 400,000 and this figure. Basing his calculations on the *Notitia Dignitatum*, Heather estimated that the western army had been substantially destroyed in the early fifth century, some 76 of 160 regiments (47.5 per cent).[205]

This was still, in theory, an effective fighting force, but as we have seen, this portion of the empire was overwhelmed on every quarter by Alans, Alamanni, Burgundians, Huns, Sueves, Vandals, Visigoths, and other barbarian tribes. The fact that the army had nearly halved, and the numbers were not replenished, suggests that the state lacked the financial resources to rebuild in this crucial period, and it is probably the case that *foederati* could not be afforded. This is borne out by the tax relief granted to the provinces of Italy at this time and also by the systematic loss of agricultural productivity in Gaul and the Iberian peninsula. The latter is attested by the apparent reduction of agricultural sites across the broader region, coupled with those that were lost as a result of barbarian settlements. In those cases where the archaeology indicates a continuity of productivity, notably in North Africa, this was used for the economic benefit of the new world order, in this case the Vandal kingdom.

To return to the massive military expenditure demanded by maintaining a vast army and navy, it is appropriate to reemphasize that around 60 to 70 per cent of state expenditure was consumed to maintain an effective militia. This takes into account a pyramidal scale of pay for both *auxilia* and legionaries, discharge payments (*praemia*), bonuses (*donativa*), the cost of equipment, and other logistical costs.[206] In previous chapters the point was made that the Roman army was always overstretched, and even in the era of the so-called *Pax Romana* – widely regarded as Rome's golden era – it came close to defeat on several occasions. The military commitment was both imperative and perilous. Taking military spending to a logical conclusion, the state could only spend what it could afford, so that by the first decades of the fifth century it is realistic to suggest that the threshold of military spending was at an all-time low – way under its critical 60 to 70 per cent threshold. That the west was struggling with its military capability is clear from its Vandal campaigns for which it enlisted substantial support from the eastern empire.

It is certainly the case that grain requisitions were an important factor in the late Roman period and that soldiers received food in kind as part of their pay. However, the high estimations of this proportion of salaries has been exaggerated and a closer scrutiny of textual evidence indicates that the army continued to be a huge strain on the budget of the state even in the sixth century, largely an era of great prosperity in the eastern Roman empire.

Also, consideration has been given to the division of economic product, which is as relevant and serious as its loss. In the third century, the Roman empire split into three parts, the Gallic empire, central empire, and eastern empire, and this represented a three-fold split in productivity and tax revenue, the situation being resolved by Aurelian, who unified the empire once more. However, in the early fifth century, there were nine usurpers in the western empire alone, often with barbarian support, and this factor – perhaps above all – allowed the invaders a crucial opportunity to combat several smaller armies, each usurper lacking sufficient product and mineral wealth to raise a large enough army to counter the peril afoot, and thereby ceding more territory in Gaul and the Iberian peninsula.

In tandem with a loss of economic product was the crippling reduction of mineral resources. As outlined above, gold and silver production was lost in Wales when Britain was relinquished in the early fifth century, while production elsewhere of both metals diminished and ceased at mines in the Balkan provinces, Gaul, and the Iberian peninsula. This impacted on the mints in those regions and the ability of the western empire to pay its militia in coinage was effectively hamstrung.

It should also be borne in mind that the fifth century was devoid of Roman booty campaigns by contrast with the era of the Principate and the earlier part of the so-called Dominate. This is clear from the cessation of great public building programmes. The imperial fora and thermae, and other monuments that were bankrolled by the spoils of war, were but a distant memory, as were the massive cash surpluses that poured into the imperial coffers of victorious emperors.

The net result was a drastically reduced army and a concomitant military capability pitted against a range of barbarian armies with a sufficient or more than sufficient number of men at arms in several theatres of conflict. Clearly, in this sense, the issue is more to do with a reduced efficiency for numeric reasons rather than a military failure based on individual discipline, prowess, or disloyalty of those of barbarian origin serving under the Roman state.

Most instructive are the archaeological data for agricultural sites across the western empire. While it is true to say this is only evidence by proxy, it is nonetheless highly suggestive of a decline after a peak in the first two centuries of the Principate, progressively moving towards economic unsustainability in an undesirable harmony with demographic decline. This 'fits', in part with a Malthusian economy, but this model is not appropriate for the loss of the entire western empire, rather only in those areas afflicted in Europe and North Africa.

Archaeological data indicate that Roman villas, the main loci of elite dominance in the countryside, progressively disappeared from rural landscapes of the western empire, and its former territories in the fourth, fifth, and sixth centuries. This appears to correspond with political pressures as well as the increasing militarization of aristocrats. In the urban sphere, civic spaces transformed in response to the same threats: defensive walls were installed, and churches increasingly dominated city landscapes under imperial patronage, and also that of bishops and other ecclesiastics.

By contrast, in the eastern empire, notwithstanding the Hunnic impact of the fifth century, there is a range of archaeological and epigraphic data that points to demographic and economic growth, especially in the later part of that period (the reign of Anastasius), gathering pace in the early half of the sixth century (the age of Justinian).[207] For instance, the French archaeologist Claudine Dauphin has demonstrated that, between the fourth and mid-sixth centuries, Palestine witnessed a dramatic demographic and economic expansion evidenced by the density of settlement in specific geographical zones.[208] Rural and urban settlement patterns based on the archaeological data culled by the Archaeological Survey of Israel indicate that the population of Palestine increased markedly from the Roman to the Byzantine period.[209] Also the quantitative approach applied to building inscriptions in Arabia, Palestine, and southern Phoenicia by Di Segni showed a similar economic pattern. One of the most important studies conducted in the Levant was conducted by the French archaeologist Georges Tchalenko. His work entailed an extensive programme of survey of a number of well-preserved villages in the hinterland of Antioch in northern Syria (today, the ancient city is located just over the border in southern Turkey). These settlements were prosperous, consisting of a number of public buildings and houses constructed from local limestone. The villages were also a thriving olive oil producer, as attested by the great many presses recorded there. This area flourished from the late third century through to the Muslim conquest of the seventh century.[210]

It is often claimed that the eastern Roman empire continued until the fall of Constantinople in 1453.[211] Strictly speaking, this is not the case, since from 636–641, the Muslim conquest resulted in the loss of the eastern provinces, and later those in North Africa, which had been reconquered by Justinian. Territorially, therefore, the empire was a pale shadow of its former self, and its economic fortunes tended to decline in the so-called Byzantine Dark Ages, wax in the middle Byzantine period, and wane in the late Byzantine period until the Ottoman conquest.[212]

Also instructive is the numismatic record, because it provides a useful 'index' of how the emerging kingdoms spread their powerbases in the former provincial territories of the western empire in the fifth century, and later in the Roman provinces of Italy. Initially, the pattern is one of minting pseudo-imperial issues in the name of contemporary emperors. Thereafter, they are struck with issues of the ruling kings. In many studies of the period, archaeologists and historians have tended not to integrate numismatic studies, and endless debates pertaining to the ethnicity of various tribes has raged on based on the evidence, or lack thereof, that links burials and material culture with specific tribes. However, as stated above, ethnicity is largely irrelevant for the purposes of my arguments, and the overarching hegemony of individual kingdoms as they emerged is more important than assigning particular ethnic 'micro' identities, the macro picture being of particular relevance here. Coins, more than any other media, give the relative precision as to when individual tribes were seizing power in particular regions and developing their powerbases.

Conclusion

The basic arguments have been presented through the lens of historical, but especially archaeological, epigraphic, and numismatic, sources. Taking the calculations of several specialists into account, the army was the largest component of state expenditure and consumed around three-quarters of the budget. The Roman empire was therefore dependent on a significant proportion of booty to fund it, and this is manifest in building inscriptions in the urban sphere. Epigraphic and material evidence points to a general correspondence between reigns bankrolled by booty and building in Rome, Italy, and the western provinces.

Generation of agricultural product was a second essential component, and an overarching system may be envisaged, in which tenant farmers sold their surplus produce in urban market-places, paying a proportion of tax from the proceeds and a portion to their landlords in rent. The latter, in the western empire, often resided in rural villas, the aristocratic loci of their estates, and they were usually *decurions*, city officials, and later ecclesiastical officials, who sponsored civic building projects from their own purse and also paid a proportion of the money accrued from tenants in tax. Extraction of precious metals, especially gold, was crucial to the economy, especially in the late Roman period, in the sense that *solidi* became the universal currency and was an important element of military pay. Also, the dependence on grain requisitions as a part of soldiers' pay, appears to be exaggerated, since successive governments struggled to pay the militia in hard cash.

The Roman economy was integrated intra-regionally and inter-regionally through short-, medium-, and long-distance trade, and it is possible to discern shifting patterns of production, especially with the oil *annona*, moving from Baetica to Africa Proconsularis. Economic theory is persuasive in viewing this as a fully-fledged market economy. This peaked in the first two centuries AD, with a relative decline in the third as a consequence of the turbulent political situation and plague, and flourished once again in the fourth century, but with a relative decline, plummeting in the fifth, due to shrinking economic product as a consequence of barbarian settlements and incursions, internecine warfare, the loss of the 'booty economy', and the steady decline of available precious metal resources.

It seems clear that taxation may be regarded as considerably higher and manifold than a number of traditional studies have regarded it. As successive barbarian tribes seized Roman territories in the western empire, it is possible to plot an administrative decline across many former provinces by equating the territorial extent of *civitates* in Gaul with territories wrested by the invaders, and also in North Africa with bishoprics. This is supported by the disappearance of villas, diminished cities, and archaeological evidence for hostile takeover at military sites, and at cemeteries in the military and urban sphere. The available documentation of the administrative structure is especially germane for the purposes of this study. These units of the 'imperial beehive', comprising cities and their territories, were the economic units – the very lifeblood – of the imperial system of taxation. Their basic concept of generating a rural-based product that fed the imperial infrastructure is crucial to understanding how the western empire became unsustainable. One by one, in some cases more rapidly than others, the individual cells of the 'honeycomb' ceased to function; product diminished, as did tax revenue and its complex infrastructure, and the size of the military apparatus; and the 'imperial beehive', along with its last 'bee' – Romulus Augustulus – ceased to be of relevance; and Rome fell, so ending the most momentous and hotly debated episodes of western civilization, and one that continues to echo down the centuries and haunt us into the modern era.

Notes

1 Gibbon on the Gothic sack of Rome in 410, III.31.290.
2 They are perhaps originally the Xiongnu, Kim, 2013, 35–39.
3 Written sources are numerous for Roman and Persian histories in the late fourth and fifth centuries, Greatrex and Lieu, 2002, 1–19, 20–30, 31–52.
4 *ZNH*, V.1–5.
5 *ZNH*, V.34.5.
6 Orientius of Auch, *Commonitorum* (lines 179–184). In *Poeti Christianae Minores*. Edited by R. Ellis. 1888. *Corpus Scriptorum Ecclesiasticorum Latinorum*, Vol. XVI. Vienna: U. Hoeplius. Translated here by Ward-Perkins 2005, 22–23.
7 Lactantius, *Divine Institutes* (VII.25.6–8). 2003. Translated by A. Bowen and P. Garnsey. Liverpool: Liverpool University Press.
8 Jerome, *Select Letters of St. Jerome* (CXXVII). 1933. Translated by F.A. Wright. LCL 262. For a biography, vii–xvi.
9 Augustine. *City of God*. Books 1–3. 1957. Translated by G.E. McCracken. LCL 411. For a biography, vii–lxxxii.
10 It seems that Caesar did not in fact say this, rather: 'Gaul is a whole divided into three parts, one of which is inhabited by the Belgae, another by the Aquitani, and a third by a people called in their own tongue Celtae, in the Latin Galli.' '*Galia est pacata*' ('Gaul is subdued'). Caesar, *The Gallic War* (I.1, II.2). 1917. Translated by H.J. Edwards. LCL 72. For a critique, x–xviii.
11 *Narratio de imperatoribus domus Valentinae et Theodosianae*. In *Chronica Minora* (IV, V, VI, VII). 1894 (1961). Edited by T. Mommsen, Monumenta Germaniae Historica, Auctores Antiquissimi, IX. Berlin: APVD Weidmannos. Translation after Ward-Perkins 2005, 44. This anonymous source comprised a series of short biographies from the reign of Valentinian I (364) to the death of Theodosius II (450).
12 Ward-Perkins, 2005, 42–43; *Theodosian Code*, VII.13.16–17.
13 Heather, 2005, 246; *Theodosian Code*, XI.28.7, 12.
14 Strabo, *Geography*, IV.5.2.
15 Burnham, Burnham, and Annels, 2004, 1.
16 Lewis and Jones, 1969, 244–272.
17 Boon, 1971, 453–503.

18 *Theodosian Code*, X.19.7, X.19.12.
19 Hirt, 2010, 51–81.
20 Edmondson, 1989, 92.
21 Wilson, 2012, 134.
22 *PNH*, XXXIII.21.68–69.
23 *PNH*, XXXIII.21.78.
24 McLaughlin, 2014, 13.
25 In the British Museum, the Hermopolis (R1904, 0530.1) and Sirmium bars (R1894, 1207.1), in the Cabinet des Médailles, Bibliothèque nationale de France, the Krazsna bars (Inv. BnF 56.18). For the use of currency bars, Lapatin, 2014, 128–129, Figure 75.
26 Jones, 1964, Map III.
27 *Notitia Dignitatum*. 2014. Roma: Istituto della Enciclopedia Italiana.
28 Heather, 2005, 247.
29 Herz, 2007, 314–315.
30 Howgego, 2014, 311.
31 Kehne, 2007, 330.
32 Elton, 1996, 120–125.
33 For pay, Jones, 1964, II, 623–649.
34 MacMullen, 1984, 571–580; Duncan-Jones, 1994, 45–46.
35 Potter, 2015, 32.
36 Treadgold, 1995, 166–167, 195–197; Shaw, 1999, 141.
37 *Peri Strategias* II.18–21. 1985. Translated by G.T. Dennis. *Three Byzantine Military Treatises. Corpus Fontium Historiae Byzantinae*, 25, Dumbarton Oaks Texts 9. Washington DC: Harvard University Press: 86–89.
38 Simpson and Speake, 2015, 9.
39 Jones, 1964, 712–714; Hopkins, 1980, 101–125.
40 Bowman, 2017, 5–6.
41 Ward-Perkins, 2005, 41.
42 Esmonde Cleary, 2013, 352–394.
43 Hydatius (Olympiad 302.6). *The Chronicle of Hydatius and the Consularia Constantinopolitana: two contemporary accounts of the final years of the Roman empire*. 1993. Translated by R. Burgess. Oxford: Oxford Clarendon Press.
44 Goffart, 1980; 1981, 275–306; 1989, 87–107. Prosper. 'Prosperi Tironis epitoma chronicon ed. primum a. CCCCXXXIII, continuata ad a. CCCLV'. In *Chronica minora saec. IV, V, VI, VII*, Vol. 1, *MGH Scriptores. Auctores Antiquissimi 9*. 1892. Edited by T. Mommsen, 469, entry 1271. Berlin: Weidmann.
45 Ward-Perkins, 2005, 13–15.
46 Prosper, entry 1290; *CH*, Olympiad 302.6, Olympiad 303.12.
47 Wolfram, 1988, 175–181. For the peace agreement of 439, Sidonius Apollinaris (I.VII.490–504; II.V.12.2). Poems. Letters, 1–2. 1936. Translated by W.B. Anderson. LCL 296.
48 *CH*, Olympiad 302.7.
49 Esmonde Cleary, 2013, 357–358.
50 Barnish, 1986, 170–195; Durliat, 1997; Goffart, 1980, Chapter 4; 2006, Chapter 7; Liebeschuetz, 1997; Halsall, 2007, 422–447.
51 Esmonde Cleary, 2013, 359–364.
52 Kazanski, 1991, 11–25, 89–95; Kazanski and Legoux, 1988, 7–53.
53 Grierson and Blackburn, 1986, 44–46.
54 *Chronica Gallica a*. CCCCLII. Entries 124, 127, 128, p. 660. See also Wood, 1997, 534. Translation after Ward-Perkins 2005, 55.
55 Esmonde Cleary, 2013, 381.
56 *PL*, X.5.1.

57 *CG*, entries 124, 127, 128.
58 Lasko, 1971, 13–24.
59 *PL*, X.10.3–6, XI.7.2.
60 Esmonde Cleary, 2013, 376.
61 Lasko, 1971, 13–24.
62 James, 1988, 51–58.
63 Esmonde Cleary, 2013, 376–386.
64 Wood, 2001, 502–503.
65 *CH*, CCCVI Olympi XII, 19 (p. 97).
66 *CH*, *Chronicle*, Olympiad 307.25 (p. 99).
67 *CG*, entry, 117.
68 Salvianus, *De gubernatione dei, Epistulae, Ad ecclesiam* (V.22, 24–26). Edited by C. Halm. *MGH Scriptores. Auctores Antiquissimi* 1.1 1877. Berlin: Weidmann.
69 Wood, 2001, 503.
70 Wolfram, 1997, 162–167.
71 Jacobsen, 2012, 1–5.
72 Esmonde Cleary, 2013, 364–376.
73 Grierson and Blackburn, 1986, 77–80.
74 Wolfram, 1997, 162–167.
75 Possidius, *Vita Augustini* (XXVIII–XXXI). 2006. Translated by W. Geerlings. Paderborn: Schöningh. For a biography of Possidius, 7–23. Victor of Vita (I.3–7), *History of the Vandal Persecution*. 1992. Translated by J. Moorhead. Liverpool: Liverpool University Press. For a biography, xi–xx.
76 Wolfram, 1997, 165–166. For the treaty of 435, Courtois, 1955, 155–171; Martindale, 1980, 166.
77 For the treaty of 442, Procopius, *Wars* (III.4.13–4.15). A foremost study of Procopius and the variability of his texts is presented by Cameron, 1985, 3–18. The full series, translated by Dewing is *History of the Wars*. Books 1–2 (Persian War). 1914. LCL 48. Books 3–4 (Vandalic War). 1916. LCL 81. Books 5–6.15, 6.16–7.35, 7.36–8 (Gothic War). 1916, 1924, 1928. LCL 107, 173, 217. *The Anecdota or Secret History*. 1935. LCL 290. *On Buildings*. 1940. LCL 343.
78 *Novels of the Emperor Theodosius II* (XXXIV: July 451). *The Theodosian Code and Novels, and the Sirmondian Constitutions*. 1952. Translated by C. Pharr. Princeton: Princeton University Press.
79 Merrills and Miles, 2014, 63–64.
80 J. Given. *The Fragmentary History of Priscus: Attila, the Huns and the Roman Empire, AD 430–476*. 2014. Merchantville, NJ: Evolution Publishing. For a biography of Priscus, xi–xxxvii. For the translation, *The Fragmentary Classicising Historians of the Later Roman Empire: Eunapius, Olympiodorus, Priscus, and Malchus*, Vol. 2. 1982. Translated by R.C. Blockley. Liverpool: Liverpool University Press.
81 Priscus, Fragments 2, 6, 9.1–4.
82 *Marcellinus Comes* (447.2). *The Chronicle of Marcellinus*. 1995. Translated by B. Croke. Sydney: Australian Association for Byzantine Studies. For a biography, xix–xxvii.
83 Priscus, Fragments 21.1–21.2, 22.1–22.3, 23.1–23.3, 24.1–24.2, 25. Thompson, 1999, 137–174.
84 Nagy, 2010, 137–175.
85 Heather, 2005, 331.
86 Vagi, II, 1999, 143–146.
87 Howgego, 2014, 311.
88 Vagi, II, 1999, 159.
89 Shaw, 1999, 135.
90 *AMH*, I.XV.12.3, 355–357.

91 *Theodosian Code*, VII.13.4–5, 367.
92 Ferrill, 1986, 164–169.
93 Vegetius, *Epitoma rei militaris* (I.3). 2004. Translated by M.D. Reeve. Oxford: Oxford University Press.
94 Watson, 1985, 26.
95 Jordanes, *The Getica* (XXXIX, 204). *The Gothic History of Jordanes*. 1915. Translated by C.C. Mierow. Cambridge: Speculum Historiale. For a biography of Jordanes, 1–6.
96 Blöndal, 1978.
97 Goldsworthy, 2009, 409.
98 Goldsworthy, 2003, 214.
99 *CH*, p. 105.
100 Prosper, entry 1375.
101 *Wars*, III.5.1–4. For the Vandal sack of Rome in 455.
102 Victor of Vita, I.24 for sack of Rome; the capture of Eudocia and her daughters, Evagrius Scholasticus, *Ecclesiastical History* (II.7). 2000. Translated by M. Whitby. Liverpool: Liverpool University Press.
103 Sidonius, *Poems*, II, *Panegyric on Anthemius*. Book 1. 1936. Translated by W.B. Anderson. LCL 296. For a biography, ix–lxvii.
104 Candidus, Fragment 2. (193). C.D. Gordon. 1960. *The Age of Attila: fifth-century Byzantium and the barbarians*. Ann Arbor: The University of Michigan Press. Fragment 2 in Suda X, 245 (χειρίζω). In Candidus, R.C. Blockley. 1982. *The Classicising Historians of the Later Roman Empire: Eunapius, Olympiodorus, Priscus, and Malchus*, Vol. 2, 464–473. Liverpool: Liverpool University Press.
105 Procopius, *Wars*, III.6.16–24. Heather, 2005, 399–406.
106 Candidus, Fragment 1, Gordon, 141–143, derives from *Corpus Scriptorum Historiae Byzantinae* (472–477). 1829. Translated by B.G. Niebuhr. Bonn: ED Weseri; *Fragmenta Historicum Graecorum*, Vol. IV (135–137). 1868. Translated by C. Müller. Paris: Firmin Didot. Jacobsen, 2012, 157–161.
107 Bowman and Wilson, 2011, 1–4; Witcher, 2011, 36–75; Mattingly, 2011, 76–96; Attema and de Haas, 2011, 97–140; Morley, 2011, 143–160; Wilson, 2011, 161–195; Marzano, 2011, 196–228; Hanson, 2011, 229–275; Keay and Earl, 2011, 276–316; Bowman, 2011, 317–358.
108 Temin, 2013.
109 Jacobsen, 2012, 298.
110 De Vos, 2013, 143–218.
111 Jacobsen, 2012, 286–287.
112 Grierson and Blackburn, 1986, 17–23, 418–422.
113 Grierson and Blackburn, 1986, 74–75.
114 Lasko, 1971, 25–32.
115 Hamerow, 2002, 31–35; Esmonde Cleary, 2013, 279.
116 Lewit, 1991, 195–219.
117 Ouzoulias, Pellecuer, Raynaud, van Ossel, and Garmy, 2001. These data are also presented by Esmonde Cleary, 2013, 271–282.
118 Gandini, 2008; Esmonde Cleary, 2013, 282–286.
119 Grierson and Blackburn, 1986, 111–122, 463–495.
120 Heather, 1996, 202–208.
121 Raynaud, 1996, 189–212; Fiches, 2002; Van der Leeuw, Favory, and Fiches, 2003; Esmonde Cleary, 2013, 286–290.
122 Marzano, 2013b, 113.
123 Petit, 1989, 53–79.
124 Carr, 1997, 421–433.
125 Lewit, 1991.

126 Gurt i Esparraguera and Palet Martínez, 2001, 303–329.
127 Carreté i Nadal, Keay, and Millett 1995.
128 Ponsich, 1974–1991.
129 Carr, 2002, Chapters 2–4.
130 Marzano, 2013b, 121.
131 Lewit, 1991.
132 Grierson and Blackburn, 1986, 46–49, 436–441.
133 *Marcellinus Comes*, 487, 489; Heather, 1996, 216–221.
134 Bovini, 1978, 26–38, pl. 25.
135 Marzano, 2013a, 89–91.
136 Attema and de Haas, 2011, 97–140; Figures 5.3 and 5.4.
137 Attema and de Haas, 2011, Table 5.2, Figure 5.7.
138 Potter, 1976, 207–219; 1978, 99–116; 1979; 1980, 73–81; Dyson, 1981.
139 Ward-Perkins, 2001, 354–355.
140 Ward-Perkins, 1981, 179–190.
141 Hodges, Barker, and Wade, 1980; Lloyd and Barker, 1981.
142 Wightman, 1981, 257–287; Greene, 1986, 103–109.
143 Lewit, 1991.
144 Christie, 2016, 146–147.
145 Grierson and Blackburn, 1986, 24–38, 422–435.
146 Parker, 1992; Wilson, 2009, 219–221.
147 Van der Meer and Mohrmann, 1958, 75.
148 HD018446 (410–420), HD018449 (410–420), HD027290 (410–423), HD008808 (412–423), HD009437 (408–423).
149 HD027296 (425–426), HD032819 (441–445), HD032828 (448).
150 HD063643 (425–455).
151 HD032849 (456).
152 HD005658 (431–475).
153 Christie, 2016, 146–147.
154 Wickham, 2005, 466–481.
155 Pollard, 2016, 332.
156 Hansen, 1987, 171–200; Nissen-Jaubert, 1996; Ethelberg, 1988, 119–154; Tornbjerg, IV, 1985, 147–156; Nielsen, 1980, 173–208.
157 Dietz, Seba, and Ben Hassen, 1995–2000.
158 Whittaker, 1994, 243–278.
159 Gillett, 2001, 131–167.
160 Coccia, 1996; Keay, Millett, Paroli, Strutt, 2005, 291–295; Augenti, 2010, 39–43.
161 DeLaine, 2016, 433.
162 Dey, 2011, 111–131.
163 Christie, 2016, 140–143.
164 Esmonde Cleary, 2013, 97–149; Reddé, Brulet, Fellmann, Haalebos, and von Schnurbein, 2006.
165 Merrony, 2013, 33–52.
166 Di Segni, 1999,149–178.
167 For instance the provinces of Phoenicia and Palestine, Merrony, 2013, 101–128.
168 Mathisen, 1993, 98.
169 Trout, 2009, 181–182.
170 *Corpus Inscriptionum Latinarum* XIII 128; Colin, 2008, 55–80.
171 Sivan, 1989, 103–113.
172 Godoy Fernández, 1995, 227–237.
173 Arce, 2002.
174 Fernández-Galiano Dimas, 2001.
175 Lapart and Paillet, 1991, 171–180.

176 Février, 1995, 175–180.
177 Pellecuer, 1996, 277–292.
178 Pirenne, 1939; Brown, 1971; 1978.
179 Ward-Perkins, 2005; Heather, 2005.
180 Brodribb, Hands, and Walker, 2005, 408–416.
181 Gerrard, 2013, 63–69.
182 Pirling, 1986; Pirling, Siepen, Galsterer, Noeske-Winter, Tegtmeier, 2000.
183 Drack and Fellmann, 1988, 300–312, 411–414.
184 Oldenstein, 1986.
185 The trends at these sites are discussed by Esmonde Cleary, 2013, 344–348.
186 Bowman and Wilson, 2011, 5.
187 Temin, 2013, 232–234.
188 Saller, 2002, 251–269.
189 Jones, 1964, II, 767–823.
190 Duncan-Jones, 1994, 45–46.
191 Collectively these settlements are regarded as cities by Jones, 1964, 712–718; Map V.
192 For dioceses and provinces, Jones, 1964, Map II.
193 Harries, 1978, 26–43.
194 Ward-Perkins, 2005, 15.
195 Ward-Perkins, 2005, 54–55.
196 Bachrach, 1967, 476–489; 1969, 166–171.
197 Jones, 1964, Map V. He discusses bishoprics, 1964, 874–879. Mesnage, 1912.
198 Jones, 1964, 769.
199 Ward-Perkins, 1997, 375.
200 Whittow, 1990, 3–29.
201 Bowman, 2017, 1–31.
202 Ward-Perkins, 1997, 371–410.
203 MacMullen, 1984, 571–580; Duncan-Jones, 1994, 45–46; Potter, 2015, 32.
204 Lee, 1997, 219–220, 232–237.
205 Heather, 2005, 246–247.
206 Duncan-Jones, 1994, 33–37.
207 Merrony, 2013, 44–52.
208 Dauphin, 1998.
209 Kingsley, 1999, 48–50, Table 1.
210 Tchalenko, 1953–1958.
211 Ward-Perkins, 2005, 58.
212 Mango, 2002, 1–16. For the Byzantine Dark Ages, Decker, 2016.

Appendix
Timeline of events

44 BC	Assassination of Julius Caesar.
44–42	Liberators' War.
44–36	Sicilian revolt.
41–40	Perusine War.
32–30	Final War of the Roman Republic.
AD 6–9	Illyrian revolt.
9	Battle of the Teutoburg Forest, *Legio XVII, XVIII*, and *XIX* destroyed.
15	Battle of the Long Bridges, Germanicus Caesar defeats the Cherusci under Armenius.
16	Battle of Idistavius, Germanicus Caesar defeats the Cherusci.
16	Battle of the Angrivar Barrier, Germanicus Caesar defeats the Cherusci.
17–23	Revolt of Tacfarinas, crushed by Publius Dolabella.
40	Gaius' 'abortive' invasion of Britannia.
43	Claudian invasion of Britannia.
61	Campaign against the Druids in north Wales.
61	Boudiccan revolt of the Iceni.
64	Great Fire of Rome.
66–73	First Jewish–Roman War.
68–69	Year of the Four Emperors.
70	Revolt of the Batavi in the Rhine Delta, *Legio V Alaudae* and *XV Primigenia* destroyed.
84	Battle of Mons Graupius under the command of Caius Agricola and defeat of the Caledonians in Scotland.
85–89	Dacian War, *Legio V Alaudae* destroyed at the First Battle of Tapae.
101–102, 105–106	Dacian Wars.
114–117	Persian War.
115–117	War of Quietus.
121	*Legio IX Hispania* destroyed in northern Britannia?
121–122	Hadrian's Tour of Britannia.
122–139	Construction of Hadrian's Wall.
132–135	Second Jewish–Roman War, *Legio X Fretensis* and *VI Ferrata* destroyed.
139–155	Hadrian's Wall abandoned; construction and first occupation of the Antonine Wall.

155–158	Possible revolt in northern Britain; first withdrawal from the Antonine Wall; reoccupation of Hadrian's Wall.
158–163	Second abandonment of Hadrian's Wall; second occupation of the Antonine Wall.
161–166	Parthian War.
162	Battle of Elegeia, forces under Parthian general Khusro destroy *Legio XXII Deiotariana*.
163	Second withdrawal from the Antonine Wall; reoccupation of Hadrian's Wall.
166–190	Antonine Plague.
167–175, 177–180	Germanic Wars.
193	Year of the Five Emperors.
231	Battle of the Euphrates River, Sasanian king Ardashir I defeats Roman forces under Severus Alexander.
235–284	Crisis of the third century.
238	Year of the Six Emperors.
250–271	The Plague of Cyprian.
250–272	The Palmyrene empire.
259	Battle of Edessa, Sasanian king Shapur I defeats Roman forces under Valerian, capturing the emperor, unknown legions lost.
259–273	Gallic empire.
284–305	Diocletian and the Tetrarchy implement administrative, economic, fiscal, and military reforms.
309	Constantine introduces the gold *solidus*.
312	Battle of the Milvian Bridge, Constantine defeats Maxentius; Edict of Milan, recognizing the official toleration of Christianity; Praetorian Guard disbanded, overarching military reforms implemented.
323	Battle of Adrianople, Constantine defeats Licinius to become sole ruler of the Roman empire.
324	Foundation of Constantinople.
337	Constantine baptized to Christianity just before his death.
357	Battle of Argentoratum, Julian as Caesar defeats the Alamanni confederacy led by king Chonodomar.
362	Julian invades Mesopotamia.
363	Death of Julian after the Battle of Samarra, Roman withdrawal from Mesopotamia under Jovian.
364	Division of western and eastern empires, Valentinian I emperor in the west and Valens in the east.
376	Goths, fleeing from the Huns, cross the Danube and are settled in Thrace.
378	Battle of Adrianople, Valens killed along with a substantial contingent of the eastern Roman field army.
380	Edict of Thessalonika under Theodosius I, Nicene Christianity becomes the official religion of the Roman empire.
395–408	Supremacy of Stilicho.
401	Goths, led by Alaric, arrive in Italy after ravaging the Balkans.
403	Goths under Alaric are driven out of Italy by Stilicho, defeated at the Battles of Pollentia and Verona.
405–406	Gothic coalition under Radagaisus invades Italy but is defeated at the Battle of Faesulae by Stilicho, Radagaisus executed.

406–409	Alans, Vandals, and Sueves cross the Rhine and ravage Gaul.
407	Usurper Constantine III supported by the army in Britain and Gaul; Britain under pressure from Anglo-Saxons, Irish, and Picts.
408	Goths return to Italy under Alaric.
408	The Huns attack the eastern empire.
409	The Vandals and Alans enter the Iberian peninsula.
410	Gothic sack of Rome under Alaric.
410–440s	*Bacaude* uprisings in Gaul and the Iberian peninsula.
411	The Iberian peninsula is divided between the Alans, Sueves, and Vandals.
416, 418	First and second Gothic settlement treaties in Gaul (Garonne valley ceded).
420s, 430s	Hunnic empire established north of the Danube.
429	Vandal invasion of North Africa under Gaiseric.
430, 435	Vandals defeat Bonifatius in North Africa.
435	First Vandal settlement treaty (parts of Mauretania and Numidia ceded).
440–442	First and second Alan settlement treaties in Gaul (middle Rhône and Loire valleys ceded).
442	Second Vandal settlement treaty (Africa Proconsularis, Byzacena, and western Tripolitania ceded).
After 443	Burgundian settlement treaty in southern Gaul (Sapaudia).
451	The Battle of the Catalaunian Plains, Roman-Alan, Visigoth alliance under Flavius Aetius defeat Hun-Gepid-Ostrogoth alliance under Attila, Theoderic killed.
452	Huns invade Italy and capture the city of Aquileia.
453	Death of Attila and gradual breakup of the Hunnic empire.
455	Vandal sack of Rome.
456	The Visigoths expand their powerbase in the Iberian peninsula, controlling it by the end of the century.
468	Western and eastern imperial Roman fleet marshalled by Anthemius and Leo, under the command of Basiliscus, defeated by the Vandal fleet at the Battle of Cape Bon.
476	Romulus Augustulus deposed by Theoderic and sent into exile (conventional date for the Fall of Rome).
480 (circa)	Frankish king Clovis establishes an increasing powerbase in northern and central Gaul.
489–493	Theoderic the Ostrogoth wrests Italy from Odovacer and replaces him as king.
507	Clovis defeats the Visigoths at the Battle of Vouillé and establishes hegemony over much of Gaul.

Bibliography

Adams, Robert McCormick. 1965. *Land Behind Baghdad: a history of settlement on the Diyala Plains*. Chicago: University of Chicago Press.

Adams, Robert McCormick. 1981. *Heartland of Cities: surveys of ancient settlement and land use on the central floodplain of the Euphrates*. Chicago: University of Chicago Press.

Alföldy, Géza. 1974. 'The Crisis of the Third Century as Seen by Contemporaries'. *Greek, Roman, and Byzantine Studies* 15 (1): 89–111.

Alföldy, Géza. 1995. 'Eine Bauinschrift aus dem Colosseum'. *Zeitschrift für Papyrologie und Epigraphik* 109: 195–226.

Arce, Javier, ed. 2002. *Centcelles: el monumento tardorromano: iconografía y arquitectura*. Rome: L'Erma di Bretschneider.

Attema, Peter and Tymon de Haas. 2011. 'Rural Settlement and Population Extrapolation: a case study from the *Ager* of Antium, Central Italy (350 BC – AD 400)'. In *Settlement, Urbanization, and Population*, edited by Alan Bowman and Andrew Wilson, 97–140. Oxford: Oxford University Press.

Auden, Wystan Hugh. 2009. *Poems Selected by John Fuller*. London: Faber.

Augenti, Andrea. 2010. *Città e porti dall'antichità al medioevo*. Rome: Carocci editore.

Bachrach, Bernard. 1967. 'The Alans in Gaul'. *Traditio* 23: 476–489.

Bachrach, Bernard. 1969. 'The Origin of Armorican Chivalry'. *Technology and Culture* 10 (2): 166–171.

Ball, Larry. 2003. *The Domus Aurea and the Roman Architectural Revolution*. Cambridge: Cambridge University Press.

Balty, Janine. 1993. 'Les Mosaïques'. In *Splendeur des Sassanides: L'empire perse entre Rome et la Chine (224–642)*, edited by Bruno Overlaet and Micheline Ruyssinck, 67–69. Brussels: Musées royaux d'Art et d'Histoire.

Banaji, Jairus. 2007. *Agrarian Change in Late Antiquity: gold, labour, and aristocratic dominance*. Oxford: Oxford University Press.

Bardill, Jonathan. 2012. *Constantine: Divine Emperor of the Christian Golden Age*. Cambridge: Cambridge University Press.

Barnish, Samuel. 1986. 'Taxation, Land and Barbarian Settlement in the Western Empire'. *Papers of the British School at Rome* 54: 170–195.

Barrett, John. 1997. 'Romanization: a critical comment'. In *Dialogues in Roman Imperialism: power, discourse & discrepant experience in the Roman Empire*, Journal of Roman Archaeology Supplementary Series 23, edited by David Mattingly, 51–64. Portsmouth, RI: Journal of Roman Archaeology.

190   *Bibliography*

Bayless, William. 1976. 'The Treaty with the Huns of 443'. *American Journal of Philology* 97 (2): 176–179.

Beckmann, Martin. 2011. *The Column of Marcus Aurelius: the genesis and meaning of a Roman imperial monument*. Chapel Hill, NC: University of North Carolina Press.

Beltrán Lloris, Francisco. 2015. 'Latin Epigraphy: the main types of inscriptions'. In *The Oxford Handbook of Roman Epigraphy*, edited by Christer Bruun and Jonathan Edmondson, 91–110. Oxford: Oxford University Press.

Bingham, Sandra. 2013. *The Praetorian Guard: a history of Rome's elite special forces*. London: I.B. Tauris.

Birley, Anthony R. 1999. *Septimius Severus: The African Emperor*. London: Routledge.

Biró, Mária. 1974. 'Roman Villas in Pannonia'. *Acta Archaeologica Academiae Scientiarum Hungaricae* 26: 23–57.

Bloch, Herbert. 1959. 'The Serapeum of Ostia and the Brick-Stamps of 123 AD: a new landmark in the history of Roman architecture'. *American Journal of Archaeology* 63 (3): 225–240.

Blockley, Roger. 1997. 'The Dynasty of Theodosius'. In *The Cambridge Ancient History, Volume 13: The Late Empire, AD 337–425*, edited by Averil Cameron and Peter Garnsey, 111–137. Cambridge: Cambridge University Press.

Blöndal, Sigfús. 1978. *Varangians of Byzantium: an aspect of Byzantine military history*. Translated by Benedikt Benedikz. Cambridge: Cambridge University Press.

Blouin, Katherine. 2013. 'The Agricultural Economy of the Mendesian Nome under Roman Rule'. In *The Roman Agricultural Economy: organization, investment, and production*, edited by Alan Bowman and Andrew Wilson, 255–272. Oxford: Oxford University Press.

Boak, Arthur. 1955. *Manpower Shortage and the Fall of the Roman Empire in the West*. Ann Arbor, MI: University of Michigan Press.

Boatwright, Mary. 2000. *Hadrian and the Cities of the Roman Empire*. Princeton, NJ: Princeton University Press.

Bodei Giglioni, Gabriella. 1974. *Lavori pubblici e occupazione nell' antichita classica*. Bologna: Pàtron.

Boon, George. 1971. 'Aperçu sur la production des métaux non ferreux dans la Bretagne romaine'. *Apulum* 9: 453–503.

Bovini, Giuseppe. 1978. *Ravenna Mosaics: the Mausoleum of Galla Placidia, the Cathedral Baptistery, the Archiepiscopal Chapel, the Baptistery of the Arians, the Basilica of Sant' Appollinare Nuova, the Church of San Vitale, the Basilica of Sant' Appolinare in Classe*. Oxford: Phaidon.

Bowersock, Glen. 1974. 'The Social and Economic History of the Roman Empire by Michael Ivanovitch Rostovtzef'. *Daedalus* 103 (1): 15–23.

Bowersock, Glen. 1996. 'The Vanishing Paradigm of the Fall of Rome'. *Bulletin of the American Academy of Arts and Sciences* 59 (8): 29–43.

Bowersock, Glen. 2007. *Lorenzo Valla: On the Donation of Constantine* (I Tatti Renaissance Library 24). Cambridge, MA: Harvard University Press.

Bowersock, Glen, Peter Brown, and Oleg Grabar, eds. 1999. *Late Antiquity: a guide to the postclassical world*. Cambridge, MA: Belknap Press of Harvard University Press.

Bowman, Alan. 2005. 'Diocletian and the First Tetrarchy, AD 284–305'. In *The Cambridge Ancient History, Volume 12: The Crisis of Empire, AD 193–337*, 2nd ed., edited by Alan Bowman, Averil Cameron, and Peter Garnsey, 67–89. Cambridge: Cambridge University Press.

Bowman, Alan. 2011. 'Ptolemaic and Roman Egypt: population and settlement'. In *Settlement, Urbanization, and Population*, edited by Alan Bowman and Andrew Wilson, 317–358. Oxford: Oxford University Press.

Bowman, Alan. 2013. 'Agricultural Production in Egypt'. In *The Roman Agricultural Economy: organization, investment, and production*, edited by Alan Bowman and Andrew Wilson, 219–253. Oxford: Oxford University Press.

Bowman, Alan. 2017. 'The State and the Economy'. In *Mining, Metal Supply and Coinage in the Roman Empire*, edited by Alan Bowman and Andrew Wilson, 1–31. Oxford: Oxford University Press.

Bowman, Alan and Andrew Wilson. 2009. *Quantifying the Roman Economy: methods and problems*. Oxford: Oxford University Press.

Bowman, Alan and Andrew Wilson. 2011. 'Introduction'. In *Settlement, Urbanization, and Population*, edited by Alan Bowman and Andrew Wilson, 1–4. Oxford: Oxford University Press.

Bowman, Alan and Andrew Wilson. 2013. 'Introduction: qualifying Roman agricultural production'. In *The Roman Agricultural Economy: organization, investment, and production*, edited by Alan Bowman and Andrew Wilson, 1–32. Oxford: Oxford University Press.

Bradley, Keith. 2014. 'Slaves'. In *The Oxford Companion to Classical Civlization*, edited by Simon Hornblower, Antony Spawforth, and Esther Eidinow, 736–737. Oxford: Oxford University Press.

Breeze, David John. 2006. *Hadrian's Wall*. London: English Heritage.

Brilliant, Richard. 1967. *The Arch of Septimius Severus in the Roman Forum*. Rome: American Academy in Rome.

Brodribb, Arthur, Anthony Hands, and David Walker. 2005. *The Roman Villa at Shakenoak Farm, Oxfordshire Excavations 1960–1976*. BAR British Series 395. Oxford: Archaeopress.

Brown, Peter. 1971. *The World of Late Antiquity: from Marcus Aurelius to Muhammad*. London: Thames & Hudson.

Brown, Peter. 1978. *The Making of Late Antiquity*. Cambridge, MA: Harvard University Press.

Brun, Jean-Pierre. 2004. *Archéologie du vin et de l'huile dans l'Empire romain*. Paris: Errance.

Burnham, Barry, Helen Burnham, and Alwyn Annels. 2004. *Dolaucothi-Pumsaint: survey and excavation at a Roman gold-mining complex (1987–1999)*. Oxford: Oxbow.

Bury, John Bagnell. 1958. *History of the Later Roman Empire: from the death of Theodosius I to the death of Justinian*, 2 vols. New York: Dover Publications.

Caballos, Antonio, and Leon Pilar, eds. 1997. *Italica MMCC: actas de las Jornadas del 2.200 Aniversario de la Fundación de Itálica (Sevilla, 8–11 noviembre 1994)*. Sevilla: Junta de Andalucía.

Cameron, Averil. 1985. *Procopius and the Sixth Century*. London: Duckworth.

Cameron, Averil. 2005. 'The Reign of Constantine, AD 306–337'. In *The Cambridge Ancient History, Volume 12: The Crisis of Empire, AD 193–337*, 2nd ed., edited by Alan Bowman, Averil Cameron, and Peter Garnsey, 90–109. Cambridge: Cambridge University Press.

Campbell, Brian. 2005. 'The Army'. In *The Cambridge Ancient History, Volume 12: The Crisis of Empire, AD 193–337*, 2nd ed., edited by Alan Bowman, Averil Cameron, and Peter Garnsey, 110–130. Cambridge: Cambridge University Press.

Carr, Eva. 1997. 'Les Francs, les Wisigoths et la "longue durée"'. In *Clovis: histoire et memoire*, Vol. 1 (Actes du Colloque International d'Histoire de Reims, du 19 au 25 septembre, 1996), edited by Michel Rouche, 421–433. Paris: Presses de l'Université de Paris-Sorbonne.

Carr, Eva. 2002. *Vandals to Visigoths: rural settlement patterns in early medieval Spain*. Ann Arbor, MI: University of Michigan Press.

Carreté i Nadal, Joseph Ma, Simon Keay, and Martin Millett. 1995. *A Roman Provincial Capital and Its Hinterland: the survey of the territory of Tarragona, Spain, 1985–1990*, Journal of Roman Archaeology Supplementary Series 15. Ann Arbor, MI: Journal of Roman Archaeology.

Carrié, Jean-Michel. 1999. 'Annona'. In *Late Antiquity: A Guide to the Postclassical World*, edited by Glen Bowersock, Peter Brown, and Oleg Grabar, 301–302. Cambridge, MA: The Belknapp Press of Harvard University Press.

Çeçen, Kâzım. 1996. *The Longest Roman Water Supply Line*. Istanbul: Türkiye Sınai Kalkınma Bankası.

Christie, Neil. 2016. 'Late Roman and Late Antique Italy: from Constantine to Justinian'. In *A Companion to Roman Italy*, edited by Alison Cooley, 133–153. Oxford: Wiley Blackwell.

Coccia, Stefano. 1996. 'Il *Portus Romae* alla fine dell'antichità nel quadro del sistema di approvvigionamento della città di Roma'. In *'Roman Ostia' Revisited: archaeological and historical papers in memory of Russell Meiggs*, edited by Anna Gallina Zevi and Amanda Claridge, 293–307. Rome: British School at Rome.

Colin, Marie-Geneviève. 2008. *Christianisation et peuplement des campagnes entre Garonne et Pyrénées IVᵉ–VIIᵉ siècles* (Archéologie du Midi Médiéval, Supplement 5). CAML: Carcassone.

Courtois, Christian. 1955. *Les Vandales et l'Afrique*. Paris: Arts et Métiers Graphiques.

Cowper, Henry Swainson. 1897. *The Hill of the Graces: a record of investigation among the trilithons and megalithic sites of Tripoli*. London: Methuen & Co.

Creighton, John. 2006. *Britannia: the creation of a Roman province*. London: Routledge.

Crow, James, Jonathan Bardill, Richard Bayliss, and Paolo Bono. 2008. *The Water Supply of Byzantine Constantinople*. Journal of Roman Studies Monograph 11. London: Society for the Promotion of Roman Studies.

Curry, Andrew. 2015. 'Trajan's Amazing Column'. *National Geographic* 227 (4):116–129.

Dando-Collins, Stephen. 2010. *The Legions of Rome: the definitive history of every imperial Roman legion*. London: Quercus.

Dauphin, Claudine. 1998. *La Palestine byzantine: peuplement et populations*, 3 vols. BAR international series 726. Oxford: Archaeopress.

De Blois, Lukas. 1975. 'Odaenathus and the Roman–Persian War of 252–264 AD'. *Talanta* 6: 7–23.

De Blois, Lukas. 2002a. 'Monetary Policies, The Soldiers' Pay and the Onset of Crisis in the First Half of the Third Century AD'. In *The Roman Army and the Economy*, edited by Paul Erdkamp, 90–107. Amsterdam: Gieben.

De Blois, Lukas. 2002b. 'The Crisis of the Third Century AD in the Roman Empire: a modern myth?' In *The Transformation of Economic Life Under the Roman Empire: proceedings of the second workshop of the international network Impact of Empire (Roman Empire, c. 200 BC – AD 476), Nottingham, July 4–7, 2001*, edited by Lukas de Blois and John Rich, 204–227. Leiden: Brill.

Decker, Michael. 2016. *The Byzantine Dark Ages*. London: Bloomsbury Academic.

Deguignes, Joseph, Charles Saillant, and Laurent Durand. 1756–1824. *Histoire générale des Huns, des Turcs, des Mogols, et des autres Tartares occidentaux, avant et depuis Jesus-Christ jusqu'a present: Précédée d'une introduction contenant des tables chronol. & historiques des princes qui ont regné dans l'Asie. Ouvrage tiré des livres chinois, & des manuscrits orientaux de la Bibliotheque du Roi*, 5 vols. Paris: Chez Desaint & Saillant.

DeLaine, Janet. 2016. 'Ostia'. In *A Companion to Roman Italy*, edited by Alison Cooley, 417–439. Oxford: Wiley Blackwell.

Delile, Hugo, Janne Blichert-Toft, Jean-Philippe Goiran, Simon Keay, and Francis Albarède. 2014. 'Lead in Ancient Rome's City Waters'. *Proceedings of the National Academy of Sciences of the United States of America* 111 (18): 6594–6599.

Demant, Alexander. 1984. *Der Fall Roms: die auflösung des römischen reiches im urteil der nachwelt*. Munich: Beck.

Depeyrot, Georges. 2006. 'Economy and Society.' In *The Cambridge Companion to the Age of Constantine*, edited by Noel Lenski, 226–252. Cambridge: Cambridge University Press.

Dessau, Hermann. 1889. 'Über Zeit und Persönlichkeit der Scriptores historiae Augustae'. *Hermes* 24 (3): 337–392.

Dessau, Hermann. 1892–1916. *Inscriptiones Latinae Selectae*, 3 vols. Berlin: Apud Weidmannos.

De Ste. Croix, Geoffrey. 1981. *The Class Struggle in the Ancient Greek World: from the Archaic age to the Arab conquests*. London: Duckworth.

De Vos, Mariette. 2000. *Rus Africum: terra a qua olio nell'Africa settentrionale: scavo e recognizione nei dintorni di Dougga (alto Tell tunisino)*. Trento: Università degli studi di Trento.

De Vos, Mariette. 2013. 'The Rural Landscape of Thugga: farms, presses, mills and transport'. In *The Roman Agricultural Economy: organization, investment, and production*, edited by Alan Bowman and Andrew Wilson, 143–218. Oxford: Oxford University Press.

Dey, Hendrik. 2011. *The Aurelian Wall and the Refashioning of Imperial Rome, AD 271–855*. Cambridge: Cambridge University Press.

Dietz, Søren, Laila Ladjimi Seba, and Habib Ben Hassen. 1995–2000. *Africa Proconsularis: regional studies in the Segermes Valley of Northern Tunisia*, 3 vols. Aarhus: Aarhus University Press.

Dijkstra, Roals, Sanne van Poppel, and Daniëlle Slootjes, eds. 2015. *East and West in the Roman Empire of the Fourth Century: an end to unity?* Leiden: Brill.

Di Segni, Leah. 1999. 'Epigraphic Documentation on Building in the Provinces Palaestina and Arabia, 4th to 7th centuries'. In *The Roman and Byzantine Near East II*, Journal of Roman Archaeology Supplementary Series 31, edited by John Humphrey, 149–178. Ann Arbor, MI: Journal of Roman Archaeology.

Drack, Walter and Rudolf Fellmann. 1988. *Die Römer in der Schweiz*. Stuttgart: Theiss.

Drinkwater, John. 1987. *The Gallic Empire: separatism and continuity in the north-western provinces of the Roman empire, AD 260–274* (Historia Einzelschriften LII). Wiesbaden: Steiner.

Dubos, Jean-Baptiste. 1734. *Histoire critique de l'établissement de la monarchie francaise dans les Gaules*, 3 vols. Paris: Chez Osmont.

Dunbabin, Katherine. 1999. *Mosaics of the Greek and Roman World*. Cambridge: Cambridge University Press.

Duncan-Jones, Richard. 1990. *Structure and Scale in the Roman Economy*. Cambridge: Cambridge University Press.

Duncan-Jones, Richard. 1994. *Money and Government in the Roman Empire*. Cambridge: Cambridge University Press.

Durliat, Jean. 1997. 'Cité, impôt et intégration des barbares'. In *Kingdoms of the Empire: the integration of barbarians in Late Antiquity*, edited by Walter Pohl, 153–179. Leiden: Brill.

Dyson, Stephen. 1981. 'Settlement Reconstruction in the Ager Cosanus and the Albegna Valley: Wesleyan University research, 1974–1979'. In *Archaeology and Italian Society: prehistoric, Roman and medieval studies*, edited by Graeme Barker and Richard Hodges, 269–274. Papers in Italian Archaeology. BAR International Series 102. Oxford: BAR. II.

Edmondson, Jonathan. 1989. 'Mining in the Later Roman Empire and Beyond: continuity or disruption?' *Journal of Roman Studies* 79: 84–102.

Elkington, David. 1976. 'The Mendip Lead Industry'. In *The Roman West Country: classical culture and Celtic society*, edited by Keith Branigan and Peter Fowler, 183–198. Newton Abbot: David and Charles.

Elton, Hugh. 1996. *Warfare in Roman Europe, AD 350–425*. Oxford: Clarendon Press.

Errington, Robert. 2006. *Roman Imperial Policy from Julian to Theodosius*. Chapel Hill, NC: University of North Carolina Press.

Esmonde Cleary, Simon. 2013. *The Roman West, AD 200–500: an archaeological study*. Cambridge: Cambridge University Press.

Ethelberg, Per. 1988. 'Die eisenzeitliche Besiedlung von Hjemsted Banke, Skaerbaek sogn, Sønderjyllands Amt'. *Offa* XLV: 119–54.

Faulkner, Neil. 2004. *The Decline and Fall of Roman Britain*. Stroud: Tempus.

Fernández-Galiano, Dimas, ed. 2001. *Carranque, centro de Hispania romana: Museo Arqueológico Regional, Alcalá de Henares, 27 de abril a 23 de septiembre de 2001*. Alcalá de Henares: Museo Arqueológico Regional.

Ferrill, Arther. 1986. *The Fall of the Roman Empire: the military explanation*. London: Thames & Hudson.

Février, Paul-Albert. 1995. 'Saint-Maximin: Mausolée antique'. In *Les premiers monuments chrétiens de la France 1. Sud-Est et Corse. Sous la direction scientifique de Noël Duval*, edited by Noël Duval, 175–180. Paris: Picard.

Fiches, Jean-Luc, ed. 2002. *Les agglomerations gallo-romaines en Languedoc-Rousillon*, 2 vols. Lattes: Lattara.

Finley, Moses. 1973. *The Ancient Economy*. Berkeley, CA: University of California Press.

Fortini Brown, Patricia. 1997. *Venice & Antiquity: the Venetian sense of the past*. New Haven: Yale University Press.

Frank, Tenney. 1933. *An Economic Survey of Ancient Rome, Volume 1: Roman and Italy of the Republic*. Baltimore, MD: Johns Hopkins University Press.

Frank, Tenney. 1940. *An Economic Survey of Ancient Rome, Volume 5: Rome and Italy of the Empire*. Baltimore, MD: Johns Hopkins University Press.

Frere, Sheppard. 1967. *Britannia: a history of Roman Britain*, 3rd ed. London: Routledge & Kegan Paul.

Fulford, Michael. 2000. 'Britain'. In *The Cambridge Ancient History, Volume 11: The High Empire, AD 70–192*, 2nd ed., edited by Alan Bowman, Peter Garnsey, and Dominic Rathbone, 559–576. Cambridge: Cambridge University Press.

Gandini, Cristina. 2008. *Des campagnes gauloises aux campagnes de l'Antiquité tardive: la dynamique de l'habitat rural dans la cité des Bituriges Cubi (IIe s. av. J.-C. – VIIe s. ap. J.-C.)* (33e Suppl. À la *Revue Archéologique du Centre de la France*). Tours: Ferac Editions.

Garnsey, Peter. 1974. 'Aspects of the Decline of the Urban Aristocracy in the Empire'. In *Aufstieg und Nidergang der römischen Welt: Geschichte und Kultur Roms im Spiegel der neueren Forschung*, Vol. 2.1, edited by Hildegard Temporini, 229–252. Berlin: Walter de Gruyter.

Gerrard, James. 2013. *The Ruin of Roman Britain: an archaeological perspective*. Cambridge: Cambridge University Press.

Ghirshman, Roman. 1956. 'Mosaïque de l'Iwan', 'Cour à Mosaïques', 'Étude comparative de la Mosaïque de l'Iwan'. In *Bîchâpour. Vol. II: les mosaïques sassanides*, Musée du Louvre, Départment des Antiquités Orientales, Tome VII, edited by Roman Ghirshman and Georges A. Salles, 37–75, 78–88, 89–148. Paris: Librarie Orinetaliste Paul Geuthner.

Giardina, Andrea. 2012. 'The Transition to Late Antiquity'. In *The Cambridge Economic History of the Graeco-Roman World*, edited by Walter Scheidel, Ian Morris, and Richard Saller, 743–768. Cambridge: Cambridge University Press.

Gibbon, Edward. 1776–1789. *The History of the Decline and Fall of the Roman Empire*, 6 vols. London. Extracts from a modern edition. 1993. New York: Alfred A. Knopf.

Gibson, McGuire. 1972. *The City and Area of Kish*. Miami, FL: Field Research Projects.

Gignoux, Philippe. 1993. 'Introduction socio-culturelle'. In *Splendeur des Sassanides: L'empire perse entre Rome et la Chine (224–642)*, edited by Bruno Overlaet and Micheline Ruyssinck, 31–43. Brussels: Musées royaux d'Art et d'Histoire.

Gilfillan, Seabury Colum. 1965. 'Lead Poisoning and the Fall of Rome'. *Journal of Occupational Medicine* 7: 53–60.

Gilfillan, Seabury Colum. 1990. *Rome's Ruin by Lead Poison*. Long Beach, CA: Wenzel Press.

Gillett, Andrew. 2001. 'Rome, Ravenna and the Last Western Emperors'. *Papers of the British School at Rome* 69: 131–167.

Godoy Fernández, Cristina. 1995. *Arqueologia y liturgía: iglesias Hispánicas (siglos IV al VIII)*. Barcelona: Universitat de Barcelona.

Goffart, Walter. 1980. *Barbarians and Romans AD 418–584: the techniques of accommodation*. Princeton, NJ: Princeton University Press.

Goffart, Walter. 1981. 'Rome, Constantinople, and the Barbarians'. *American Historical Review* 86 (2): 275–306.

Goffart, Walter. 1989. 'The Theme of "the Barbarian Invasions in Late Antique and Modern Historiography."' In *Das Reich und die Barbaren*, edited by Euangelos Chrysos and Andreas Schwarcz, 87–107. Vienna: Böhlau.

Goldsworthy, Adrian. 2003. *The Complete Roman Army*. London: Thames & Hudson.

Goldsworthy, Adrian. 2009. *How Rome Fell: the death of the Roman superpower*. London: Weidenfeld & Nicolson.

Goldsworthy, Adrian. 2016. *Pax Romana: war, peace, and conquest in the Roman world*. London: Weidenfeld & Nicolson.

Gorges, Jean Gérard. 1979. *Les villas hispano-romaines: inventaire et problématique archéologiques*. Paris: E. de Boccard.

Grant, Michael. 1976. *The Fall of the Roman Empire: a reappraisal*. Radnor, PA: Annenberg School Press.

Greatrex, Geoffrey and Samuel Lieu. 2002. *The Roman Eastern Frontier and the Persian Wars, Part II, AD 363–630: a narrative sourcebook*. London: Routledge.

Greene, Kevin. 1986. *The Archaeology of the Roman Economy*. London: Batsford.

Gregory, Timothy and Anthony Cutler. 1991. 'Arianism'. In *The Oxford Dictionary of Byzantium*, Vol 1, edited by Alexander Kazhdan, 167. Oxford: Oxford University Press.

Grierson, Philip and Mark Blackburn. 1986. *Medieval European Coinage, 1: the early Middle Ages (5th–10th centuries)*. Cambridge: Cambridge University Press.

Grig, Lucy and Gavin Kelly. 2012. 'Introduction: from Rome to Constantinople'. In *Two Romes: Rome and Constantinople in Late Antiquity*, edited by Lucy Grig and Gavin Kelly, 3–30. Oxford: Oxford University Press.

Gros, Pierre. 2011. *L'Architecture Romaine du début du IIIe siècle av. J.-C. à la fin du Haut-Empire, Volume 1: Les monuments publics*, 3rd ed. Paris: Picard.

Gurt i Esparraguera and Josep Palet Martinez. 2001. 'Structuration du territoire dans le nord-est de l'Hispanie pendant l'Antiquité tardive: transformation du paysage et dynamique du peuplement'. In *Les campagnes de la Gaule à la fin de l'Antiquité, Actes du colloque de Montpellier*, edited by Pierre Ouzoulias, Christophe Pellecuer, Claude Raynaud, Paul van Ossel, and Pierre Garmy, 303–329. Antibes: Éditions APDCA, Association pour la promotion et la diffusion des connaissances archéologiques.

Gyles, Mary Francis. 1947. 'Nero Fiddled While Rome Burned'. *Classical Journal* 42 (4): 211–217.

Halsall, Guy. 2007. *Barbarian Migrations and the Roman West, 376–568*. Cambridge: Cambridge University Press.

Hamerow, Helena. 2002. *Early Medieval Settlements: the archaeology of rural communities in north-west Europe 400–900*. Oxford: Oxford University Press.

Hansen, Torben. 1987. 'Die eisenzeitliche Siedlung bei Nørre Snede, Mitteljütland'. *Acta archaeologica* LVIII: 171–200.

Hanson, John. 2011. 'The Urban System of Roman Asia Minor and Wider Urban Connectivity'. In *Settlement, Urbanization, and Population*, edited by Alan Bowman and Andrew Wilson, 229–275. Oxford: Oxford University Press.

Harl, Kenneth. 1996. *Coinage in the Roman Economy, 300 BC to AD 700*. Baltimore, MD: Johns Hopkins University Press.

Harries, Jill. 1978. 'Church and State in the Notitia Galliarum'. *The Journal of Roman Studies* 68: 26–43.

Hatt, Jean-Jacques. 1966. *Histoire de la Gaule romaine (120 av. J.-C. – 451 ap. J.-C.). Colonisation ou Colonialisme?*, 2nd ed. Paris: Payot.

Haynes, Ian. 2013. *Blood of the Provinces: the Roman auxilia and the making of Provincial society from Augustus to the Severans*. Oxford: Oxford University Press.

Heather, Peter. 1991. *Goths and Romans 332–489*. Oxford: Oxford University Press.

Heather, Peter. 1996. *The Goths*. Oxford: Oxford University Press.

Heather, Peter. 2005. *The Fall of the Roman Empire: a new history of Rome and the barbarians*. London: Macmillan.

Heather, Peter. 2010. *Empires and Barbarians: the fall of Rome and the birth of Europe*. Oxford: Oxford University Press.

Henig, Martin. 2003. 'Roman Religion and Roman Culture in Britain'. In *A Companion to Roman Britain*, edited by Malcolm Todd, 220–241. Oxford: Wiley Blackwell.

Herz, Peter. 2007. 'Finances and Costs of the Roman Army'. In *A Companion to the Roman Army*, edited by Paul Erdkamp, 306–322. Oxford: Wiley Blackwell.

Hetland, Lise. 2006. 'Dating the Pantheon'. *Journal of Roman Archaeology* 20: 95–112.

Hirt, Alfred. 2010. *Imperial Mines and Quarries in the Roman World: organizational aspects 27 BC – AD 235*. Oxford: Oxford University Press.

Hitchner, Robert. 2009. 'Roman Republican Imperialism in Italy and the West'. *American Journal of Archaeology* 113 (4): 651–655.

Hodge, A. Trevor. 2002. *Roman Aqueducts and Water Supply*. London: Duckworth.

Hodges, Richard, Graeme Barker, and Keith Wade. 1980. 'Excavations at D85 (Santa Maria in Città): an early medieval hilltop settlement in Molise'. *Papers of the British School at Rome* 48: 70–124.

Holloway, Ross. 1987. 'Some Remarks on the Arch of Titus'. *L'antiquité classique* 56: 183–191.

Hong, Sungmin, Jean-Pierre Condelone, Clair Patterson, and Claude Boutron. 1994. 'Greenland Ice Evidence of Hemispherical Lead Pollution Two Millennia Ago by Greek and Roman Civilizations'. *Science* 265 (5180): 1841–1843.

Hopkins, Keith. 1980. 'Taxes and Trade in the Roman Empire (200 BC – AD 400)'. *The Journal of Roman Studies* 70: 101–125.

Horbury, William. 2014. *Jewish War under Trajan and Hadrian*. Cambridge: Cambridge University Press.

Horden, Peregrine and Nicholas Purcell. 2000. *The Corrupting Sea: a study of Mediteranean history*. Oxford: Blackwell.

Howard-Johnston, James. 1994. 'The Official History of Heraclius' Persian Campaigns'. In *The Roman and Byzantine Army in the East*, edited by Edward Dóbrowa, 57–87. Kraków: Drukarnia Uniwersytetu Jagiellońskiego.

Howard-Johnston, James. 1995. 'The Two Great Powers in Late Antiquity: a comparison'. In *The Byzantine and Early Islamic Near East. III: states, resources and armies*, edited by Averila Cameron, 157–226. Princeton, NJ: Darwin Press.

Howard-Johnston, James. 1999. 'Heraclius' Persian Campaigns and the Revival of the Eastern Empire, 622–630'. *War in History* 6 (1): 1–44.

Howard-Johnston, James. 2002. 'Armenian Histories of Heraclius: an examination of the aims, sources, and working-methods of Sebeos and Movses Daskhurantsi'. In *The Reign of Heraclius (610–641): Crisis and Confrontation*, edited by Gerrit Reinink and Bernard Stolte, 41–62. Leuven: Peeters Publishers.

Howard-Johnston, James. 2004. 'Pride and Fall: Khusro II and his regime, 626–628'. In *La Persia e Bisanzio (Atti dei Convegni Lincei 201)*, edited by Gherardo Gnoli, 93–113. Rome: Accademia Nazionale dei Lincei.

Howard-Johnston, James. 2006. *East Rome, Sasanian Persia and the End of Antiquity*. Ashgate Publishing Limited: Aldershot.

Howgego, Christopher. 2014. 'Questions of Coin Circulation in the Roman Period'. In *Proceedings: First International Congress of the Anatolian Monetary History and Numismatics, 25–28 February 2013*, edited by Kayhan Dörtlük, Tekin Oğuz, and Remziye Boyraz Seyhan, 307–317. Istanbul: Suna & İnan Kıraç Research Institute on Mediterranean Civilizations.

Huff, Dietrich. 1993. 'Architecture Sassanide'. In *Splendeur des Sassanides: l'empire perse entre Rome et la Chine (224–642)*, edited by Bruno Overlaet and Micheline Ruyssinck, 45–65. Brussels: Musées royaux d'Art et d'Histoire.

Hunt, David. 1997. 'Julian'. In *The Cambridge Ancient History, Volume 13: The Late Empire, AD 337–425*, edited by Averil Cameron and Peter Garnsey, 44–77. Cambridge: Cambridge University Press.

Jacobsen, Torsten Cumberland. 2012. *A History of the Vandals*. Yardley, PA: Westholme.

James, Edward. 1988. *The Franks*. Oxford: Blackwell.

Johnson, Stephen. 1983. *Late Roman Fortifications*. London: Batsford.

Jones, Arnold Hugh Martin. 1964. *The Later Roman Empire 284–602: a social, administrative, and economic survey*, 3 vols. Oxford: Blackwell.

Jones, Donald. 2014. *Economic Theory and the Ancient Mediterranean*. Oxford: Wiley Blackwell.

Kazanski, Michel. 1991. *Les Goths (Ier – VIIe siècles après J.-C.)*. Paris: Errance.

Kazanski, Michel and René Legoux. 1988. 'Contribution à létude des témoignages archéologiques des Goths en Europe orientale à lépoque des Grandes Migrations: la chronologie de la culture de Černjahov récente'. *Archeologia Medievale* 18: 7–53.

Keay, Simon and Graeme Earl. 2011. 'Towns and Territories in Roman Baetica'. In *Settlement, Urbanization, and Population*, edited by Alan Bowman and Andrew Wilson, 276–316. Oxford: Oxford University Press.

Keay, Simon and Nicola Terrenato. 2001. *Italy and the West: comparative issues in Romanization*. Oxford: Oxbow.

Keay, Simon, Martin Millett, Lidia Paroli, and Kristian Strutt. 2005. *Portus. An Archaelogical Survey of the Port of Imperial Rome*. London: Archaeological Monographs of the British School at Rome 15.

Kehne, Peter. 2007. 'War- and Peacetime Logistics: Supplying Imperial Armies in East and West'. In *A Companion to the Roman Army*, edited by Paul Erdkamp, 323–338. Oxford: Wiley Blackwell.

Kim, Hyun Jin. 2013. *The Huns, Rome and the Birth of Europe*. Cambridge: Cambridge University Press.

Kingsley, Sean. 1999. *Specialized Production and Long-Distance Trade in Byzantine Palestine*, 2 vols. D. Phil thesis: University of Oxford.

Kingsley, Sean. 2006. *God's Gold*. London: John Murray.

Kobert, Rudolph. 1909. 'Chronische Bleivergiftung im klassischen Altertum'. In *Die Beiträge aus der Geschichte der Chemie. Dem Gedächtnis von Georg W A Kahlbaum*, edited by Paul Diergart, 103–119. Leipzig: Franz Deuticke.

Kovács, Péter. 2013. 'Constantine, the Sarmatians, the Goths, and Pannonia'. In *More Modoque: Die Wurzeln der europäischen Kultur und deren Rezeption im Orient und Okzident. Festschrift für Miklós Maróth zum siebzigsten Gegurtstag*, edited by Pál Fodor, Gyula Mayer, Martina Monostori, Kornél Szovák, and László Tackács, 193–211. Budapest: Forschungszentrum für Humanwissenschaften der Ungarischen Akademie der Wisssenschaften.

Krautheimer, Richard and Slobodan Ćurčić. 1986. *Early Christian and Byzantine Architecture*, 4th ed. New Haven, CT: Yale University Press.

Lapart, Jacques and Jean-Louis Paillet. 1991. 'Ensemble paléochrétien et mérovingien du site de Séviac à Monréal-du-Gers'. In *Gallo-Romains, Wisigoths et Francs en Aquitaine, Septimanie et Espagne: actes des VIIe journées internationales d'archéologie mérovingienne, Toulouse, 1985*, edited by Patrick Périn, 171–180. Rouen: Association française d'Archéologie mérovingienne.

Lapatin, Kenneth, ed. 2014. *The Berthouville Silver Treasure and Roman Luxury*. Los Angeles: J. Paul Getty Museum.

Lasko, Peter. 1971. *The Kingdom of the Franks: north-west Europe before Charlemagne*. London: Thames & Hudson.

Le Bohec, Yann. 1994. *The Imperial Roman Army*. London: Batsford.

Leclercq, Henri. 1907. *Les Martyrs: recueil de pieces authentiques sur les martyrs depuis les origins du christianisme jusqu'au XXe siècle, Volume 4: Juifs, sarrasins, iconoclasts*. Paris: Oudin.

Lee, Douglas. 1997. 'The Army'. In *The Cambridge Ancient History, Volume 13: The Late Empire, AD 337–425*, edited by Averil Cameron and Peter Garnsey, 211–237. Cambridge: Cambridge University Press.

Lee, Douglas. 2007. 'Warfare and the State'. In *The Cambridge History of Greek and Roman Warfare, Volume 2*, edited by Philip Sabin, Hans van Wees, and Michael Whitby, 379–423. Cambridge: Cambridge University Press.

Lemprière, John. 1793. *Bibliotheca Classica; or, A Classical Dictionary: containing a full account of all the proper names mentioned in antient authors. To which are subjoined, tables of coins, weights and measures, in use among the Greeks and Romans*. Dublin: Tegg and Company.

Lenski, Noel. 2002. *Failure of Empire: Valens and the Roman state in the fourth century AD*. Oxford: Oxford University Press.

Lenski, Noel, ed. 2012. *The Cambridge Companion to the Age of Constantine*. Cambridge: Cambridge University Press.

Levick, Barbara. 2015. *Claudius*, 2nd ed. London: Routledge.

Lewis, Peter and Geraint Jones. 1969. 'The Dolaucothi Gold Mines 1: the surface evidence'. *The Antiquaries Journal* 49 (2): 244–272.

Lewit, Tamara. 1991. *Agricultural Production in the Roman Economy AD 200–400*. Series: BAR International Series 568. Oxford: Tempus Reparatum.

Liebeschuetz, Wolf. 1997. 'Cities, Taxes and the Accommodation of the Barbarians: the theories of Durliat and Goffart'. In *Kingdoms of the Empire: the integration of barbarians in Late Antiquity*, edited by Walter Pohl, 135–151. Leiden: Brill.

Lightfoot, Christopher. 1990. 'Trajan's Parthian War and the Fourth-Century Perspective'. *The Journal of Roman Studies* 80: 115–126.

Littman, Robert, and Maxwell Littman. 1973. 'Galen and the Antonine Plague'. *The American Journal of Philology* 94 (3): 243–255.

Lloyd, John, and Graeme Barker. 1981. 'Roman Settlement in Rural Molise: problems of archaeological survey'. In *Archaeology and Italian Society: prehistoric, Roman and medieval studies, Papers in Italian Archaeology*, Vol. 2, edited by Graeme Barker and Richard Hodges, 289–304. BAR International Series 102. Oxford: BAR.

Lo Cascio, Elio. 2007. 'The Early Roman Empire: the state and the economy.' In *The Cambridge Economic History of the Greco-Roman World*, edited by Walter

Scheidel, Ian Morris, and Richard Saller, 619–647. Cambridge: Cambridge University Press.

Loseby, Simon. 2005. 'The Mediterranean Economy'. In *The New Cambridge Medieval History. Volume 1: c.500–c.700*, edited by Paul Fouracre, 605–638. Cambridge: Cambridge University Press.

Loseby, Simon. 2009. 'Mediterranean Cities'. In *A Companion to Late Antiquity*, edited by Philip Rousseau, 139–55. Oxford: Wiley Blackwell.

Luce, James. 1989. 'Ancient Views on the Causes of Bias in Historical Writing'. *Classical Philology* 84 (1): 16–31.

Luttwak, Edward. 1979. *The Grand Strategy of the Roman Empire: from the first century A.D. to the third*. Baltimore, MD: Johns Hopkins University Press.

MacDonald, William. 2002. *The Pantheon. Design, Meaning, and Progeny.* Cambridge, MA: Harvard University Press.

Macdonald, William, and John Pinto, 1995. *Hadrian's Villa and Its Legacy*. New Haven, CT: Yale University Press.

McLaughlin, Raoul. 2014. *The Roman Empire and the Indian Ocean: the ancient world economy and the kingdoms of Africa, Arabia and India*. Barnsley: Pen & Sword Books.

MacMullen, Ramsay. 1980. 'How Big was the Roman Imperial Army?' *Klio* 62 (2): 451–460.

MacMullen, Ramsay. 1982. 'The Epigraphic Habit in the Roman Empire'. *American Journal of Philology* 103 (3): 233–246.

MacMullen, Ramsay. 1984. 'The Roman Emperors' Army Costs', *Latomus* 43 (3): 571–580.

McNeill, William. 1976. *Plagues and Peoples*. New York: Anchor Books Doubleday.

Mallan, Christopher. 2013. 'The Style, Method, and Programme of Xiphilinus' Epitome of Cassius Dio's Roman History'. *Greek, Roman, and Byzantine Studies* 53 (3): 610–644.

Maloney, Stephanie, and John Hale. 1996. 'The Villa of Torre del Palma (Alto Alentejo)'. *Journal of Roman Archaeology* 9: 275–294.

Malthus, Thomas. (1798) 1826. *An Essay on the Principle of Population*. London: John Murray.

Mango, Cyril. 1995. 'The Water Supply of Constantinople'. In *Constantinople and its Hinterland*, edited by Cyril Mango and Gilbert Dagron, 9–18. Aldershot: Variorum.

Mango, Cyril. 2002. 'Introduction'. In *The Oxford History of Byzantium*, edited by Cyril Mango, 1–16. Oxford: Oxford University Press.

Martindale, John, ed. 1980. *The Prosopography of the Later Roman Empire. Volume 2: AD 395–527*. Cambridge: Cambridge University Press.

Marzano, Annalisa. 2011. 'Rank-Size Analysis and the Roman Cities of the Iberian Peninsula and Britain: some considerations'. In *Settlement, Urbanization, and Population*, edited by Alan Bowman and Andrew Wilson, 196–228. Oxford: Oxford University Press.

Marzano, Annalisa. 2013a. 'Agricultural Production in the Hinterland of Rome: wine and olive oil'. In *The Roman Agricultural Economy: organization, investment, and production*, edited by Alan Bowman and Andrew Wilson, 85–106. Oxford: Oxford University Press.

Marzano, Annalisa. 2013b. 'Capital Investment and Agriculture: multi-press facilities from Gaul, the Iberian peninsula, and the Black Sea region'. In *The Roman*

Agricultural Economy: organization, investment, and production, edited by Alan Bowman and Andrew Wilson, 107–141. Oxford: Oxford University Press.

Masson, Vadim, Bail Puri, Clifford Edmund, and Irfan Habib. 1992. *History of Civilizations of Central Asia*. Paris: Unesco.

Mathisen, Ralph. 1993. *Roman Aristocrats in Barbarian Gaul: strategies for survival in the age of transition*. Austin, TX: University of Texas Press.

Matthews, John. 2012. 'The Notitia Urbis Constantinopolitanae'. In *Two Romes: Rome and Constantinople in Late Antiquity*, edited by Lucy Grig and Gavin Kelly, 81–115. Oxford: Oxford University Press.

Mattingly, David. 2006. *An Imperial Possession: Britain in the Roman empire, 54 BC – AD 409*. London: Penguin.

Mattingly, David. 2011. 'Calculating Plough-Zone Demographics: some insights from arid-zone surveys'. In *Settlement, Urbanization, and Population*, edited by Alan Bowman and Andrew Wilson, 76–96. Oxford: Oxford University Press.

Meates, Geoffrey. 1987. *The Lullingstone Roman Villa. Volume II: The Wall Paintings and Finds*, Monograph Series of the Kent Archaeological Society 3. Maidstone.

Merrills, Andrew, and Richard Miles. 2014. *The Vandals*. Oxford: Wiley Blackwell.

Merrony, Mark. 1998. 'The Reconciliation of Paganism and Christianity in the Early Byzantine Mosaic Pavements of Arabia and Palestine'. *Liber Annuus* XLVIII: 441–82.

Merrony, Mark. 2002. 'Sasanian Silver: the art of tribute'. *Minerva* 13 (5): 52–54.

Merrony, Mark. 2005. 'Nemesis of the Caesars'. *Minerva* 16 (1): 33–35.

Merrony, Mark. 2009. 'Water from Afar'. *Minerva* 20 (2): 30–34.

Merrony, Mark. 2013. *Socio-economic Aspects of the Late Roman Mosaic Pavements of Phoenicia and Northern Palestine*, BAR International Series 2530. Oxford: Archaeopress.

Mesnage, Joseph. 1912. *L'Afrique Chrétienne: evéchés & ruines antiques*. Paris: Ernest Leroux.

Millett, Martin. 1990. *The Romanization of Britain*. Cambridge: Cambridge University Press.

Mitrofan, Dragoş. 2014. 'The Antonine Plague in Dacia and Moesia Inferior'. *Journal of Ancient History and Archeology* 1 (2): 9–13.

Momigliano, Arnaldo and Antony Spawforth. 2012. 'Sulpicius Severus'. In *The Oxford Classical Dictionary*, edited by Simon Hornblower, Antony Spawforth, and Esther Eidenow, 1358. 4th ed. Oxford: Oxford University Press.

Morley, Neville. 2011. 'Cities and Economic Development in the Roman Empire'. In *Settlement, Urbanization, and Population*, edited by Alan Bowman and Andrew Wilson, 143–160. Oxford: Oxford University Press.

Murphy, Cullen. 2007. 'Are We Rome?': *The Fall of an Empire and the Fate of America*. Boston: Houghton Mifflin Co.

Nagy, Margit. 2010. 'A Hun-Age Burial with Male Skeleton and Horse Bones Found in Budapest'. In *Neglected Barbarians: studies in the early Middle Ages*, Vol. 32, edited by Florin Curta, 137–175. Turnhout: Brepols.

Neal, David, and Stephen Cosh. 2005. *Roman Mosaics of Britain, Volume 2: South-West Britain*. London: Society of Antiquities of London.

Needleman, Lionel, and Diane Needleman. 1985. 'Lead Poisoning and the Decline of the Roman Aristocracy'. *Classical Views* 4 (1): 63–94.

Neuburger, Albert. 1930. *Technical Arts and Sciences of the Ancients*. London: Methuen.

Nielsen, Leif Christian. 1980. 'Omgård. A Settlement from the Late Iron Age and the Viking Period in West Jutland'. *Acta Archaeologica* L: 173–208.

Nischer, Ernst. 1923. 'The Army Reforms of Diocletian and Constantine and Their Modifications Up To the Time of the Notitia Dignitatum'. *The Journal of Roman Studies* 13 (1–2): 1–55.

Nissen-Jaubert, Anne. 1996. *Peuplement et structures d'habitat au Danemark durant les IIIe–XIIe siècles dans leur contexte nord-ouest européen*. Thèse de doctorat, École des hautes études en sciences sociales. Paris: EHESS.

Nixon, Richard. 1998. *Victory Without War*. London: Sidgwick & Jackson.

Nriagu, Jerome. 1983a. *Lead and Lead Poisoning in Antiquity*. New York: Wiley.

Nriagu, Jerome. 1983b. 'Occupational Exposure to Lead in Ancient Times'. *The Science of the Total Environment* 31 (2): 105–116.

Nriagu, Jerome. 1983c. 'Saturnine Gout Among Roman Aristocrats: did lead poisoning contribute to the fall of the empire?' *The New England Journal of Medicine* 308 (11): 660–663.

Oates, David. 1953. 'The Tripolitanian Gebel: settlement of the Roman period around Gsar ed-Daun'. *Papers of the British School at Rome* 21: 81–117.

Odahl, Charles. 2004. *Constantine and the Christian Empire*. London: Routledge.

Oldenstein, Jürgen. 1986. *Neue Forschungen im spätrömischen Kastell von Alzey: Vorbericht über die Ausgrabungen 1981–1985*. Mainz am Rhein: Verlag Philipp von Zabern.

Opper, Torsten. 2008. *Hadrian: empire and conflict*. London: The British Museum Press.

Ouzoulias, Pierre, Christophe Pellecuer, Claude Raynaud, Paul van Ossel, and Pierre Garmy, eds. 2001. *Les campagnes de la Gaule à la fin de l'Antiquité, Actes du colloque de Montpellier*. Antibes: Éditions APDCA, Association pour la promotion et la diffusion des connaissances archéologiques.

Papadakis, Aristeides. 1991. 'Councils of Nicaea'. In *The Oxford Dictionary of Byzantium*, edited by Alexander Kazhdan, 1464–1465. Oxford: Oxford University Press.

Parker, Anthony. 1992. *Ancient Shipwrecks of the Mediterranean and the Roman Provinces*. BAR International Series 580. Oxford: Tempus Reparatum.

Parker, Anthony. 2008. 'Artifact Distributions and Wreck Locations: the archaeology of Roman commerce'. In *The Maritime World of Ancient Rome*, edited by Robert Hohlfelder, 177–196. Ann Arbor, MI: University of Michigan Press.

Pellecuer, Christophe. 1996. 'Villa et domaine'. In *Le IIIe siècle en Gaule Narbonnaise, données régionales sur la crise de l'Empire* (Actes de la table ronde du GDR 954 'Archéologie de l'espace rural méditerranéen dans l'antiquité et le haut Moyen Age', Aix-en-Provence, La Baume, 15–16 septembre 1995), edited by Jean-Luc Fiches, 277–292. Sophia-Antipolis: Editions APDCA.

Petit, Catherine. 1989. 'La prospection archéologique dans la vallée de l'Arrats (Gers et Tarn-et-Garonne), approche d'un espace rural de l'Aquitaine méridionale'. *Aquitania* 7: 53–79.

Pirenne, Henri. 1937. *Mohammed and Charlemagne*. Translated by Bernard Miall. New York: W.W. Norton.

Pirenne, Henri. 1939. *A History of Europe from the Invasions to the XVI Century*. London: G. Allen & Unwin, Ltd.

Pirenne, Henri. 1952. *Medieval Cities: their origins and the revival of trade.* Translated by Frank Halsey. Princeton: Princeton University Press.

Pirling, Renate. 1986. *Römer und Franken am Niederrhein : Katalog-Handbuch des Landschaftsmuseums Burg Linn in Krefeld.* Mainz am Rhein: P. von Zabern.

Pirling, Renate, Margareta Siepen, Brigitte Galsterer, and Barbara Noeske-Winter. 2000. *Das Römisch-fränkische Gräberfeld von Krefeld-Gellep: 1983–1988.* Stuttgart: Franz Steiner.

Pitassi, Michael. 2012. *The Roman Navy: ships, men & warfare 350 BC – AD 475.* Barnsley: Seaforth Publishing.

Platner, Samuel, and Thomas Ashby. 1926. *A Topographical Dictionary of Ancient Rome.* London: Oxford University Press.

Pohl, Walter. 2005. 'Justinian and the Barbarian Kingdoms'. In *The Cambridge Companion to the Age of Justinian*, edited by Michael Maas, 448–476. Cambridge: Cambridge University Press.

Pohl, Walter. 2015. 'Migrations, Ethnic Groups, and State Building'. In *The Cambridge Companion to the Age of Attila*, edited by Michael Maas, 247–263. Cambridge: Cambridge University Press.

Pollard, Nigel. 2003. *Soldiers, Cities, and Civilians in Roman Syria.* Ann Arbor, MI: University of Michigan Press.

Pollard, Nigel. 2010. 'The Roman Army'. In *A Companion to the Roman Empire*, edited by David Potter, 206–227. Oxford: Blackwell.

Pollard, Nigel. 2016. 'Villas.' In *A Companion to Roman Italy*, edited by Alison Cooley, 330–354. Oxford: Wiley Blackwell.

Ponsich, Michel. 1974–1991. *Implantation rurale antique sur le Bas-Guadalquivir*, 4 vols. Madrid: Laboratoire d'archéologie de la Casa de Velázquez (Vols 1, 4); E. de Boccard: Paris (Vol. 2); E. de Boccard: Madrid (Vol. 3).

Potter, David. 1990. *Prophecy and History in the Crisis of the Roman Empire: a historical commentary on the Thirteenth Book of the Sibylline Oracle.* Oxford: Clarendon Press.

Potter, David. 2004. *The Roman Empire at Bay AD 180–392.* London: Routledge.

Potter, David. 2015. 'Measuring the Power of the Roman Empire'. In *East and West in the Roman Empire of the Fourth Century: an end to unity?* Radboud Studies in Humanities 5, edited by Roald Dijkstra, Sanne van Poppel, Daniëlle Slootjes, 26–48. Leiden: Brill.

Potter, Timothy. 1976. 'Valleys and Sediment: some new evidence'. *World Archaeology* 8 (2): 207–219.

Potter, Timothy. 1978. 'Population Hiatus and Continuity: the case of the South Etruria survey'. In *Papers in Italian Archaeology*, Vol. 1, pt. i, edited by Hugo Blake, Timothy Potter, and David Whitehouse, 99–116. BAR Supplementary Series 41 (ii). Oxford: BAR.

Potter, Timothy. 1979. *The Changing Landscape of South Etruria.* London: Elek.

Potter, Timothy. 1980. 'Villas in South Etruria: some comments and contexts'. In *Roman Villas in Italy: recent excavations and research*, edited by Kenneth Painter 73–81. British Museum Occasional Papers 24. London: The British Museum.

Quidde, Ludwig. 1894. *Caligula: Studie über römischen Caesarenwahnsinn.* Leipzig: Friedrich.

Rathbone, Dominic. 1991. *Economic Rationalism and Rural Society in Third-Century Egypt: the Heroninos archive and the Appianus estate.* Cambridge: Cambridge University Press.

Rathbone, Dominic. 2001. 'The Muziris papyrus (SB XVIII 13167): financing Roman trade with India'. *Bulletin de la Société d'Archéologie d'Alexandrie* 46 (Festschrift for Prof. Mostafa el-Abbadi): 39–50.

Raynaud, Claude. 1996. *Les campagnes rhodaniennes: quelle crise?, La crise du IIIème siècle*, Actes de la Table-Ronde d'Aix-en-Provence.

Raynaud, Claude. 2002. 'Les campagnes rhodaniennes: quelle crise?' In *Les agglomerations gallo-romaines en Languedoc-Rousillon*, 2 vols, edited by Jean-Luc Fiches, 189–212. Lattes: Lattara.

Reddé, Michel, Raymond Brulet, Rudolf Fellmann, Jan-Kees Haalebos, and Siegmar von Schnurbein, ed. 2006. *L'Architecture de la Gaule Romaine: les fortifications militaires*. Documents d'archéologie française 100. Éditions de la Maison des Sciences de l'Homme. Paris.

Reece, Richard. 1981. 'The Third Century: crisis or change?' In *The Roman West in the Third Century: contributions from archaeology and history*, edited by Anthony King and Martin Henig, 27–38. BAR International Series 109. Oxford: BAR.

Revell, Louise. 2009. *Roman Imperialism and Local Identities*. Cambridge: Cambridge University Press.

Robertson, Anne, and Lawrence Keppie. 2015. *The Antonine Wall: a handbook to Scotland's Roman frontier*, 6th ed. Glasgow: Glasgow Archaeological Society.

Rohrbacher, David. 2013. *The Historians of Late Antiquity*. New York: Routledge.

Rossini, Orietta. 2007. *Ara Pacis*. Milan: Electa.

Rostovtzeff, Michael. 1926. *The Social and Economic History of the Roman Empire*, 2 vols. Oxford: Clarendon Press.

Roth, Leland. 1994. *Understanding Architecture: its elements, history and meaning*. London: Herbert Press.

Ryberg, Inez. 1949. 'The Procession of the Ara Pacis'. *Memoirs of the American Academy in Rome* 19: 77–101.

Saller, Richard. 2002. 'Framing the Debate over Growth in the Ancient Economy'. In *The Ancient Economy*, edited by Walter Scheidel and Sitta von Reden, 251–269. New York: Routledge.

Salway, Peter. 1993. *A History of Roman Britain*. Oxford: Oxford University Press.

Sarris, Peter. 2002. 'The Eastern Roman Empire from Constantine to Heraclius (306–641)'. In *The Oxford History of Byzantium*, edited by Cyril Mango, 19–70. Oxford: Oxford University Press.

Scarborough, John. 1984. 'The Myth of Lead Poisoning Among the Romans: an essay review', *Journal of the History of Medicine and Allied Sciences* 39 (4): 469–475.

Scheidel, Walter. 2015. 'State Revenue and Expenditure in the Han and Roman Empires'. In *State Power in Ancient China and Rome*, edited by Walter Scheidel, 150–180. Oxford: Oxford University Press.

Scott, Sarah. 2010. 'Review Article: local responses to Roman imperialism', *American Journal of Archaeology* 114 (3): 557–561.

Scullard, Howard. 1991. *Roman Britain: outpost of the empire*. London: Thames & Hudson.

Sear, David. 2000. *Roman Coins and their Values: the millennium edition, Volume I: The Republic and the Twelve Caesars 280 BC – AD 96*. London: Seaby.

Shaw, Brent. 1999. 'War and Violence'. In *Late Antiquity: A Guide to the Postclassical World*, edited by Glen Bowersock, Peter Brown, and Oleg Grabar, 130–169. Cambridge, MA: The Belknapp Press of Harvard University Press.

Shaw, Beth, Nicholas Ambraseys, Philip England, Michael Floyd, Gerard Gorman, Thomas Higham, James Jackson, Jean-Mathieu Nocquet, Christopher Pain, and Matthew Piggott. 2008. 'Eastern Mediterranean Tectonics and Tsunami Hazard Inferred from the AD 365 Earthquake'. *Nature Geoscience* 1 (4): 268–276.

Sherman, Irwin. 2006. *The Power of Plagues*. Washington DC: ASM Press.

Sim, David. 2011. 'A Terrible Weapon'. *Minerva* 22 (6): 48–50.

Simpson, St John. 2000. 'Mesopotamia in the Sasanian Period'. In *Mesopotamia and Iran in the Parthian and Sasanian Periods: rejection and revival c. 238 BC – AD 642*, edited by John Curtis, 57–66. London: The British Museum Press.

Simpson, John, and Jennifer Speake, eds. 2015. *Oxford Dictionary of Proverbs*, 6th ed. Oxford: Oxford University Press.

Sivan, Hagith. 1989. 'Town, Country and Province in Late Roman Gaul: the example of CIL XIII 128'. *Zeitschrift für Papyrologie und Epigraphik* 79: 103–113.

Smith, William. 1851. *A New Classical Dictionary of Greek and Roman Biography, Mythology, and Geography: partly based upon the Dictionary of Greek and Roman Biography and Mythology*. New York: Harper & Brothers.

Speidel, Alexander. 1992. 'Roman Army Pay Scales'. *The Journal of Roman Studies* 82: 87–106.

Sutherland, Carol. 1955. 'Diocletian's Reform of the Coinage: a chronological note'. *The Journal of Roman Studies* 45 (1–2): 116–118.

Syme, Ronald. 1930. 'The Imperial Finances under Domitian, Nerva and Trajan'. *The Journal of Roman Studies* 20 (1): 55–70.

Syme, Ronald. 1969. *Tacitus*, 2 vols. Oxford: Clarendon Press.

Syme, Ronald. 1979. 'Problems about Janus'. *The American Journal of Philology* 100 (1): 188–212.

Taylor, Donathan. 2016. *Roman Empire at War: a compendium of Roman battles from 31 BC to AD 565*. Barnsley: Pen & Sword Military.

Tchalenko, Georges. 1953–1958. *Villages antiques de la Syrie du nord: Le massif du Belus a l'epoque romaine*, 3 vols. Paris: Institut français d'archéologie de Beyrouth.

Temin, Peter. 2013. *The Roman Market Economy*. Princeton: Princeton University Press.

Terrier, Jean. 2005. 'Bilan des recherches archéologiques sur les églises rurales en Suisse Occidental'. In *Aux origines de la paroisse rural en Gaule méridionale (IVᵉ–IXᵉ siècles)*, edited by Christine Delaplace, 72–81. Paris: Editions Errance.

Testa, Rita. 2009. 'The Late Antique Bishop'. In *A Companion to Late Antiquity*, edited by Philip Rousseau, 525–538. Oxford: Wiley Blackwell.

Thompson, Edward. 1999. *The Huns*. Oxford: Wiley.

Tiradritti, Francesco. 2015. 'Of Kilns and Corpses: Theban plague victims', *Egyptian Archaeology* 44: 15–18.

Tornbjerg, Svend. 1985. 'Bellingegård, a Late Iron Age settlement site at Køge, East Zealand'. *Journal of Danish Archaeology*, IV (1): 147–156.

Treadgold, Warren. 1995. *Byzantium and its Army, 284–1081*. Stanford, CA: Stanford University Press.

Trout, Dennis. 2009. 'Inscribing Identity: the Latin epigraphic habit'. In *A Companion to Late Antiquity*, edited by Philip Rousseau, 170–186. Oxford: Wiley Blackwell.

Vagi, David. 1999. *Coinage and History of the Roman Empire, c. 82 BC – AD 480*, Vol. II. Sidney, OH: Amos Press.

Vanden Berghe, Louise. 1993. 'La Sculpture'. In *Splendeur des Sassanides: L'empire perse entre Rome et la Chine (224–642)*, edited by Bruno Overlaet and Micheline Ruyssinck, 71–88. Brussels: Musées royaux d'Art et d'Histoire.

Van der Leeuw, Sander, François Favory, and Fiches, Jean-Luc. 2003. *Archéologie et systèmes socio-environnementaux: etudes multiscalaires sur la vallée du Rhône dans le programme Archaeomedes*. Centre d'études Préhistoire-Antiquité-Moyen Âge. Paris: CNRS.

Van der Meer, Frederik, and Christine Mohrmann. 1958. *Atlas of the Early Christian World*. Translated and edited by Mary Hedlund and Harold Rowley. London: Nelson.

Vogel, Alexius. 1987. 'Die historische Entwicklung der Gewichtsmauer'. In *Historische Talsperren*, Vol. 1, edited by Günther Garbrecht, 47–56. Stuttgart: Wittwer.

Ward-Perkins, Bryan. 1981. 'Luni: the prosperity of the town and its territory'. In *Archaeology and Italian Society: prehistoric, Roman and medieval studies*, edited by Graeme Barker and Richard Hodges, 179–190. Papers in Italian Archaeology, BAR International Series 102. Oxford: BAR.

Ward-Perkins, Bryan. 1997. 'The Cities'. In *The Cambridge Ancient History Volume 13: The Late Empire, AD 337–425*, edited by Averil Cameron and Peter Garnsey, 371–410. Cambridge: Cambridge University Press.

Ward-Perkins, Bryan. 2001. 'Specialized Production and Exchange'. In *Cambridge Ancient History, Volume 14, Late Antiquity: empire and successors, AD 425–600*, edited by Averil Cameron, Bryan Ward-Perkins, and Michael Whitby, 346–391. Cambridge: Cambridge University Press.

Ward-Perkins, Bryan. 2005. *The Fall of Rome and the End of Civilization*. Oxford: Oxford University Press.

Ward-Perkins, Bryan. 2012. 'Old and New Rome Compared: the rise of Constantinople'. In *Two Romes: Rome and Constantinople in Late Antiquity*, edited by Lucy Grig and Gavin Kelly, 53–80. Oxford: Oxford University Press.

Ward-Perkins, John, Barri Jones, Roger Ling, and Philip Kenrick. 1993. *The Severan Buildings of Leptis Magna: an architectural survey*. London: Society for Libyan Studies.

Warden, Gregory. 1981. 'The Domus Aurea Reconsidered'. *Journal of the Society of Architectural Historians* 40 (4): 271–278.

Watson, Alaric. 1999. *Aurelian and the Third Century*. London: Routledge.

Watson, George. 1985. *The Roman Soldier*. Ithaca, NY: Cornell University.

Wenke, Robert. 1975–1976. 'Imperial Investments and Agricultural Developments in Parthian and Sasanian Khuzestan: 150 BC to AD 640'. *Mesopotamia* 10–11: 31–221.

Whitby, Michael. 2008. *Rome at War AD 293–696*. Oxford: Osprey Publishing.

Whittaker, Richard. 1976. 'Agri deserti'. In *Studies in Roman Property*, edited by Moses Finley, 137–166. Cambridge: Cambridge University Press.

Whittaker, Richard. 1994. *Frontiers of the Roman Empire*. Baltimore, MD: Johns Hopkins University Press.

Whittow, Mark. 1990. 'Ruling the Late Roman and Early Byzantine City: a continuous history'. *Past and Present* 129 (1): 3–29.

Wickham, Chris. 2005. *Framing the Early Middle Ages: Europe and the Mediterranean, 400–800*. Oxford: Oxford University Press.

Wightman, Edith. 1981. 'The Lower Liri Valley: problems, trends and peculiarities'. In *Archaeology and Italian Society: prehistoric, Roman and medieval studies*, edited by Graeme Barker and Richard Hodges, 257–287. Papers in Italian Archaeology, Vol. 2. BAR International Series 102. Oxford: BAR.

Wilkes, John. 1985. 'Review of *The Making of the Roman Army: From Republic to Empire* by Lawrence Keppie; *The Development of the Roman Auxiliary Forces from Caesar to Vespasian (49 BC–AD 79)* by Dennis Saddington; *Roman Army Studies 1* by Michael Speidel; *The Emperor and the Roman Army: 31 BC – AD 235* by J. Brian. Campbell'. *Journal of Roman Studies* 75: 239–243.

Wilson, Andrew. 2002. 'Machines, Power and the Ancient Economy'. *Journal of Roman Studies* 92: 1–32.

Wilson, Andrew. 2009. 'Approaches to Quantifying Roman Trade'. In *Quantifying the Roman Economy: methods and problems*, edited by Alan Bowman and Andrew Wilson, 213–249. Oxford: Oxford University Press.

Wilson, Andrew. 2011. 'City Sizes and Urbanization in the Roman Empire'. In *Settlement, Urbanization, and Population*, edited by Alan Bowman and Andrew Wilson, 160–195. Oxford: Oxford University Press.

Wilson, Andrew. 2012. 'Raw Materials and Energy'. In *The Cambridge Companion to the Roman Economy*, edited by Walter Scheidel, 133–155. Cambridge: Cambridge University Press.

Winterling, Aloys. 2011. *Caligula: a biography*. Oakland: University of California Press.

Witcher, Robert. 2011. 'Missing persons? Models of Mediterranean Regional Survey and Ancient Populations'. In *Settlement, Urbanization, and Population*, edited by Alan Bowman and Andrew Wilson, 36–75. Oxford: Oxford University Press.

Witschel, Christian. 2004. 'Re-evaluating the Roman West in the 3rd c. AD', *Journal of Roman Archaeology* 17: 251–281.

Wolfram, Herwig. 1988. *History of the Goths*. Translated by Thomas Dunlap. Berkeley, CA: University of California Press.

Wolfram, Herwig. 1997. *The Roman Empire and its Germanic Peoples*. Translated by Thomas Dunlap. Berkeley, CA: University of California Press.

Wolters, Reinhard. 1999. *Nummi Signati: Untersuchungen zur römischen Münzprägung und Geldwirtschaft*. Munich: C.H. Back.

Wood, Ian. 1997. 'The Barbarian Invasions and First Settlements'. In *The Cambridge Ancient History, Volume 13: The Late Empire, AD 337–425*, edited by Averil Cameron and Peter Garnsey, 516–537. Cambridge: Cambridge University Press.

Wood, Ian. 2001. 'The North-Western Provinces'. In *Cambridge Ancient History, Volume 14, Late Antiquity: empire and successors, AD 425–600*, edited by Averil Cameron, Bryan Ward-Perkins, and Michael Whitby, 497–524. Cambridge: Cambridge University Press.

Woolf, Greg. 1998. *Becoming Roman: the origins of provincial civilization in Gaul*. Cambridge: Cambridge University Press.

Yavetz, Zvi. 1996. 'Caligula, Imperial Madness and Modern Historiography'. *Klio* 78 (1): 105–129.

Yegül, Fikret. 1992. *Baths and Bathing in Classical Antiquity*. London: MIT Press.

Zanker, Paul. 1988. *The Power of Images in the Age of Augustus*. Translated by Alan Shapiro. Ann Arbor, MI: University of Michigan Press.

Index